Empowering Your Life with
with
NATURAL MAGIC

Sirona Knight

ALPHA

A member of Penguin Group (USA) Inc.

This book is dedicated to Midnight.

International Standard Book Number: 1-59257-207-3
Library of Congress Catalog Card Number: 2004106738

06   05   04   8   7   6   5   4   3   2   1

Interpretation of the printing code: The rightmost number of the first series of numbers is the year of the book's printing; the rightmost number of the second series of numbers is the number of the book's printing. For example, a printing code of 04-1 shows that the first printing occurred in 2004.

Printed in the United States of America

Note: This publication contains the opinions and ideas of its author. It is intended to provide helpful and informative material on the subject matter covered. It is sold with the understanding that the author and publisher are not engaged in rendering professional services in the book. If the reader requires personal assistance or advice, a competent professional should be consulted.

The author and publisher specifically disclaim any responsibility for any liability, loss, or risk, personal or otherwise, which is incurred as a consequence, directly or indirectly, of the use and application of any of the contents of this book.

Publisher: Marie Butler-Knight
Product Manager: Phil Kitchel
Senior Managing Editor: Jennifer Chisholm
Senior Acquisitions Editor: Randy Ladenheim-Gil
Development Editor: Lynn Northrup
Production Editor: Janette Lynn
Copy Editors: Molly Schaller and Sara Fink
Cover/Book Designer: Trina Wurst
Indexer: Tonya Heard
Layout/Proofreading: Ayanna Lacey

Contents

Appendixes

Introduction

After our family put a small down payment on a piece of property in Northern California, we began visiting the property on the weekends and spending most of our time in nature. We brought picnics with us, walked the property for hours on end, and discovered the animals and plants on the land (including, unfortunately, the poison oak!). All in all, we enjoyed being in nature so much that a couple of years later, we decided to make it our permanent home.

The land was mostly unspoiled and the plant and animal life were abundant. Because of this, we felt it was important to be careful and work with the natural energies. We blessed any trees that had to be cut to make room for our home, and we made every effort to retain the harmonic balance that was present in each environmental setting.

An old and gnarled ash tree proudly guarded the area at the creek, just below the house. I sensed a nature deva (you'll learn more about these magical energies in Chapter 3) in the tree, whom I came to call "the lady in the tree." I could sense her displeasure when we started to build, and for a while I found it extremely unpleasant to go down to this spot in the creek.

Eventually I did a ritual at the spot, and I assured "the lady in the tree" that we would not disturb her area around the creek. We have kept our word and the energy has dramatically changed for the better. Now the area by the creek is a family favorite for meditating and becoming One with nature.

Moving to the country put me in touch with nature and the energies of natural magic. Now I experience natural magic every time I walk out my front door. I've been impressed by the importance of experiencing nature and its magic firsthand in order to fully appreciate it.

When our family moved to the country, the main problems we encountered were not due to nature, wild animals, or harsh weather. The main problems were due to the backward-thinking people who littered the countryside, killed the wildlife, and clear-cut the forests for profit. The land was—and unfortunately still is—commonly used as a dumping ground where people haul garbage and junk cars onto undeveloped land and bury them.

A couple of years ago, we were drawn to restoring the natural beauty of a couple of acres of land about five miles from us that had been totally trashed by the former tenants. There were 17 junk cars, waist-high piles of garbage, a surplus of broken appliances, and a mostly burned-down house. The land seemed to be weeping as we walked on it. The land itself seemed to be calling to us. It not only called, it screamed in agony!

Part of the cleaning process involved healing the land, which had been seriously abused. When we first started visiting the property, the energy in the land was severely depleted. I felt a sadness that came from Earth herself as I walked among the broken glass, rusty appliances, and pieces of junked-out cars.

In time, the junk was cleared away and nature's beauty returned. I did several healing rituals to help bring back the natural energy that had been lying dormant underneath all the debris. After the long process of clearing away the trash bit by bit, we discovered what used to be a beautiful garden with fruit trees, daffodils, rose and quince bushes, painted ladies, irises, lupines, and a variety of other vegetation.

The next spring was magical in that the land had almost completely transformed back to its natural beauty. It seemed to be smiling and the nature spirits of the land were especially pleased. There were carpets of golden daffodils in the spring, followed by blue-violet lupines in the early summer. One afternoon, I quietly watched as a large doe walked through the restored acreage and two squirrels ran up a large pine tree. The land was beautiful once again and a true expression of natural magic.

Restoring the land was a learning experience on several levels. As our family took on the task of cleaning up and healing the land, we felt something inside ourselves being healed as well. It opened a doorway within that connected us with both the sacred and natural energies of Earth and the Oneness of all things.

Although I had always felt connected to the energies of Earth, these feelings only became real when I began having more contact with nature. I became aware of a form and flow. I was inspired by the natural power around me.

Nature seemed to be a connecting point for both the sciences, such as biology and geometry, with their modern explanations for everything, and the ancient spiritual traditions, such as the Celtic and Native American, with their reverence for the cycles of Earth. This is also the vortex of natural magic.

Written with this combination of science and spirituality in mind, *Empowering Your Life with Natural Magic* helps you boost your wellness, encourage healing, and bring balance into your relationships. Included is information and techniques on using sacred geometry, feng shui, aromatherapy with essential oils, stones, herbs, nature devas, and faeries. Instructions for tree magic, planting a peace rose for world peace, and communing with the elements of Earth, Air, Fire, Water, and Spirit are provided, as well as planting an organic healing light garden and working with the energies of nature.

Through affirmations, meditations, rituals, blessings, and exercises, you embark upon a natural magic quest. You follow this quest through to completion as you progress through the chapters of this book, which are formulated in three categories: relationships, wellness, and enrichment. In the process, you empower your life!

What You'll Find in This Book

The first three chapters in this book help you prepare for your natural magic quest. In Chapter 1, you explore your natural self and get an idea of what natural magic is. Information and hands-on exercises are provided on sacred geometry, setting up your personal sacred space, and bringing in the divine energy of the Goddess and God. Chapter 2 helps you understand and identify your natural magic goals. This includes beginning your personal quest and working with the elements. In Chapter 3, you map out your quest by creating your natural magic plan. In the process, you learn to work with natural energies in the form of nature devas and faeries.

The next three chapters explain how to get ready for and begin your natural magic quest. Chapter 4 covers empowerment tools for natural magic such as flower essences, herbs, and stones. Chapter 5 provides methods for aligning yourself with your natural magic goals by using the concepts of Feng Shui. And in Chapter 6, you enact your natural magic plan and begin the quest that you have mapped out. In the process, you also plant your healing light garden.

Progressing on your natural magic quest is emphasized in the next three chapters. You actually go on your natural magic quest using the map and tools you've gathered. Chapter 7 addresses the idea of building natural magic relationships. Within this framework are animal, spirit, and energetic allies and the ideas of competition and cooperation. Finding natural magic all around you is the focus of Chapter 8. This includes the healing energies of plants and tree magic. Chapter 9 explains how to stick to your natural magic plan so that you can attain your natural magic empowerment goals.

The last three chapters deal with manifesting and enjoying the fruits of your endeavors. Chapter 10 shows you how to manifest your natural magic empowerment goals, which includes creating a sacred cave for meditating and dreaming. After manifesting your goals, Chapter 11 describes how you can celebrate and enjoy your accomplishments. This is the essence of empowerment. This chapter also includes ideas for Earth-friendly nuptials. In Chapter 12, you reflect on your natural magic process and learn to save seeds and set the stage for future generations. The process in natural magic is continual in that you are always setting, attaining, and resetting your goals. This is how you evolve.

Taken in its totality, natural magic is about strengthening your connection to the energies of Earth. She is the Goddess of creation and the Mother to us all. We are all part of Earth. When you begin to understand and work with Earth's natural patterns, your life will flow in the direction you desire.

I invite you now to venture out into nature, seek out its natural wisdom, and tap into its wonders. Really *look* at the divine beauty around you. Within that beauty is the power of natural magic, a power that you can use to strengthen your relationships, improve your health, and enrich your life.

Acknowledgments

I would like to gratefully acknowledge and sincerely thank Randy Ladenheim-Gil, senior acquisitions editor at Alpha Books, for empowering me to write this book! Thank you, Randy, for your continued encouragement, support, and enthusiasm. Many heartfelt thanks to Lynn Northrup, my development editor, for her fine editing job, for her patience, and for helping to make my book even better! I would also like to respectfully thank my publisher, Marie Butler-Knight, for the opportunity to write this book. And many genuine thanks to my senior managing editor Jennifer Chisholm, my production editor Janette Lynn, my copy editors Molly Schaller and Sara Fink for their excellent editing efforts, product manager Phil Kitchel, book designer Trina Wurst, and everyone at Alpha Books for their time and splendid work!

I'd also like to thank Mother Nature for her divine gifts, and thank my many dear pet companions for their unconditional love. Loving thanks and gratefulness to my family and friends, especially Michael, Skylor, and my parents. And I would like to extend an empowering THANK YOU! to each person who reads this book and uses the natural magic methods within it to empower his or her life. May we all learn to respect, honor, and enjoy the natural beauty of Earth and work with Mother Nature rather than destroy her and her many gifts. Blessed be!

Trademarks

All terms mentioned in this book that are known to be or are suspected of being trademarks or service marks have been appropriately capitalized. Alpha Books and Penguin Group (USA) Inc. cannot attest to the accuracy of this information. Use of a term in this book should not be regarded as affecting the validity of any trademark or service mark.

Chapter One

Exploring Your Natural Self

Natural magic essentially revolves around the dynamic relationship you have with Earth as a living and nurturing entity. This relationship moves from the cellular to the divine. You are like a flower growing in a magical garden, and natural magic is the cyclic but ever-changing relationship you have with this garden as the divine creatrix/creator of your life. The relationship happens on many levels simultaneously. The basic idea in natural magic is to harmonize your energy to the natural energy around you and in doing so, to manifest the things you want and need in life.

Natural magic happens everywhere, but some places embody the overall idea more than others. One place I have found that provides a great example of natural magic is Yosemite Valley in California. Every time I visit Yosemite, I am awed by the natural splendor and also overtaken by an excitement that permeates every cell of my body. There's a high level of natural energy that you can feel the moment you enter the valley. Part of it is being surrounded by such powerful natural elements, such as the magnificent rock formations, waterfalls, and lush greenery. I invariably wind up among the giant sequoias whose size dwarfs all other living things, including myself. When I put my hands on the enormous tree trunks and feel the texture of the bark, I sense an energy that is very ancient and tied intricately to the energy of Earth. From my perspective on the ground, the giant sequoia is like a natural link between the elemental powers of Earth and those of the sky.

In the realm of natural magic, Yosemite represents a power spot, where the energies of Earth are stronger and more pronounced. When you enter one of these power spots, the energy in your body is affected by the natural energy of the area. As Gregg Braden, author of *Awakening to Zero Point: The Collective Initiation*, writes, "Energetically, we are electrical in nature. Each cell within each component of our body generates a charge of approximately 1.17 volts at a specific frequency for that organ." This means that when you enter a place where Earth's energies have coalesced, the cells of your body are actually electrically affected in a very physical and measurable way.

This concept can help explain the effect that certain places have on your body. Some places invigorate and excite your cells and organs, while other places literally seem to drain the energy right out of you. This is why it is important to make the environment around you empowering rather than draining. Your home—including your yard, if you have one—should be a power spot for you in that it recharges your batteries so you can go out and face the world again. Some of the ways you can make your personal space more conducive to natural magic is by using sacred geometry and feng shui, working with nature devas or spirits and animal allies, and creating a natural sacred space.

By creating a natural sacred space, you create an area that resonates with the energy emanating from each part of your body as well as the whole of your being. For the most part, natural magic is a personal experience in that it is happening to your body and no one else's. Your natural sacred space is your personal power spot where you can go whenever you need to be revitalized, and is also a place for doing the rituals, meditations, and other natural magic techniques, including communing with the elements and the faery kingdom, doing tree magic, and working with oils, herbs, stones, and flowers. The idea in doing natural magic is to have fun while improving your life in terms of your relationships, wellness, and enrichment.

Different Views on the Original Energy of Creation

One of the reasons that natural energy is good for manifesting things in your life is because of its connection to the original energy of creation. These are the building blocks that make up everything in the universe. From this original source, all energy moved universally outward, creating a world that has uniformity within the diversity. This uniformity of shape and form is the basic premise behind sacred geometry.

Before creation, everything existed within a primordial soup. This soup had no ordered form or structure and as such was dimensionless. Like an immense womb of Oneness, it was unaffected and free of polarities and boundaries. It was the "unmanifested," waiting to give birth to all of eternity.

Greek mythology describes this birth of all creation as beginning with Gaea, Earth, who comes into being as a result of the "unmanifested" beginning to settle and take form. The cosmic soup becomes Gaea, making the transition from the primordial to the ethereal. Keep in mind this is still before actual creation, when time and space have yet to come into being. Rather than being physical, the concept was more of the divine Earth, a Mother Goddess of creation and birth. She contained the seed of all that now exists in the manifested world, and as such, her seed and spirit is in all things.

The Mother Goddess Gaea longed to experience love, so she created a son, Uranus, who became the heavens. As her horizons expanded, she desired to experience more things; she created more offspring, including time, space, and the polarities of energy. As each of her offspring had offspring of their own, the world became more populated and defined in terms of form and structure.

The defining process included all the natural features, such as the oceans and mountains, as well as the flora and fauna that were created. And although everything became more diversified and evolved, it still retains the energy and spirit of creation. In this way, every rock, tree, flower, insect, animal, and person contains the energy that finds its roots in the Mother Goddess and original womb of Oneness. Natural magic is about learning to work in cooperation with this energy.

In the Norse tradition, the primordial soup before creation was perceived more in terms of "chaos" because of its lack of order. In Norse mythology, structure only occurs when Ymir, the cosmic cow, begins licking the unmanifested and giving it form. The various parts of the cosmic cow then become all the aspects of manifested reality. In this way, death is not an end, but instead a rebirth or transition to another level of being. This sequence of life, death, and rebirth is an essential concept that continually arises in natural magic.

In the Egyptian cosmology, the Gods and Goddesses left the earthly plane long ago; those beings left behind were less divine. By being reborn in earthly form, these beings have the opportunity to once again rejoin and become one with the divine energy of their ancestors.

Some ancient spiritual traditions believe that not only the animate things on Earth but also the inanimate things have an energetic connection to the divine stage that came before creation. The most notable of these traditions is the Aborigines' concept of "dreamtime." It refers to the time beyond memory when ancestral beings began roaming Earth and in the process formed its features.

To the Aborigines, these ancestral beings represented the divine. They left their mark all over Earth in what have come to be called *sacred sites*. They believe their ancestors left an energetic spirit in the rock, earth, and other natural objects. Derived from a primal power called *djang*, this creative energy can be evoked through rituals and merging with the ancestors, who are like an infinite metaphysical database.

In the Japanese Shinto spiritual tradition, the rocks, trees, rivers, and other aspects of the natural world are imbued with spirit life. This energy is connected to origins of creation and the source of all natural energy. Because the rocks, trees, and rivers are unevenly dispersed throughout the earth, it makes for energy vortexes and ley lines within the energy configurations of Earth. Energy vortexes are the power spots, such as Yosemite and Yellowstone, whereas ley lines are the energetic arteries within the earth that connect all the power spots to each other. As with power spots, the energy of ley lines has a profound effect on the human body.

The Aborigines believe that ley lines are the paths taken by the ancestral beings. They call these energetic paths *dreaming tracks* or *song lines*. As the ancestral spirits moved along the path, they imparted their divine energy into the landscape. When people follow these energetic paths, they then harmonize themselves with this ancestral energy that has roots extending back before creation.

The Celts and other ancient cultures had a tendency to build large stone structures such as Stonehenge and Callanish along the "ley of the land." In addition, they built their places of worship and homes along these same energetic paths. Later the Christians built their churches on the same sites because they were on ley lines that either were, or had become, energy vortexes.

One way to find ley lines is by looking at the land for places where there is an accumulation of natural elements such as rocks, water in the form of creeks and springs, and large assemblages of plant and wildlife. There's something about energy that attracts everything around it, both inanimate and animate. Everything has an innate drive to move toward higher levels of energy. With ley lines, what you see are lines across the landscape, energy lines that tie the accumulations of rocks, water, and everything else together in a way similar to connecting the dots.

The study of sacred geometry has shown that Earth has meridians of energy that extend around the globe. In addition, many sacred sites and natural power spots can be found on these meridians, showing that ancient cultures were very aware of the natural energy around them. The understanding and utilization of this natural energy and power is now coming back to the forefront. Almost as if encoded in our DNA and cell structure, people are becoming more aware of the natural magic around them.

One of the best ways to experience this natural energy is to visit these energy vortexes and power spots. Along with the major power spots such as Yosemite and Yellowstone, which are spread throughout the country, there are many energy vortexes within each local area. Any large body of water, mountain, giant rock formation, lush vegetation, and area of diversified wildlife qualifies as a potential power spot. Go to these places, and be aware of the energetic effect that the area has on your body. While visiting these power spots, begin establishing a dynamic and energetic relationship with Earth.

Sacred Geometry

I had an opportunity to visit Alaska, which was incredible in terms of the energy I sensed coming from the land. I don't know if its proximity to the North Pole gives Alaska a buildup of natural energy or not, but the sensation is both euphoric and grounding at the same time. One of the ways you know something is happening energetically is because all of the wildlife in Alaska is larger than everywhere else. Flying in, I saw a raven at the airport that was by far the biggest I had ever seen. It was the first sign that I had entered the land of the giants.

As if the enormous amount of energy emanating from the land wasn't enough, what I saw in the sky was better than any fireworks display. I was at the lodge when people suddenly started leaving in droves. I asked one of the people leaving what was going on. He said something about "northern lights." Sensing something incredible was happening, I made a beeline for the front door and ran out into the brisk Alaskan night air. When I looked up, I was greeted by a magical display of white, green, gold, and blue cloudlike streaks of mysterious lights flowing here and there against the backdrop of the night sky.

As I stood watching the mysterious lights on that cold March night, I realized that I was seeing one of the natural wonders of the world. I watched in awe as streaks and bizarre shapes of light danced around the sky in ways that make fireworks seem like mundane child's play. Shimmering greens, blues, and golds lit up the night sky in patterns that seemed divine in origin.

Named after the Roman Goddess of the dawn and the Greek God of the north wind, the aurora borealis has delighted the imaginations of northern cultures fortunate enough to be able to view its spectacle. Visible only in the very northern latitudes, to the Norse it was the flashing of the armor of the Valkyries who looked after the heroes who had died in battle. To the Finns, it was the shimmering fur of the foxfire, sending messages that spread out between dimensions. Various Native American cultures, such as the Athabascan and Tlinquit, saw the lights as divine communications with their ancestors.

The aurora borealis, also called the northern lights, results from the interplay between Earth and the Sun, the two celestial bodies that nature-based spiritual traditions symbolically refer to as Goddess and

God. The northern lights begin life as part of the tremendous amount of energy that is generated by the Sun. The Sun's energy creates a solar wind that bursts from the Sun's surface at speeds of up to five hundred miles per second.

When this solar wind, with its capacity to kill on contact, reaches Earth, it is repelled and neutralized by Earth's magnetic field, one of many ways Earth protects and nurtures life. Small streams of light make it through and become trapped at the points of the North and South poles. As this energy moves up out of the poles into the upper ionosphere and encounters atmospheric gases, it creates shapes and flowing patterns of lights, whose colors are determined by types of gases, speed, and other related factors.

After the astral light show died down, I found myself alone looking up at the night sky. I became astounded because I had never seen that many stars. Looking up at all of them, I was overwhelmed by the perception that I was one of myriad points of light that make up the whole of the cosmos. For a moment I sensed my personal relationship with the whole of Oneness, and felt not only at peace with myself, but also with everything around me. I knew in my heart that even though things are different, they are linked by a commonality that binds everything together.

Within sacred geometry, also termed the *language of light,* this commonality is known as the *Principle of Oneness.* The Principle of Oneness underlies all geometry that permeates the architecture of universal form in its infinite diversity. In other words, nature contains patterns, designs, and structures that extend from the minute to the cosmic. These patterns follow geometrical archetypes that reveal the nature of each form in conjunction with its vibrational resonances and essential energy patterns. Without the Principle of Oneness there would no sacred geometry.

Drunvalo Melchizedek, who is known for his books and teachings on sacred geometry, the Flower of Life, and the Mer-ka-ba fields around the human body, writes about the need for creating an energy field of complete harmony. He indicates that there is an energetic space within the heart where we can experience life without the constraints of polarities. When you enter this space, everything is whole, complete, and perfect as it is. Everything is exactly the way it's supposed to be. Rather than being focused on thoughts and logic, one is able to focus on dreaming, feelings, and emotions.

Also known as the "language of creation," sacred geometry is about universal forms and their relation to energy, something that happens on every level from the cellular to the cosmic. Three of the most common universal forms are the point, the circle, and the sphere. They are the basic forms that are the stepping-stones into natural magic.

The Point

At the center of a circle or sphere is always the point. It represents the source of creation. Because the point is one-dimensional, it transcends the illusions of time and space. The point also symbolizes the eternal now, forever unfolding. As such, it is continually empowering itself as it reveals each new aspect of creation.

Within natural magic, the point symbolizes the self, with all of its expectations and desires. From an inward point, energy is moved outward. Every point added to creation gives things form, dimension, and pattern. Each point is like a star in the night sky. Alone, it is a pinpoint of light overwhelmed by the darkness, but when added with all the other stars, each point becomes part of larger patterns in the form of constellations and galaxies.

The Circle

As the point represents one-dimensional reality, the circle represents two-dimensional reality. In Sanskrit, the word *mandala* means circle, which is the first enclosed archetype of sacred geometry. The single point at the center of the circle is called the *Bindu*. The circle symbolizes the Goddess and God, and in turn represents the spiritual realms. As such, it is very good for working with divine energies, and it's used extensively by many spiritual traditions throughout the world.

Within natural magic, the circle is the symbol of Oneness and the sacred union of the Goddess and God. The circle also represents the cycles of nature in their complete form, with no beginning or end. Because of its divine energetic properties, the circle is used as the platform when doing natural magic rituals and other techniques.

The Sphere

Representing three-dimensional reality, the sphere symbolizes the ultimate expression of unity, completeness, and integrity. Everything is an equal distance from the center and has the same importance. The sphere is the primal container of energy and consciousness. Cells, seeds, and globular star systems all mirror the form of the sphere. In terms of creation, it is symbolic of the first cell of life that replicated itself in the process of creating all the life on this planet.

Within terms of natural magic, the sphere represents Earth. As Earth revolves around another larger sphere, the Sun, the effect creates the seasons and the cycle of life. The idea in natural magic is to replicate the natural harmonies and rhythms found in nature and to become One with the harmony of creation. When you reach this place, you can then begin manifesting whatever you want in your life.

Opening the Doors of Perception

The other night I dreamt of a giant gold-colored bird, whose purpose was to watch over everything. The bird did this from his perch on the top of a group of mountain peaks that stood high above the surrounding landscape. From this vantage point, the bird could see all things in all realms of reality. It oversaw the cycles of nature, making sure every part worked together to make everything happen as it should. In this capacity, it balanced the polarities so that they knotted together. Eventually they looked like a gnarly tree whose branches extended together into a single weave, like a giant tapestry.

After waking from the dream, I realized the mountain peaks where the giant bird in my dream watched over the world was in reality the Sutter Buttes—a small mountain range in Yuba County, California, close to where I live. Realizing this made me want to go and learn what I could about this power spot. One of the first bits of information I found was that in native Maidu legend the buttes are the home of Earthmaker, who has a spirit dance house on the highest peak, South Butte. It was from this place that Earthmaker and coyote sang the world into being.

The Maidu name for the Sutter Buttes is *Esto-Yamani*, meaning Mountain-Set-in-the-Center, coming from their location in the center of the Sacramento Valley, one of the most fertile places in California.

To the Maidu, these mountains were more than a sacred site and natural wonder; they were one of Earthmaker's greatest vantage points for observing the natural cycles of Earth and the heavens, and how they all connect and influence one another. It was there that the doors of perception were opened and one could easily see how the elements of Earth, Air, Fire, Water, and Spirit reveal themselves within the many interlinking, natural cycles.

After reflection, I made two decisions based on my dream: to observe and harmonize with the cycles of nature, and to raise my awareness or perception to a height where it escapes the confines of polarities and views everything as One.

Since the beginning of humankind, human beings have observed the interaction of Earth and the Sun. As people became more interested in planting seeds and growing things, it became even more important to learn the relationship between Earth and the Sun.

Many ancient nature-based traditions such as Wicca celebrate the cycle of Earth (the Goddess) and the Sun (the God) as they traverse the heavens in an annual cycle that brings continual birth, life, death, and rebirth. This cycle happens on many levels, often simultaneously. The days when the cycles of Earth and the Sun coincide are traditionally called "Great Days." Observing them was a way ancient peoples harmonized with the cycles of nature, the energy source of their magic. These eight "Great Days" relate to the two equinoxes, two solstices, and the four cross-quarter days that are the points in between the equinoxes and solstices.

The death of the "old self" and rebirth of the "new self" is a universal concept in most spiritual traditions, mainly because it is such an intricate part of the overall natural cycle. In terms of Earth, this natural cycle is played out every year when seeds germinate and sprout in the spring, then plants grow tall and plentiful in the summer, then the harvest and seeds for next year come in fall, and the winter serves as a dormant period. The seeds and dormant plants wait for the next spring, when the entire cycle starts again.

The basic concept of birth, life, death, and rebirth is a pivotal part of natural magic. As with nature and Earth, this cycle is continually happening on many levels simultaneously. Some cycles happen hourly or daily, whereas others can take hundreds, thousands, even millions of years.

In Egyptian mythology, the fabled Benu (a yellow and red bird with green eyes) had many magical qualities, including teardrops with the power to heal. The mythical Benu symbolized the rising and regeneration of the Sun. Like an Egyptian version of the Phoenix, it lived for 500 years, at which time the "old" Benu died. From its embalmed body was born the "new" Benu, which goes on to live for another 500-year cycle.

Along with observing and harmonizing with the natural cycles of Earth, the second part of my dream was about moving perception beyond the confines of polarities to a place where everything is One. To do this, one needs to perceive everything for what it is as a whole within Oneness rather than judging everything and seeing it as black or white. Human nature is to perceive things in terms of polarities—light or dark, sweet or sour, soft or hard. These polarities become a conditioned part of reality until everything is either black or white, with no in between. When this happens, you begin to see things in terms of your template of polarities and not as they really are.

If you view polarities in terms of a circle rather than as linear, you realize that at some point within the circle every polarity meets its opposite, and at that point there is no definition between the two, just as it was at the inception of creation. White and black become gray, and hot and cold become warm, with varying degrees. Within the whole everything eventually meets its opposite and becomes One. You move forward by integrating and balancing these polarities so that they work within the context of your life.

The idea when opening up your doors of perception is to begin to view things as a whole as well as in terms of their separate parts. Be aware of the polarities, but also be aware of the connection and Oneness that binds everything together into a whole.

The basic concept of Oneness is a concept in which all things— animate and inanimate, domestic, foreign, and alien—are One. Oneness is the whole of everything, including time, space, matter, and polarities. Oneness encompasses everything and nothing at the same time. It embodies both the manifested and the unmanifested.

With regard to the divine polarity, Oneness is the sacred union of the Goddess and God. When the polarities come back together as they were originally in the primordial soup, they complete a cosmic circuit with an endless reservoir of energy. This energy can be used for natural magic and making your life the best it can be. The idea is to shift your awareness and open your doors of perception so that you can become more in tune with the subtle energies of Earth and Oneness.

Learning to Shift Your Awareness

By shifting your awareness you begin to view things in a more expanded and holistic way. You notice how the polarities of energy balance and become One. You also realize that the benefits from your cooperative and naturally compassionate efforts are oftentimes much broader sweeping and longer lasting than those gleaned from competitive efforts.

The creative artist and the shaman have common ground in that both shift their awareness in such a way as to move across dimensions to the source of creation. They both use rhythm and tone to enter altered states of being where the doors of perception become windows to the divine spirit, an immense pool of knowledge that contains the energetic imprint of everything. When an artist, shaman, or any person shifts awareness so that it is in tune with the natural energy of Oneness, information and inspiration become readily accessible.

The idea of Oneness is to live in harmony with nature rather than struggle against it. It can help you begin to understand and harmonize with the natural cycles, making your life flow like a river rather than damming it up with obstructions. Whenever you feel your attitude sinking to an all-time low, that's the time to begin shifting your awareness to a place where things do work out. In natural magic, energetic entities rise to their highest potential, and as a result, anything is possible.

In natural magic, you learn to connect to this pool of creative energy as well as the divine cycles of nature. By doing so, you can produce tremendous results within the context of your life. Natural magic comes from your human relationship with these forces and energies that you perceive as divine. When the energy is with you, then everything seems to come together in magical ways. You can write that beautiful melody, build your dream home, or find true love in your life!

In natural magic, Earth is a living entity that has a sacred source of vitality that harmoniously energizes all who come into contact with it. As you learn to work with the energies of natural magic, you bring more harmony into your life and begin realizing those goals that are truly important with respect to who you are as a person.

Exploring your natural self is about figuring out ahead of time what you want, so that when you go after it and get it, it provides a positive influence in your life. Like the foundation of a house, it gives stability and support for everything that comes after. If your foundation is weak, your plan eventually falls apart. This is why this first step in empowerment is so important. Make your foundations strong and the rest of your plans will benefit and be more likely to succeed.

An Awareness-Shifting Exercise

This easy-to-do exercise can be used for shifting your awareness and merging with the all, with totality, with Oneness. Begin by selecting a plant or animal to aid you in your awareness shift. When selecting an animal, choose one that doesn't move very much, as you will be using the animal as a focal point during the awareness-shift exercise.

Put the plant or animal you have selected in front of you as you get in a comfortable position. Take a few deep and complete breaths to relax and center your attention. As you breathe in and out, imagine letting go of any tension you may be feeling and allowing your thoughts to calmly flow through your mind.

Begin staring at the plant or animal, noticing all of its details. Start at the bottom and move slowly upward. In the case of a plant, notice how its roots extend into the ground, providing support for the rest of the plant. Look at the shapes and hues of its foliage. Move your awareness around the plant, continuing to notice all of the individual details. In the case of an animal, notice the feet and legs and how they connect to the torso. Does the animal have fur? Notice the color and texture of the animal's outside surface, whether it's fur or something else. Continue moving your awareness up toward the top of the plant or animal, until you have scanned every part and aspect of your subject.

After you have finished looking at the individual parts, shift your perception so that you see the plant or animal as a whole entity. Observe how each part works with the others to form the total organism. From the bottom to the top, all the pieces fit together and work together as one. Be aware of how each part interacts with the others and how the parts are inseparable from the whole in the same way that the whole is inseparable from them.

Continue shifting your awareness until you can sense the subtle energy body that surrounds the plant or animal. There is energy being emitted by every part of your subject, and this all combines to create a field of energy. Feel your awareness expanding in a way similar to zooming out on a picture. Now fine-tune the image so that you become aware of the energy field around your focal point. Notice any characteristics and changes that occur within the energy field.

Now, move your awareness up to the next level and sense your energy becoming One with the energy of your subject. Your essences intertwine together, and for a moment you merge and become One. You perceive the world in terms of your subject. Let the experience expand your awareness and stretch the bounds of your beliefs.

From this point, you flow into a magical awareness where you and your subject are part of a giant ocean of energy, with streams that connect the whole of things together. Imagine a beam of light moving from you to your subject and then expanding outward in all directions. This light continues to expand until it encompasses everything. Through your connection to the light, you have a connection to all of creation and the powers of natural magic.

After a few minutes, take a few deep breaths to bring your awareness back to the present moment and into your physical body. Stretch your body and take a few moments to thank the plant or animal spirit that you used as a focal point.

Setting Up Your Natural Magic Sacred Space

You deserve some time for flying free and easy, unencumbered by the stress and responsibilities of modern life. It's important to give yourself some well-deserved time to unwind and enjoy the natural power and beauty of nature. Creating a natural magic sacred space can help you do just that!

In addition to being a practical place for doing affirmations, meditations, rituals, blessings, and exercises for empowerment such as those you'll find in these chapters, your natural magic sacred space represents the connecting ground between you and the divine. Your sacred space should resonate with the elements and energies of Earth so you can send and receive the natural power. Like a personal sacred site, this space should also resonate with your energy, making it the ideal place for you to practice natural magic.

Depending upon your need and situation, you can create your natural magic sacred space in a variety of locations. It depends on where you find yourself and what is possible. The best location is outdoors in nature. If you own acreage or have a garden, a large backyard, or access to natural areas, you will be able to easily determine and build your natural magic sacred space.

In an urban environment your choices are more limited, yet you can still find and create small natural havens. If you live in an apartment with a small balcony, you can grow container gardens, create living screens, and enjoy small garden rooms by planting flowers, ornamentals, vegetables, and small trees in clay pots and other containers. Even if you have no space for a garden on a balcony, patio, or a window box, you can create an indoor garden retreat by using containers and indoor growing lights. Just make the best use of what you have and what's readily available.

Your natural sacred space should contain representations of the elements of Earth, Air, Fire, Water, and Spirit. For example, a pot and soil could be used to represent the earth, a whirlybird or small garden flag could signify the element of air, a candle or a grow-lamp could represent fire, and a fountain, small pool, or a large bowl of water with colored pebbles could be used to depict the water element. Spirit is represented by every living thing and being in your natural magic sacred space—including yourself. After all, you are the embodiment of the divine spirit.

Your Natural Magic Altar

Traditionally the altar is either set up in the north quadrant (because north represents the ancestors) or in the east quadrant (because the Sun rises in the east) of your sacred space. You can actually use any of the four directions and elements to orient your altar, depending on your personal inclinations. If you like, you can position your natural magic altar in the middle of your natural sacred space as a representation of the Great Spirit that connects us all together as One.

Within your natural sacred space, it is important to find your "sweet spot." Cats and dogs always gravitate toward these places because they are attuned to the spots with the most energy. You need to find your personal sweet spot so that you can occupy the spot and put your altar nearby. Focus on what's convenient and what works.

In musical recording, an engineer moves a microphone around an area until he or she finds a spot where the singer's voice is optimally picked up by the microphone. In terms of your sacred space, you are looking for a spot where you are most in accordance with the energies of natural magic. One method for doing this is to begin by completely clearing your mind of all thoughts. Move around your sacred space, trying out different spots until you find a place in which you feel comfortable and receptive to the energies of natural magic. When you discover your sweet spot you will naturally feel more energized, uplifted, and inspired when you stand, sit, or recline in it. It is your spot or place of natural magic power.

Your natural magic altar is a meeting place of the mundane and divine. It's like a dining table at which you sit on one side and the divine spirit sits on the other. At that divine table or altar, you are able to communicate with those energies present. In many spiritual traditions the left side of the altar represents the Goddess (feminine energies) and the right side represents the God (masculine energies). The center of the altar is where these energies converge into one.

Your natural magic altar also holds the tools that you will need for rituals and exercises. Some tools are such intricate parts of natural magic that they are always included on the altar; others are used only in specific rituals or exercises.

Your natural magic tools include the following:

- **A candle and candleholder.** The candle and holder on the altar represent the element of Fire, which can both fuel your efforts for success and light your way thorough the darkness.

- **A ceramic bowl.** This bowl should be filled with the earth to bring the Earth element into your magical circle. Earth is useful for grounding, when you want to give stability to what you're doing, and fertility, when you want the seeds you have planted to grow.

- **A ceramic incense burner and smudge stick.** Symbolizing the element of Air, the smudge stick is made of sage and cedar and used for purifying the sacred space. If you do not like or are allergic to smoke, you can use a feather as your spirit wand to purify your sacred space. The element of air gives your ideas the breath of life and the wings to fly.

- **A cup.** Fill the cup with water to bring this element into your magical circle. Water has the property of fluidity and cleansing.

- **A quartz crystal point.** This tool represents the element of Spirit, both personal and universal. Use the crystal to amplify your energy in drawing a circle of light for doing natural magic.

Be particularly careful when burning anything, especially when you're outdoors. Keep candles securely in their holders when lit, and make sure the smudge stick is in the incense burner when lit. Always make sure anything that has been burning in a natural magic ritual or exercise is thoroughly extinguished before leaving the area.

As you progress through the rituals and exercises in each chapter, you will be adding to your natural sacred space and to your altar. Your tools are essential because they give added energy and focus to your natural magic. Use what you have learned about the various elements to amp up the level of the energy in your circle so that when you release it, you can sense its effects. The more you use your tools, the more they resonate with your energy and empower your practice of natural magic.

Doing the Rituals and Exercises

The affirmations, meditations, rituals, blessings, and exercises that come at the latter half of each chapter are intended to help you as you move through the stages of empowerment. In the case of this first chapter, these rituals and exercises revolve around the theme of exploring your natural self. The better you understand who you are in a natural sense, the easier it will be to set your goals for what you want in life.

When you begin to explore your natural self, you are reawakening and reconnecting a part of your self that has been sleeping. The natural magic rituals and exercises will facilitate this process and help you to realize your full power. You have the ability to set your mind on a goal, direct your energies toward it, and make it come true. This is in many ways the true measure of any magic.

Before beginning the rituals and exercises, create a Natural Magic Empowerment Journal so that you have somewhere to record your progress in empowering your life with natural magic. It's important to write things down because later on you might not remember specifics of the rituals you performed. Also, when you see things in writing, it gives another dimension to the whole experience. And most of all, it gives focus to your natural magic process by giving you something to refer to and ground yourself with in times of crisis when you need reassurance. Your journal can be like a best friend; you can confide your innermost thoughts within it without fear of being laughed at or frowned upon.

Make or buy a notebook to use for your Natural Magic Empowerment Journal with pages that are at least 8½" by 11". (You can also keep your journal on the computer if you prefer.) Decorate the cover with images, designs, and quotations that express your natural self. Write on the front cover a title such as "Natural Magic Empowerment Journal," and then below it write your name. Keep it with you when doing the rituals and exercises in this book, and remember to tuck a pen into it or attach one with a string. Keep the journal in a safe, private place when you are not writing in it or referring to your notes.

With regards to the blessings in each section, write each one down in your Natural Magic Empowerment Journal. Say each blessing aloud when you go to sleep and when you wake up. These are the two best times. Saying the blessing before you go to sleep gives the blessing access to your dream world, and repeating it when you wake up gives it access to your waking world. In the words of author Gregg Braden, "Prayer is the most ancient of all sciences, as it represents our opportunity to directly access the creative forces of our world, as well as our bodies. Prayer is to our lives as water is to the seed of a plant. In the presence of prayer, we blossom to an even greater possibility."

Take as much time as you need to work through each chapter and stage in natural magic empowerment. You might take 28 days (a moon cycle) to work through each set of affirmations and the accompanying exercises and rituals. Or you can take longer if you prefer. Go at your own pace. The idea is to give the natural energy enough time to make its magic happen. You know better than anyone when you're ready to move on to the next stage of empowerment.

Trust your instincts as they relate to your natural self. Because of the way it was created, the natural or primordial world is only a flicker of perception away. When you learn to tap into it at will, it becomes a powerful and practical resource.

Relationships

Within natural magic, relationships are threefold—your relationship with the earth, your relationship with yourself, and your relationship with other people. Your relationship with the earth is your relationship with the divine. Because relationships, wellness, and enrichment all deal with your interaction with the earth; in a sense wellness and enrichment also have aspects that have to do with your relationship with the earth, yourself, and other people, thus creating an overlap between the three areas.

What separates relationships from wellness and enrichment is that that area deals with how relationships affect your life overall, whereas the other two areas perceive relationships as they affect particular aspects of your life—wellness and enrichment. If you carry this perception further, relationships are the primal source from which the other two are derived. Without a relationship with nature, there would be no natural magic. Without a relationship with the earth, there would be no life.

Natural Magic Affirmation for Relationships

Write the following affirmation in your Natural Magic Empowerment Journal. Then repeat it aloud three times:

Today and every day, my intention is to explore and become familiar with all of the aspects of my natural self.

Write the affirmation on a small note card and carry it with you throughout the day, reviewing it from time to time as a way to unleash your natural powers and explore your natural self.

At bedtime, set the card by your bed so that you will see and read the affirmation just before you go to sleep and first thing in the morning.

Natural Magic Meditation for Relationships

Begin by lying or sitting down in your natural sacred space and getting in a relaxed state of awareness. Do this by breathing in deeply and filling your lungs with air. Feel them expand like giant balloons until they are full, and for a second, sense your awareness expanding and filling the vessel of your body. As you slowly exhale, sending the breath of air out of your lungs and into the surrounding space, imagine your awareness also moving outward from your body. Expand your awareness until it fills your natural sacred space.

Now take in another deep breath, and as you hold it for a moment, sense everything in your sacred space as being a part of you. Breathing out slowly, sense your awareness expanding even further until it encompasses the area 10 feet around your natural sacred space. The next time you breathe in and out, extend your awareness to 100 feet around your natural sacred space. Continue to expand your awareness until it encompasses the entire Earth.

You are the rocks, minerals, and dirt. You are the rivers, lakes, and oceans. You are mountains. You are valleys. You are glaciers. Sense yourself becoming One with Earth, feeling all her parts as if they were part of you. The rocks are your bones, and the dirt is your flesh. The rivers, lakes, and oceans are your life's blood flowing through your veins. The breeze is your breath, and the fire represents life, death, and renewal. Your spirit is in all things—from the smallest to the largest.

You are the living Earth. You are the source of creation for everything that exists on this planet. From your flesh grow all flora, including the most beautiful parrot tulip to the largest redwood to ever grace the land. Within yourself you sense the connection between all the things that live both within and on Earth. You understand the true meaning of magic every time a seed sprouts and out pops life, ready and eager to begin the voyage.

Next expand your awareness outward until you are the Mother Goddess of Earth, who, with her consort the Sun, governs the forces of life, death, and renewal. This is the cycle governs all things—human and divine. Continue to move your awareness outward until you are the whole of Oneness. You are all things in all dimensions and all perceptions of reality.

Imagine yourself as pure energy that is born, lives, dies, and then is reborn on a continual basis, moving progressively from one level to the next. From this awareness, you can momentarily see that all the dots connect to one another, and life is not as chaotic as it seems on the day-to-day level. You sense an understanding that sends a warm glow throughout your body and the whole of Earth. For a moment you are One.

Now take several deep breaths and begin coming back to the room. Bring your awareness back to your physical body by moving your hands and feet. Next rub your arms and legs as a means of getting back into your body.

After returning to the present moment and place, take several moments to reflect on your experiences within the meditation. What did it feel like to be the Earth Mother? Write your thoughts and impressions down in your Natural Magic Empowerment Journal. What did the experience tell you about your natural self? What elements and parts of Earth do you connect with in terms of who you are as both a human and spiritual being?

Natural Magic Ritual for Relationships

The purpose of the following ritual is to gain a rapport with the elements and to bring their energy into your natural sacred space. You will need a clear quartz crystal point, a bowl of the earth, an incense burner with a smudge stick, a beeswax candle and holder, and a cup of well or spring water. Follow these steps:

1. Standing before your natural magic altar, hold the clear quartz crystal between the thumb and index finger of your right hand, with the base of the crystal resting on the thumb and the tip of the crystal extending up to your index finger. Place your left hand around the crystal, and as you do so, breathe in and imagine a clear mountain stream. Now pulse your breath out through your nose and as you do so, visualize the mountain stream running its clear water through the crystal, clearing the stone of all energy that may be embedded in it.

   After clearing the stone, you will want to impart it with new programming. Keeping the crystal secure between your thumb and index finger, breathe in, only this time visualize your spirit and natural self soaring like a giant bird through the heavens. Pulsing your breath out through your nose, move the image of your spirit into the crystal so that it vibrates in harmony with you. The more you work with the crystal, the more it will resonate with your energy. Return the crystal to its place on your altar.

2. Take the bowl of the earth from your altar and, beginning at the north point, move clockwise around the circle, sprinkling earth as you go.

21

Upon returning to the north point, say:

Watchers of the North Gate
Elemental powers of Earth
Please hear me now
I invite you into my sacred space.

Setting the bowl of the earth back down on your altar, take the incense burner containing the smudge stick from your altar. Move to the east point of your circle, and light the sage and cedar so that it smokes. Next, take the burner around the circle clockwise until you return to the east point, and then say:

Watchers of the East Gate
Elemental powers of Air
Please hear me now
I invite you into my sacred space.

Setting the incense burner back down, take the beeswax candle and holder from your altar and move over to the south point of your circle. Light the candle and then progress clockwise around the circle until you again find yourself at the south point, at which time you say:

Watchers of the South Gate
Elemental powers of Fire
Please hear me now
I invite you into my sacred space.

Set the candle and holder back down, and take the cup of water from your altar, and move to the west point of the circle. Sprinkle water onto the west point, and then circle clockwise around your sacred space until you are again at the west point. Call out:

Watchers of the West Gate
Elemental powers of Water
Please hear me now
I invite you into my sacred space.

3. After you set the cup of water back down on your altar, again pick up the crystal and move to the middle of the circle. Holding your crystal in your right hand, point it at the north point, and imagine a white beam of light moving from the tip of the crystal to the

north point. Now slowly move around the circle clockwise, imagining that beam of light connecting to each of the points until you again return to the north point. After completing this, hold the crystal in the air and say:

To the whole of Oneness
Elemental powers of Spirit
Please hear me now
I invite you into my sacred space.

With your mind's eye, imagine your entire circle being filled with divine white light. Feel the elements of Earth, Air, Fire, Water, and Spirit come together as One. At this point you are ready to do magic, in its every form derived from creation.

When you are done, thank the elemental powers and divine energies for their helpful energy. Make sure the candle and smudge stick are thoroughly extinguished before leaving the area.

Natural Magic Blessing for Relationships

Great Mother, creator and nurturer of all things
Please let me know your love
So that I might begin to understand
The true and full meaning of divine love
And begin to explore my natural self.

Natural Magic Exercises for Relationships

The objectives of the following natural magic exercise are to make Goddess and God creations that you can put in your natural sacred space and use in ritual, and to merge with the divine energy of the Goddess and God. Begin by finding two objects: one that you want to represent the divine Goddess and another that you want to represent the divine God. It can be a rock, piece of wood, shell, feather, or something you make out of mud or clay. Whatever you use should be something natural so that it can resonate with energy in such a way as to help you in your natural magic. You can decorate your Goddess and God creations in any way you desire by drawing on them, adorning them with stones, or any other way you can imagine—or you can leave them plain and natural.

After your symbols are ready, get comfortable and set your Goddess creation in front of you. Using your senses, begin scanning it from bottom to top, becoming aware of every detail. Look at it, touch it, smell it. Imagine yourself becoming one with every aspect of your Goddess creation. Now, shift your perception outward like a cloud diffusing into spirit. Sense your essence and the essence of the Goddess merge together and become One. Spend a moment merging with the energy of Goddess. Then do the same thing with your God creation, merging with it. When you are done, give your Goddess and God creations special places on your natural magic altar. Traditionally the Goddess creation would be placed on the left side and the God creation on the right side of the altar.

This second natural magic exercise helps you become aware of your perceptions of the polarities of female and male and discover more about what makes good and bad relationships. Begin by taking two pages from your Natural Magic Empowerment Journal and labeling one *Female Qualities* and the other *Male Qualities*. Starting with the Female Qualities page, write *Divine* and under it list all the qualities that you associate with the Goddess and the divine female. Now take the Male Qualities page and do the same thing; write *Divine* and under the heading list all the things you associate with the God and the divine male. Next, on both pages write the heading *Human.*

As you progress through the next few days, weeks, or months, depending on your time frame, take time to notice the qualities of female and male as exhibited by the people around you. As you observe and notice new things about women and men, write them down on the appropriate page under the Human heading.

After doing this for a while, compare the two lists. What do they tell about how you perceive the divine Goddess and God? What are the differences and similarities between the divine and the human? What are the differences and similarities between the polarities of female and male?

For the second part of this exercise, use two more pages from your Natural Magic Empowerment Journal and write at the top of one *Qualities of Good Relationships* and at the top of the other *Qualities of Bad Relationships*. Again, observe and notice the qualities of the people around you. How do they relate to one another in terms of female and male, female and female, and male and male? List the qualities that you perceive as being good on the Qualities of Good Relationships page and the qualities you think are bad on the Qualities of Bad Relationships page.

Continue doing this exercise until you get a feel for both polarities as well as a complete list for both. What do these two lists tell you about your perceptions of relationships? Don't be disappointed if you find there are more things listed on your bad relationship page; you can use this as a starting point in determining what you don't want in a relationship. Sometimes it's easier to figure out what you want by knowing what you *don't* want. What do these two lists tell you about what you want in a relationship, in terms of what is good and what works? Keep this invaluable information handy; you will use it in the next chapter when you determine your natural magic goals for relationships.

Wellness

In natural magic, wellness with Mother Earth is all about nurturing and healing. The nurturing part is preventative, much like a baby drinking mother's milk and drawing nourishment as well as the natural antibodies to ward off disease.

The healing aspects of natural magic relate to the symbiotic relationship you have with Earth; you draw strength from her being and she draws strength from your being. Your symbiosis creates an energetic bond, linking you for eternity. She keeps you strong and healthy, and you keep her strong and healthy. Together you have the potential to thrive and evolve in magical ways.

Natural Magic Affirmation for Wellness

Write the following affirmation in your Natural Magic Empowerment Journal. Then repeat it aloud three times:

> Today and every day of my life I want to explore my natural self, and how it affects the overall wellness of my being.

Write the affirmation down on a note card and put it near your bed so that you see it first thing when you awaken. As you repeat the affirmation to yourself, let your awareness move to your natural self. How does your natural self affect the overall wellness of your being?

Keep the note card with you as you move through your day, taking it out every couple of hours and repeating the affirmation to yourself while letting your awareness move to and explore the many aspects of your natural self.

Natural Magic Meditation for Wellness

Get comfortable in your natural sacred space, and begin to relax by taking a deep breath. Slowly inhale, and as you hold your breath for a few seconds, imagine all of the tensions in your body—particularly those around your neck and shoulder areas—coalesce into a single ball of energy. As you exhale the air in your lungs slowly out your nose, sense the ball of energy that represents your tensions pulsating out of your body.

Feel your neck and shoulders begin to relax, as if a giant weight had been lifted from them. Take another deep breath and do this exercise again by visualizing the tension in your entire body coming together into a single ball. When you exhale, send the ball on its way out into the ethers to dissipate into nothingness.

If certain areas of your body in particular hurt or carry a lot of tension, then concentrate on these areas. Breathe as much of the pain and tension out of your body as you can.

Once you feel fairly relaxed, imagine a beam of beautiful white light splashing down from above and flowing all over your body. Your body feels warm and glowing as the light caresses the various parts of your body. Where there was once pain and tension, you sense the light replacing it with a healing energy. Soon your whole body feels revitalized and connected. You are in harmony with the energies of nature, Earth, and the cosmic primordial source of everything—Oneness.

Imagine the white light lifting your being slowly upward. Lighter than air, you continue to ascend within the beam of light. At a certain point, there are no more directions, and it's hard to tell if you are floating up or down, left or right. The light is everywhere and permeates every part of your being. You have a strange feeling that filters through to your core—a feeling of finally returning home.

Like a child finding a parent after a long separation, you reach outward and caress your primal mother and she in turn reaches out and caresses you. She nurtures you, and you nurture her with long, soothing caresses that heal and make each of you feel complete. You feel her love and she feels yours, and the feeling gives both of you an endless sensation of joy that spreads outward through the particles of white light, filling all of Oneness.

At this moment you know you have returned home, completing a divine circle. You feel as if you have been reawakened and energized with a new vitality. You are once again in harmony with your natural self. The idea now is to explore the many aspects of your natural self and begin integrating these aspects into your life once again.

Bring this idea back with you as you begin returning your awareness back to your physical body. With your hands, rub your arms, legs, and other parts of your body until you feel your awareness has returned enough to start stretching your muscles. When standing up, give yourself a little time to fully bring your awareness back to your body before attempting movement. Write any thoughts you have in your Natural Magic Empowerment Journal, particularly with regards to exploring your natural self.

Natural Magic Ritual for Wellness

The purpose of the following ritual is to bring the healing power of the Mother Goddess and the Father God into your natural sacred space. You will need a clear quartz crystal point, a bowl of the earth, an incense burner with a smudge stick, a beeswax candle and holder, a cup of well or spring water, and your Goddess and God creations. Follow these steps:

1. Call in the elements as outlined in the relationships ritual, described earlier in the chapter. After calling Spirit and Oneness, approach your altar and point your crystal first at your Goddess creation, imagining a beam of white light moving from your crystal to the Goddess. As you do so, call out:

   From the void and nothingness
   Came creation and wholeness
   She, who is the Mother of all things
   She, who is the Goddess
   Ayea! Ayea! Ayea!

2. Point your crystal toward your God creation, and once again imagine the beam of white light moving from you, through your crystal, into your symbol for the God. Sense an energy moving back and

forth between your energy and the energy emanating from your creation. The idea is to become sensitive to energy and how it affects you on many levels. This energy is masculine, whereas before it was feminine. Sense not only the energy moving from you to your creation, but also from your creation back to you. Understand that energy and its transfer is almost always a two-way street; this is not just karma, but an energetic polarity that is in everyone and everything. This polarity is what continues to divide and subdivide us into separate groups until we finally realize our common element of spirit that ties us all back together into Oneness.

As you sense the energy moving back and forth between your crystal and your God creation, call out:

From the void and nothingness
Came creation and wholeness
He, who is the Father of all things
He, who is the God
Ayea! Ayea! Ayea!

3. Again with your crystal draw a circle of light around your natural sacred space. Finish by bringing in the healing energies of the Goddess and God:

Let the wellness of Goddess and God
Be One with this space
So that whenever this circle is open
Everyone is protected from harmful energy
Ayea! Ayea! Ayea!

When you are done, thank the elemental powers and divine energies for their helpful energy. Make sure the candle and smudge stick are thoroughly extinguished before leaving the area.

Natural Magic Blessing for Wellness

Goddess and God of Wellness
Please bring your energy into my life
Let me know the ways of Oneness
So that I might live in harmony with all of creation.

Natural Magic Exercises for Wellness

The objectives of the following natural magic exercise are to make a Oneness creation that you can place on your natural magic altar and use in rituals and to merge with the energy of Oneness. Begin by taking a natural material that you can weave into a circle, such as grape vines, willow branches, or anything else that is stiff enough to stand on its own but pliable enough to weave around itself without breaking. With your weaving material in hand, find a comfortable spot in your natural sacred space. Use the material to make a circle that is 18 to 24 inches wide. Begin weaving the material around in a circle, as if you were making a wreath or basket. (It's easier to work with smaller pieces and intertwine them into the circle.)

Watch as your Oneness creation begins to take shape, becoming a weave that becomes stronger and more complex with each piece that's added to it. After you have the circle the way you want it, add any natural decorations you might like (such as pine cones, feathers, seed pods, shells, or acorns) to your Oneness creation for wellness. Make it an expression of you and your perception of the divine.

When you are done, sit back and study every facet of your creation. See how each strand of material weaves in and out of the other strands, connecting the whole of the circle. With no beginning or end, the weaves appear to move on indefinitely.

Hold your Oneness creation in your hands and move it around. Look deep into the middle of the circle and imagine a pinpoint of white light. As you become focused on the pinpoint, the white light begins expanding like a cloud of light until it fills the whole circle. Sense your energy diffusing and becoming One with the natural energy of the cosmos. Time, space, and all the polarities of energy cease to have any effect as your spirit connects to your ancestors and divine roots of creation.

When you are done doing the exercise, find an honored place on your natural magic altar for your Oneness creation, preferably in the middle, where part of it is on the left side and part of it is on the right side.

In this second natural magic exercise, you explore your perceptions of the polaritics of "well" and "not well" in terms of your physical, mental, and spiritual wellness. Begin by taking three pages from your Natural Magic Empowerment Journal and labeling the first with the heading *Physical*, the second *Mental*, and the third *Spiritual*. Underneath the heading on each page, write the subheading *Good Wellness Habits* on the left side of the page and *Bad Wellness Habits* on the right side so that you have two columns on each page.

Now go through your daily routines and observe what works and what doesn't work in terms of wellness. Notice not only your own habits, but also the habits of other people. Things such as eating and exercise go under Physical, things like positive thinking and compulsive behavior go under Mental, and things energetic and connecting to the divine go under Spiritual. *Good* and *bad* are often subjective terms, but that's all right in terms of this exercise because what you are gauging is your personal perception of wellness, which is also subjective. So with this in mind, write each habit under either the Good Wellness Habits or Bad Wellness Habits column. If you wonder whether a habit is good or bad because maybe it's a little of both, write it down in both columns. This also applies to the Physical, Mental, and Spiritual categories; if a habit overlaps between the physical and mental or the mental and spiritual, write it down on both pages. The important thing is to list as many things as possible so that you can begin tracking your perceptions toward wellness.

As you review your three lists, be aware of what they say about you and your perceptions of wellness. Essentially this is an exploration of your attitudes toward physical, mental, and spiritual health. Be sure to merely observe; try not to judge what you are seeing with regard to your perceptions. Your perceptions can be accentuated or changed in the future by altering your habits and patterns, but for now the concept is to see them for what they are. Also, your perceptions of wellness may not at this time mirror your actions, but that is what the later chapters in this book are all about—empowering your life and altering your habits so that they are in harmony with who you are as a person. Be sure to keep these lists in your Natural Magic Empowerment Journal handy because you will be using them again in the next chapter.

Enrichment

Part of enrichment is about having great relationships and being well, connecting it to the other two sections. Beyond that, enrichment is about abundance, something that can happen on physical, mental, and spiritual levels. It all depends on your expectations, and what you set as your goals.

Natural magic is about getting what you want, and exploring your natural self is about being a little clearer about what it is you want. Fads can be wonderful at times, but at the same time they are indicative of the way many things come and go—from hula-hoops to disco. What you are looking for are patterns in your life that are long-lasting. Knowing who you are and knowing what you want are two ways you can give longevity to your empowerment goals.

Natural Magic Affirmation for Enrichment

Write the following affirmation in your Natural Magic Empowerment Journal. Then repeat it aloud three times:

Today and every day I am exploring my natural self, which gives me a better idea of who I am and what I want in life.

Write it on a small note card and keep it with you so that you can refer to the affirmation during your day, just before you go to sleep, and when you wake up.

The more times you read and say an affirmation, the more you move it from your conscious level to your subconscious. In your subconscious the affirming message truly becomes part of you, helping you change your life in a positive way, which helps you explore your natural self.

Natural Magic Meditation for Enrichment

Get comfortable in your sweet spot in your natural sacred space, and take a deep breath. As you breathe in, fill yourself full of positive energy, and as you exhale, let all the negative energy flow out of your body. Do this a few more times, until you feel relaxed and full of positive energy.

Imagine yourself walking down a tunnel. With each breath, you move further down the tunnel toward a door at the end. As you get closer to the door, you see a pale light coming from beyond the door. Taking a deep breath, you find yourself before the door, and when you exhale the door begins to open.

As you move through the door, the morning greets you with the first rays of sunlight filtering over the shadowy outline of the distant horizon. Without hesitation, you move through the door and down a tree-lined path. Covered with leaves and other droppings from the trees, the ground is spongy and gives a spring to each of your steps as you walk. Stopping to take a deep breath, your nostrils detect a moistness that includes the pungent aroma of plants and trees. Feeling energized, you continue down the path, sensing as you go that the moistness not only lingers but seems to be increasing.

Up ahead you see a ray of sunlight sparkle and dance along the path. Stepping closer, you see a line of clear quartz crystals refracting the light like six-sided prisms. The colors of the rainbow stream and weave through the trees, arcing in every direction.

For a moment, you stand at what seems to be the energetic vortex as the light whirls around you. You sense yourself moving to another level of awareness—one where your thoughts are clear and uninhibited. A rush of energy moves up from the ground into your feet and ankles and continues up your legs into the base of your spine and eventually up all the way to your crown chakra (or energy center) at the top of your head. For a moment in eternity, you become aware that you are a conduit between the earth and sky.

Your senses seem heightened, and you hear a faint rumbling intermixed with a tinkling sound, like chimes being caressed by the wind. Moving out of the vortex of light, you move toward the source of the sound, which leads you off the beaten path to one of your own choosing. The sound grows louder and the moistness in the air intensifies. In a moment of anticipation you feel a tingling sensation that has the feeling of electricity running along your skin, making your hair stand on end.

Breaking through to a clearing in the flora, you behold the sight of a pool of water, covered with a morning mist that glows yellowish-orange from the rays of the newborn sun. Looking through the mist, you see the source of the rumbling and tinkling sounds—a waterfall that cascades down a long incline of rocks on the other side of the pool.

Without hesitation, you move into the water, which feels warm and soothing to the touch. Breathing in, you detect the faint smell of sulfur and other minerals that all seem to have a healing effect on your body. Steadily you move closer to the waterfall, and as you do so, its features become more pronounced; you can see details of the rocks illuminated in the morning light as the mist clears away.

The waterfall gushes down a rock ledge that spans 300 feet down into the pool of water. Moving under it, you feel invigorated by its effervescent vitality. The water flows down from your crown chakra, streaming like beads of light that connect into a wholeness that blends into the divine Oneness. As you spread your arms out into the water, you sense a connection to your natural self where Earth, Air, Fire, and Water connect with body, mind, and spirit to evolve into another awareness of yourself and the world around you.

This awareness includes exploring your natural self with the intention of understanding what you want in life and what you should be putting your energies toward to find the path to lead you to the life you have envisioned. When you have reached this point, you will be empowered by all that is around you. In your primordial form you are all energy, one point of light in a web that stretches out over all of Oneness.

Slowly begin to bring yourself back from the meditation by breathing deeply and sensing your awareness returning to your natural sacred space. Stroke your legs, arms, and head with your hands, bringing sensation back to them. Before getting up, review in your mind the sensations and perceptions that you had during the meditation. Write these sensations and perceptions down in your Natural Magic Empowerment Journal.

Natural Magic Ritual for Enrichment

The purpose of the following ritual is to bring the blessings and natural magic of Oneness into your magical circle. Oneness is the sacred union of the Goddess and God. You will need a clear quartz crystal point, a bowl of the earth, an incense burner with a smudge stick, a beeswax candle and holder, a cup of well or spring water, your Goddess and God creations, and your Oneness creation. Follow these steps:

1. Perform the three preliminary steps outlined in the relationships ritual for bringing in the elements, and then perform the three steps in the wellness ritual for bringing in the Goddess and God, as described earlier in this chapter.

   Pick up your Oneness creation. Hold it between your hands, shift your awareness, and say:

   Power of Oneness
   Energy in all things
   I call to your power
   To my circle please bring
   The natural magic of the sacred union
   Of Goddess and God.

2. Go to the north point of your circle, and holding your Oneness creation up in the air, say:

Ayea, Ayea, Oneness
Ayea, Ayea, Natural Magic
Ayea, Ayea, Ayea!

Go to the east, south, and west points, carrying your Oneness creation and empowering it with all of the energies from all the directions. After you are done going around the circle, return your Oneness creation to your altar and pick up your crystal.

3. With crystal in hand, move to the center of the circle, and imagine a bright golden light emanating from the crystal. From the center outward, the golden light fills the circle, and you say:

Great Powers of Oneness
Help me to decide my life
Let my natural self be free
And forever be a part of me.

When you are done, thank the elemental powers and divine energies for their helpful energy. Make sure the candle and smudge stick are thoroughly extinguished before leaving the area.

Natural Magic Blessing for Enrichment

May each of my days be blessed by the light of the God, and each of my nights be blessed by the fertility and enrichment of the Goddess. Together they are the power of Oneness, which blesses every part of my being.

Natural Magic Exercises for Enrichment

In the following natural magic exercise, your objective is to make an enrichment stone and use it to connect and merge with your natural self. Begin by selecting a stone. You may want to research the energetic properties of various stones before making your choice. Malachite is for communicating with animals; amethyst is for spiritual enrichment; and rose quartz is for emotional enrichment. No matter what stone you select, you can program it for any type of enrichment.

After selecting your stone, cleanse it by cupping it between your hands and getting a vivid impression in your mind of a clear mountain stream. Pulse your breath sharply out your nose, and as you do this, imagine the image of the clear mountain stream moving into the stone in your hands. Sense the water cleansing the stone of all previously held energy. Next, keeping the stone cupped between your hands, imagine all the things you associate with enrichment—starting with the physical, moving to the mental, and finishing with the spiritual. Pulsing your breath out through your nose, imagine all of this moving into your enrichment stone. Even after you are done programming your stone for the moment, you can always go back and add to the programming. Once you have programmed the stone, you should carry it with you as a way to add enrichment into your daily life.

Find a comfortable spot in your natural sacred space and set your enrichment stone in front of you. Using your eyes and any ultrasensory perception you might have, begin scanning every aspect of the stone—its color; whether it's clear, cracked, or has indentations; its shape, surface texture, and everything else. Now pick up the stone and hold it between your hands, sensing how it feels and what energy is emanating from it. Imagine the stone in your mind's eye, and as you do so, sense it opening up into a portal that connects you to your natural self. As you move through the portal, you feel invigorated with a wave of energy that connects you with the Mother Goddess and Earth. You feel the energy of Oneness pulsating through the stone and you feel a communion with all the animals, plants, and sacred sites that exist on this planet.

Keep your enrichment stone with you or nearby because it is something that attracts enrichment into your life as well as your connection with your natural self. Whenever you want to connect with your natural self, take the stone out and place it between your hands. Use your expectation and intention to connect to your natural self.

In this second natural magic exercise you review your life in terms of past, present, and future. Begin by taking three pages from your Natural Magic Empowerment Journal, labeling them with the heads *Past, Present,* and *Future.* Underneath each head, write the subheads *Life's Successes* and *Life's Failures.* Now imagine yourself as a very old person looking back on your experiences. On the page labeled Past, list the things you have done that you considered successful and the things you considered unsuccessful. Be honest, because after all, this is for your own evolution. On the Present page, list the things that are successful and things that are unsuccessful in your current life. If something is a little of both, list it in both columns. When you get to the Future page, project your life from the present forward through time. What would you like to happen? What would you not like to happen? Given your current situation, look back on the past and make a note of the things you are happy you did and that you want to continue. Then look back and make a note of the things you did that you didn't like and don't want to continue. Pretend you are looking back on your life as it already happened, and fill out the three lists as completely as possible.

For the moment, review the three lists as a way of exploring what is important to you and your perception of enrichment. It tells you a lot about how you view your life and how you might view it in the future. This exercise is great way for looking at your expectations in life. As before, keep the lists handy, because in the next chapter when you begin determining your natural magic empowerment goals, they will be invaluable tools.

Chapter Two

Identifying Your
Natural Magic Goals

The popular animated movie *The Emperor's New Groove* tells the story of a self-absorbed and conceited prince who is turned into a llama by his royal advisor after he fires her. Left for dead in the jungle, the prince-turned-llama is forced to deal with a hostile environment filled with predators. He also finds himself in the position of having to accept the help of a peasant to survive—a peasant the prince had scorned earlier. This situation sets up a journey or quest where the prince encounters challenges along the way as he heads back to the palace. At the end of the movie, the prince battles the wicked royal advisor and her moronic henchmen, returns to human form, and in the process, transforms into a more compassionate, less self-absorbed person.

Basically this movie is a retelling of the story *Metamorphoses*, penned by the second-century Roman author and philosopher Lucius Apulieus. The rich and superficial main character of the story is changed into a donkey, instead of a llama, by his mistress. Mirroring *The Emperor's New Groove*, he then goes on a quest where he faces the hardships and challenges of a beast of burden while witnessing almost every imaginable form of human love and betrayal. His journey ends in the temple of the Goddess Isis, where he eats a rose from the hands of a priest and regains human form. As a result of his experience, he also becomes more spiritual and compassionate, and then becomes a devotee of the Goddess and divine love.

Both stories embody the theme of the quest. The main characters are self-indulgent by nature. As a result, they are magically transformed into animals. Through their experience as animals, their overall perception of life is radically altered. They are forced to view the things around them from a much different and often more humble perspective. Although the obstacles each character faces are great, they each overcome them and complete their quest successfully by once again regaining human form. As a result of the experience, each character becomes a more empowered person.

Identifying your natural magic goals works in a similar way. Once you determine your goals, it gives you a quest or focus to move your mind and energy toward. Any time you seek to achieve something, you encounter resistance and problems along the way. The idea is to overcome these challenges to become successful. In this scenario, you identify and achieve your natural magic goals, and in the process of attaining these goals, you become a better person.

The natural magic quest brings about a personal transformation during which you begin to attain your goals both mentally and physically. As a cornerstone for personal growth, the quest also enables you to transform and evolve spiritually. This is why identifying the goals for your personal quest is such an important step in empowering your life with natural magic.

Your Personal Quest

Rather than solely being a mystical experience, in his book *The Spiritual Quest*, Robert Torrance suggests that the desire for questing is rooted in our biological, psychological, linguistic, and social character. Rooted in our human impulses is the inclination to seek out our spiritual nature as a way to become whole again.

The spiritual quest is not a single quest, but instead a series of quests that merge into a main quest. The imagery here is analogous to creeks merging into streams, which merge into rivers, which in turn merge into oceans. The progression is from being small and separate to whole and universal. This is something that seems to be coded into our genetic makeup. It is an essential ingredient in the chemistry and evolution of life.

Expressed in cross-cultural myths and legends, the quest usually involves a hero or heroine who makes a journey across an unknown landscape. It usually starts when the heroine or hero decides to (or is forced to do so due to circumstances) venture into the outside world in search of a remedy. While on the quest, the individual accomplishes great deeds and overcomes difficulties. In the end, the heroine or hero returns home successful and triumphant and consequently gains knowledge from the experience. This knowledge both about the self and the outside world enables the heroine or hero to evolve as a living, spiritual being.

One of the keys to natural magic is the quest, which brings with it a tangible and practical result and also influences and drives your spiritual evolvement. Like two extremes facing off in a duel, the quest is often about experiencing and balancing these extremes so that they work within the parameters of your life. With each quest you undertake, you move closer to Oneness and the source of creation. You also become One with your past, present, and future.

Explorers on a quest are usually after something extremely precious that often represents the goal of spiritual enlightenment or self-knowledge. Adversaries who try to prevent the explorer from completing the quest are representations of the dark side of human nature. The quest happens on several levels simultaneously, from the physical to the energetic. In this context, material goals are often symbolic of more abstract goals. An example of this is someone who wishes for wealth to be happy and feel successful. The material goal of the quest might be a new car or an opulent house, but the underlying abstract goal is to be happy and successful. Ironically, the abstract goal is the actual goal and the material goal becomes the intended means for realizing, in this case, happiness and success.

Often the problems and struggles you encounter when questing are manifestations of your negative self. This refers to the aspect of each of us that is socially conditioned to feel that somehow we are not worthy of success. Every person has moments of doubt and self-conflict, particularly when personal and professional areas of life are not going well.

When beginning your personal quest, the optimum approach is to balance your negative self with your positive self. For every problem there is a solution, and for every struggle there is a way to move beyond it, especially when the struggle is within you.

Affirmations are an important part of the empowerment process. They help you erase your negative programming and replace it with positive expectations and intentions. The best way to move beyond your negative self and the self-doubt it stirs up inside is to get up each morning, take a few deep breaths to center your mind, and then tell yourself:

I naturally deserve to be happy and successful.

The quest is an evolving and dynamic process in two ways. The first way deals with how each quest by its definition takes you from one place to another. The second way involves a more holistic perception of all of your quests in life.

As one quest ends, another begins, thus giving more continuity to the progression of events in your life. When you identify a natural magic goal and go on a quest to achieve it, the experience helps you grow and evolve. As you evolve, your perceptions, needs, and desires also change; consequently, you discover that you are constantly updating your goals. In this way, your goals continue to reflect who you are and who you are becoming.

Steps for Identifying Your Natural Magic Goals

The first thing you need to do for your personal quest is to identify your natural magic goals. This gives your quest focus and form. It gives you something to direct your energies toward and a platform for bringing natural magic into your life. Here are the steps:

1. Determine your overall or long-term natural magic empowerment goals first. These are the goals that affect the overall direction of your life. Once you have done that, identify your immediate or

short-term goals. These are the goals that are essential on an immediate, day-to-day basis.

2. Now that you have identified your long-term and immediate goals, connect the two. At this point, you know where you want to be and you know where you are. Identifying your midterm goals is a matter of determining the goals you need to achieve in order to move your life from your immediate goals toward your overall goals.

3. Your overall natural magic goals deal with the more philosophic questions of life: Who do you want to be in life? What do you want to do with your life? What is your purpose or focus in life? These are the questions whose answers influence the whole scope and direction of your life. Because of their importance, spend some time searching the innermost parts of your being for the answers to these questions. They will help you identify your overall natural magic goals, both material and abstract.

4. Once you have spent some time thinking about the overall direction of your life, take the different aspects of your life and identify the overall natural magic goals associated with it. Begin with relationships and identify what kind of relationships you would like to have in your life with respect to the long-term.

5. Take a few minutes to review the pages in your Natural Magic Empowerment Journal that deal with the second exercise under "Natural Magic Exercises for Relationships" in Chapter 1. You listed female and male qualities as well as the things that make good and bad relationships.

6. After taking some time to reflect on your overall attitudes about what you would like your relationships to be in time, start on a blank sheet of paper in your Natural Magic Empowerment Journal and write your overall natural magic goals for relationships. Include both your long-term material and abstract goals. An example of a material goal would be a relationship that lasts through a long period of time. An example of an abstract goal would be wanting both you and your partner to be fulfilled physically, mentally, and spiritually by the relationship.

7. Identify your overall wellness goals. Refer to the pages in your Natural Magic Empowerment Journal that you created in the second exercise under "Natural Magic Exercises for Wellness" in Chapter 1. In this exercise you listed your perceptions of good and bad wellness habits as they relate to your physical, mental, and spiritual self.

8. On a blank page in your Natural Magic Empowerment Journal, write your overall wellness goals, both material and abstract. An example of a material wellness goal would be to stop eating animal flesh or meat. An example of an abstract wellness goal would be to be healthy and disease free.

9. Now refer to the pages in your Natural Magic Empowerment Journal that deal with the second exercise under "Natural Magic Exercises for Enrichment" in Chapter 1 and review your perceptions of the things that work in your life and the things that don't. The fact that you divided these pages into past, present, and future makes your task of identifying your overall natural magic goals for enrichment that much easier. In the exercise, you listed what you wanted in terms of enrichment for the future.

10. After reviewing these pages, turn to a blank page in your Natural Magic Empowerment Journal and write down your overall goals for enrichment.

11. Now identify your immediate goals. In contrast to your overall goals, they are much less philosophic and much more practical. Your immediate goals deal with the day-to-day issues of your life, such as food on the table, a roof over your head, and protecting your possessions. They reflect the goals you set in the morning and achieve by evening. Your immediate goals mirror who you are at a given moment in time. Because of this, your short-term goals can continually change, depending on how you evolve as a person.

12. Begin by identifying your immediate natural magic goals for relationships. You can do this by doing an evaluation of your current relationships. Cut out the ones that don't work, and accentuate the ones that do. Determine which relationships empower you and which ones drain you. Accentuate the empowering relationships in your life, and at the same time eliminate the ones that energetically drain you.

13. Now identify your immediate natural magic goals for wellness. What do you need to do to stay alive and survive? This includes your daily diet and determining which foods agree with you and which foods don't. Never ignore what your body is telling you. It knows much more than you do. If certain foods disagree with you, stay away from them. If other foods make you feel good afterward, then they are the ones you need to predominately eat. The important thing is to not struggle with who you are. If you are allergic to something, you don't go about immersing yourself in the stuff, do you? You know that it is only going to cause you problems, and as a result, impact your health.

14. Finally, identify your immediate natural magic goals for enrichment. In a practical sense, this has to do with the ways you enrich your life mentally, physically, and spiritually. Enrichment, in order to be effective, needs to happen on all three levels. When you enrich your body, mind, and spirit, you create a balance that opens the door to further enrichment and personal enlightenment. That space where you become One with your thoughts, and through an intermingling with the energies of natural magic, you learn to manifest these thoughts in the physical world. When this happens, you invoke the incredible reservoir of natural energy that resides in everything around you.

You now have six pages in front of you; three that represent your overall goals and three that represent your immediate goals. You now need to identify which goals you need to achieve to transform your life from its present situation into what you would like it to be in the future. These are your midterm goals or transition goals.

In terms of your personal quest, your immediate goals represent where you are right now at the beginning of your quest. Your long-term, overall goals represent where you would like to be at the end of the quest. Your midterm goals represent the route you take for your personal quest to be a success.

Review your immediate and overall goals for relationships. On a blank page in your journal, write down all the things that would need to happen to move from your immediate goals to your overall goals. These would be your midterm goals.

For example, if your immediate goal is to meet someone who is compatible with you and your overall goal is a lasting relationship, your midterm goals might be to join an organization, take a class or workshop, and go to places where people who share your interests might frequent. Also, there are many books, workshops, and organizations whose intention is to put people together in long-term and fulfilling relationships.

If you have an immediate relationship, and you want it to evolve into something that more meets your needs and desires, on your midterm goals page write down things that would need to happen in order for that to become a reality in your life.

Avoid struggling with this process. You know inside yourself what you need to do to make it happen. Sometimes it's just a matter of tweaking your life, and other times it necessarily involves making major changes. If your immediate situation is in any way oppressive or a source of health problems, that's an indication that you need to make definite choices and changes in order to empower your life.

After you have mapped out your midterm goals for relationships, do the same thing for wellness and enrichment. As you move along in this process, you will notice that there are overlaps between the three areas of relationships, wellness, and enrichment. A positive or negative relationship can deeply affect both your wellness and enrichment; your health can affect your relationships and enrichment; and your level of enrichment can affect your relationships and wellness.

Most times there is overlapping of your natural magic goals for these three areas. The intention in dividing the empowerment process into three distinct areas is to make the task easier. It's similar to redecorating a house in that it's easier if you do it room by room. Keep in mind that unlike the rooms of a house, relationships, wellness, and enrichment have no physical barriers that separate them. They all connect to manifest the whole of your being.

Keeping Your Focus

Keeping your focus is important in both natural magic and the empowerment process. Focus gives direction to your energy, thoughts, actions, and dreams. It boosts your forward movement in your quest for your natural magic goals. Without focus, you can wind up lost and spinning around and around without getting anywhere. With focus, you keep moving toward your goals until you become One with them—until your empowerment goals become the reality you see when you look out your window every day.

Within natural magic, you focus, gather, and direct physical, mental, and spiritual energy toward a specific goal. The idea is to get a clear expectation of what you want firmly planted in your mind. Then you take this expectation and begin focusing a tremendous amount of attention toward all of the various aspects of it.

Once the image of your expectation becomes clearly set in your mind, you merge with that image, and then with all things. You become One with your expectation and with everything. As you do this, you will find that your awareness becomes light and buoyant. Your mind diffuses into Oneness, blending into the All, like a gaseous cloud. The clearer your expectation and the more powerful your merge, the better the results.

The empowerment process is about identifying your natural magic goals and then achieving them. Within this process, you make plans, use the best tools available to you, and follow the course you have set out for your personal quest. Focus is what keeps you on course. It moves you in the direction of your goals. This is why it is an essential part of empowerment.

When you combine natural magic with empowerment in a focused and directed way, you open the door to natural energies and powers that can help you on your upcoming quest. These natural energies are the elemental powers of Earth, Air, Fire, Water, and Spirit.

Getting in Touch with the Elements

I have a special place in nature where I like to go when I want to get in touch with the elements. It's a crystal-clear lake high in the mountains. One of the reasons it's special to me is that my family has been going there every year since I was very young. No matter how everything around me changes, I can still go back to this one place and know that everything will be basically the same.

When I visit the lake, I like to relax and become One with the natural elements. I sit down next to the lake and I sense all of the elemental powers around me. I feel the sandy ground beneath me, with its cushion of deep green, needlelike grass. I smell the pine trees and wildflowers as I look all around me. I hear the blue jays nearby and the buzzing of the bees. I gaze at the rocky mountaintops high above the lake, and I am filled with the element of Earth with all of its inviting stability and strength.

I hear the water lapping softly against the banks of the lake, and I breathe in its refreshing coolness. I wade slowly along the sandy shore of the cold mountain lake, and it wakes me up completely. As I slowly wade along, the element of Water fills me with its fluidity and flow. I lie down on my air mattress and drift along the shallows with ducks, tadpoles, and hundreds of dragonflies. The warmth of the fiery sun fills me with light and energy, a soothing contrast to the biting cold of the lake water. The sun sustains me with its warmth as I drift along.

I close my eyes and hear the wind flowing down from the mountaintops and down onto the lake. The ripples push the air mattress closer to the lake bank, and the coolness of the wind balances the sun's heat as I feel the breeze on my skin. I listen to the wind as it makes its way playfully through the pine trees surrounding me. The wind becomes stronger and fills me with the element of Air with all of its movement and flight.

As I lie there drifting against the lake bank, I consecrate my being with the elements, with the earth, water, wind, and sunlight. My spirit dances with the natural elements of Earth, Air, Fire, and Water. I know once again I am home and at peace with myself, with everything.

Calling Upon the Elemental Powers

In his book *Medicine of the Cherokee,* J. T. Garrett writes about a Nachez medicine elder who once told him, "Nature is as it always was, but we as humans try to change it to make it ours." The elder goes on to point out that nature is much older than humankind and insists that we must honor nature; in doing so, we honor the spirits of our ancestors who realized the critical balance of all things and directly relied on and communed with the elements.

In natural magic, the elements provide an excellent way of regaining the intimate connection your ancestors had with the energies of creation and Mother Nature. With this connection, you awaken the natural energy within you and around you, energy that has lain dormant. This energy is ready to be accessed and used to restore balance in your life and create a much more empowered you. Specifically, the elemental powers of Earth, Air, Fire, Water, and Spirit can be called upon to help you in your quest. The elements exist both on the energetic and physical levels. They also are represented in your body through your bones, muscles, flesh, breath, body heat, blood, digestion, sight, touch, hearing, smell, and human spirit.

You naturally resonate with the elements; they are a part of you. You are one with the elements in this respect. It also means that the elemental energies affect every aspect of your being: body, mind, and spirit.

As you continue to work with the elemental energies, you will discover that you have a natural inclination toward a particular element. This is known as your power element. You can have a strong resonance with more than one element, but usually there is one that you find yourself continually gravitating toward.

Most of us can be identified by our power element. For example, certain people have earthy qualities and seem very down to earth, while others are drawn to water and water bodies and are always in the bathtub, shower, spa, pool, river, or ocean. Some people are so intense they seem to burn with an inner fire that can consume you when you are around them, while others seem to flit from one idea to another like birds flitting about from one branch of a tree to another.

It's important to use your power element and natural elemental inclinations. At the same time, and for the best results, you need to expand your connection to include all of the elements in order to restore your inner and outer balance and empower yourself with the combined energies of natural magic.

In a basic sense, you are consecrating yourself with the elemental powers when you begin to connect with the elements themselves. Through this consecration, in essence you bless yourself with the elemental energies and create a sacred union with them. To do this, you need to become familiar with the elemental properties and merge with their innate energies. You can do this in many ways, including interacting with a physical representation of the element such as a crystal for the earth or a creek for water. When doing so, direct this elemental power toward your questing journey and attaining your natural magic empowerment goals.

Let's take a closer look at the elements and how you can get in better touch with them.

Earth

The energetic qualities of Earth include a grounded character, stability, foundation, roots, strength, and substance. The correlations with the physical body include flesh, bones, and organs. The natural representations include mountains, hills, valleys, rocks, soil, and plants.

Use a large tree, rock, crystal, flowering bush, or the ground itself as an elemental doorway into the power of Earth. Use all of your senses—including touching it with your hands—to merge with it. Sense the elemental power permeating every part of your being as you move through the doorway and become One with the element of Earth.

Air

The energetic qualities of Air include thought, creative ideas, flying, "winging it," patience, and persistence. The correlations with the physical body include your breath and the gases given off by cells. Natural representations include the wind in all its many forms, from slight breezes to full-force tornadoes and hurricanes.

Go outdoors and use the wind moving through the trees and blowing against your face as an elemental doorway into the power of Air. Take a few deep and complete breaths and sense yourself becoming the wind itself as it rolls over the earth. Become the elemental power of Air as it folds you in its wings and flows with you through the elemental doorway.

Fire

The energetic qualities of Fire include ambition, drive, assertiveness, creative power, passion, desire, and warmth. The correlations with the physical body include body heat, the light that flows through your eyes, and the spark of life. The natural representations include sunlight, heat, volcanoes, and hot springs (fire combined with water).

Use a lit candle as your doorway into the element of Fire. Slowly light a special candle. Take a few minutes to gaze at the flame. Notice how it flickers and pops. One of the best ways to do so is by placing a mirror behind the candle and looking at the image. The mirror conveniently acts as a representative doorway.

Use the bright light of the sun to connect with the powers of the Fire element. Go outdoors and lie in the warm sun for a few minutes, feeling its warmth on your skin. Open your eyes ever so slightly—don't stare directly at the sun—and enjoy the patterns the sun creates on your eyelids. Breathe in the sun's warmth and smell the scents around you made stronger by the sun's warmth.

If you prefer, you can also use a fireplace with its warmth and bright embers as an elemental doorway. Sense how it feels on your skin, how the fire sounds, how it looks, and how the burning wood smells. When you move deep within the flames and embers and through the doorway, you become One with the element of Fire.

Water

The energetic qualities of Water include fluidity, adaptability, changeability, feelings, and emotions. The correlations with the physical body include the bloodstream, the water content in our bodies, sweat, saliva, and tears. The natural representations include oceans, rivers, lakes, ponds, creeks, wells, pools, and waterfalls.

Use a pool, creek, stream, river, lake, ocean, or a waterfall with its cool spray and ionization as an elemental doorway. Sense how the water feels on your skin and how it flows through your fingers. Imagine swimming through the doorway to altered states of consciousness and becoming One with the element of Water.

Spirit

The energetic qualities of Spirit include life energy, divinity, ancestral energy, and natural energy. The correlations with the physical body include the life force that animates the body and our DNA coding. The natural representations include energy in all forms.

Sense the vitality and life force that moves through a child, puppy, kitten, or a flowering rosebud. Imagine life as a new experience where everything is wonderful and alive, and as you do so, move through the elemental doorway and become One with the element of Spirit.

Relationships

In order for relationships to be long-lasting, they generally need to evolve and change. The dimension of time brings a dynamic element to life and, in turn, relationships. In this context change becomes a constant that continually needs to be included in your natural magic goals for relationships. As you and the people around you change, your relationships also change and hopefully evolve and expand.

Change is usually the aspect of relationships that determines whether they are short-term or long-term. Many of the relationships in life come to an end when those involved no longer engage in a particular activity together; for example, working at the same job or living in the same location. What makes relationships last is when they are able to change and evolve through time. This often means putting a little extra effort into the relationship, especially when changes are occurring.

These times of change are also when you need to keep your focus on your natural magic goals for relationships. It is easy to get sidetracked by other people, events, and even your own ego. The idea is to stay on your chosen path. If there are any detours, let them be of your own design and not a wild goose chase. The following techniques will help you to keep your focus on identifying your natural magic goals and questing toward their successful fruition.

Natural Magic Affirmation for Relationships

Write the following affirmation in your Natural Magic Empowerment Journal. Then repeat it aloud three times:

I am on a quest to make the relationships in my life more fulfilling. Every day I direct positive energy toward my natural magic empowerment goals for relationships in every way.

Write the affirmation on three small note cards. Each time you write it down, say the affirmation aloud three times. Then place the cards with the affirmation on them next to your telephone, front door, and computer. Every time you relate to people in your life, remember you are on a quest to create more positive relationships.

Natural Magic Meditation for Relationships

Relax in your natural sacred space by sitting or lying down in your sweet spot and taking a deep breath. As you slowly fill your lungs, sense your being becoming lighter than air. Holding your breath for a few moments, imagine beginning to rise up and gently float upward. As you release your breath, you move slightly downward, until you are buoyed up by your next breath.

With each breath, imagine rising up through layers of light. Each time you inhale and hold your breath, you float higher within the strata of light. When you exhale, you sense the energy spreading out and balancing before you again inhale and float even higher. You feel relaxed and totally at ease.

Eventually, you reach a layer that is filled with golden light. At this juncture, energy begins fanning out horizontally. You find that you are in a place where there is a group of people; some you know and some are strangers. You sense that everyone in the scene has been anticipating your arrival. They gather around you in anticipation.

You realize that you have come to a place where there is a natural magic play happening and you are the scriptwriter. The play is entitled "The Quest for Love," and the plot is a biographical account of the relationships in your life—past, present, and future. The play deals with the love that happens on many levels in life from the ancestral and romantic to the spiritual and divine. Love is an emotion that is a motivating source in every stage of life. You move toward love, and move away from that which you don't love—balancing the natural magic polarities.

You marvel at how it is up to you to write the script, with a little divine help, as to how you want the relationships of your life to work out. The past has already happened and, as such, is a learning tool. The present is forever happening and, as such, is the current playground of your life. It is what's happening right now. The future is about what will happen given input, energy, and circumstance from both the past and present.

Your relationships are often guided by the choices you make in life. You can choose to be an introvert or an extrovert, and you change this choice depending on the circumstance of your life. You can be anyone you want to be, and accordingly you choose whom to be in relationships with. It's important to know that the choice is yours to make.

As scriptwriter, you create the dialogue and actions in the play. You create the characters and direct your relationships. In your mind, play out all the sequences that you want to happen in your quest for love and meaningful relationships. Most important, make sure this play about your relationships has a happy ending. Envision your quest being successful and your life blossoming with an abundance of love. In your mind, visualize each relationship reflecting your positive expectations.

Now imagine, as the last sequence of the play ends, a feeling of empowerment spreading through your being. Each cell in your body is activated with a feeling of love. As this happens, you sense you are gradually moving back into your physical body. Rub your hands together now and come back to the present time and place.

Wait until you are fully back into your body before trying to do anything. Remember to write down any impressions and insights you might have had in the meditation, particularly as they relate to your natural magic goals for relationships, in your Natural Magic Empowerment Journal.

Natural Magic Ritual for Relationships

The purpose of the following ritual is to focus and direct energy toward your natural magic quest or goals for relationships. You will need a clear quartz crystal point, a bowl of the earth, an incense burner with a smudge stick, a beeswax candle and holder, and a cup of well or spring water. Follow these steps:

1. Bring the elemental powers into your sacred circle by doing the three steps of the natural magic ritual for relationships in Chapter 1. As you progress through each element, envision the power of the element coming into your circle and becoming available as a tool in your upcoming quest.

2. Select three divine energies to help you in this ritual. You can call them by name if you like, such as Anu, Lugh, and Bridget (Celtic); Odin, Frigga, and Frey (Norse); Hera, Zeus, and Gaea (Greek); or Jesus, Mother Mary, and the apostle Paul (Christian). If you prefer, you can mix and match your Goddesses and Gods from different spiritual traditions, or if you don't want to use specific names you can use three words such as Goddess, God, and Oneness. Invoke their energies by asking for their presence in your circle. For example, if you are going to use divine Celtic energies, you would begin at the north point and say:

Divine energy of the Goddess Anu [name of first divine energy], come into my sacred circle.
Divine energy of the God Lugh [name of second divine energy], come into my sacred circle.
Divine energy of the Goddess Bridget [name of third divine energy], come into my sacred circle.
Ayea! Ayea! Ayea!

Repeat this invitation to the divine energies you have selected in the east point, south point, and west point of the circle.

3. Stand in the middle of the circle and begin slowly turning around in a clockwise motion. As you do, begin chanting the names of the divine energies in sequences of three, for example, *"Anu, Lugh, Bridget, Anu, Lugh, Bridget, Anu, Lugh, Bridget!"* While turning and chanting, visualize in your mind's eye your overall natural magic goals for relationships. Let the image become clear and vivid. Merge and become One with your goals.

Once the energy in your circle has heightened and the image in your mind is clear, then stop turning and extend your arms and hands up as high as you can while saying:

Ayea! Ayea! Ayea!

Sense all the divine energy that you have amassed in your circle being directed up through your torso, shoulders, arms, hands, and fingers. Direct this energy toward the image in your mind of your empowerment goals for relationships. Try to keep your focus for as long as possible. Continue holding your arms up until you start to feel your focus and level of energy begin to waver.

Afterward, thank the elemental powers and divine energies for their helpful energy. Make sure that the candle and smudge stick are thoroughly extinguished before leaving the area.

Natural Magic Blessing for Relationships

Divine powers of nature, please light the way on my quest with your infinite love. Let me know this love every moment of each day.

Natural Magic Exercises for Relationships

The objectives of the following natural magic exercise are to compile a list of the people and relationships in your life, and determine which elemental power they express and whether they are active or negative.

On a blank page in your Natural Magic Empowerment Journal, write down all the people you currently have relationships with, including lovers, family, friends, neighbors, and professional acquaintances. List anyone with whom you have regular interaction or who in some way impacts your life.

Next to each name on your list, write down what element—Earth, Air, Fire, Water, or Spirit—that person most resembles. After listing your impressions of each person's power element, review each name and list, writing down whether that person is an active or passive person or a positive or negative person.

Once you have completed the exercise, sit back and reflect on the people around you. Is there a preponderance of one element or another? Are the people in your life mostly active, mostly passive, or is there a balance? Are they positive or negative? Beware of passive, negative people; they have a tendency to sap your energy and draw you into their personal problems.

In this second natural magic exercise, you create a collage that visually expresses your perceptions of your overall natural magic goal for relationships, and give yourself a focus for directing your energy.

Begin by getting a blank sheet of pink or rose-colored construction paper. Draw, paste, or stencil pictures that to you represent your overall goals for relationships. Put as little or as many pictures as you need to create a pictorial of what's inside your mind.

Once you are finished, hang it where you will see it often. I like to hang things like this in my office where I can look at them while I'm working. It helps me remember why I'm doing what I'm doing.

Wellness

When identifying your natural magic wellness goals, remember that wellness happens on a physical, mental, and spiritual (or energetic) level. As such, disease often begins on the energetic level and from there moves to the mental and physical levels. An example is when someone is mean or nasty to you. First their attitudinal energy invades your energetic space, and then it moves to your mental space. Finally it gets tucked away somewhere in your body. If the negative experience continues over time, it begins to manifest itself as physical ailments to the body. This is why many holistic health practitioners treat illness on all three levels rather than just the physical level.

In the same way that disease begins on the energetic level, so does good health and wellness. Surround yourself with a positive environment, and when you have the misfortune of encountering a nasty person, make sure you go home afterward and cleanse yourself of the negative experience.

Doing meditations and rituals are excellent ways for relaxing and releasing any unwanted energies. Affirmations and blessings can be written on note cards and carried with you for those times when you need an energetic burst of positive light.

Natural Magic Affirmation for Wellness

Write the following affirmation in your Natural Magic Empowerment Journal. Then repeat it aloud three times:

Today I begin my quest for my overall natural magic goal for wellness. Each and every day is dedicated to my questing success.

Write this affirmation on a small note card. Place the card up somewhere in your kitchen so that you can see it and read it often as you are identifying and working your natural magic goals for wellness.

Natural Magic Meditation for Wellness

Relax in your natural sacred space by taking several deep breaths. Slowly inhale while moving your shoulders gradually upward. Hold your breath for a moment and become aware of any tension and stiffness in your shoulders and neck. Release your breath while at the same time pulsing the tension and stiffness out by dropping your shoulders back down.

Repeat the breathing exercise and sense a warm relaxing sensation that begins at your neck and shoulders and then spreads throughout your body. Continue taking deep breaths until the relaxing feeling has traveled to every part of your body.

Imagine standing on a mountaintop. Sense the elemental energy of Earth as it vibrates up from the mountain into your body. The earth energy is like a tuning fork that aligns and connects the many levels of your being. Physically your skin feels energized and your bones feel strong. Mentally you feel grounded into practical reality. Spiritually you feel connected to the Earth Mother and the energies of creation. Overall you are like a seed planted in the garden of natural magic.

From the top of the mountain, you begin to move down a mountain path. With each step you take, you descend closer to the bottom of the mountain. The sweet odor of pine and cedar begins mixing with the scent of salt water and fish. The texture of the ground begins changing from the earth and rock to a terrain that is sandy. You hear a roar that sounds either like a gust of wind, a wave of water, or a combination of the two. As you approach a series of natural earth stairs that descend to the beach, you sense a transition happening that affects all aspects of your being.

Stepping down the earthen stairs and out onto a sandy beach, you feel the wind as it caresses every inch of you. The breath of life fills your being, and your spirit rises above the landscape as if buoyed with helium. Every cell of your body releases gases, the metaphysical building blocks of universes. Physically you have to breathe in order to live. Mentally it reflects the abstract and creative aspects of both art and life. Spiritually, it becomes the voice of the divine, a spiritual compass. Go where the voice directs you. It keeps you on track during your upcoming quest for wellness.

The sun warms the center of your soul as you move farther out on the sandy beach. The fire of life is pacified within the warmth of your spirit. Like a great sunflower, you come into your florescence as the life-giving beams of sunlight revitalize every cell of your being. Your leaves stretch up as far as they can and bask in the warm sunlight. Experience the physical fire of life, the mental fire of knowledge, and the spiritual fire of creation. You feel all of this as you move through the hot sand to the water's edge.

A crashing wave spills onto your feet. Moving into the water, you're immersed in a feeling of fluidity. Like a droplet of water, you evaporate into clouds and then come raining down into creeks, rivers, and finally into oceans. Water is essential to all life. Physically it is the blood that runs through your body, mentally it is the fluidity of creative thought, and spiritually it is the ocean of Oneness where you become aware of your connection to everything.

At the completion of the cycle, you sense Earth, Air, Fire, and Water coming together as one element. Fish jump up from the sea and the birds wing down from the sky. You sense the spirit of life wherever you go. Divine and mortal spirits come together as One. You are a spirit that transcends this lifetime into many lifetimes. Like the mythical Benu and Phoenix, you live, you die, and you are reborn.

Begin bringing your awareness back to the room. Stretch your muscles and become aware of the physical sensations in various parts of your body. Wait until your awareness is back to the present time and place before writing your impressions and insights in your Natural Magic Empowerment Journal.

Natural Magic Ritual for Wellness

The purpose of the following ritual is to focus and direct the elemental energies toward the wellness aspect of your natural magic goals. You will need a clear quartz crystal point, a bowl of the earth, an incense burner with a smudge stick, a beeswax candle and holder, and a cup of well or spring water. Follow these steps:

1. Bring the elemental powers into your sacred space by doing the three steps of the natural magic ritual for relationships in Chapter 1. As you face each direction, visualize the energy of each element, and then bring it into your circle. This increases the energy of your natural magic.

2. Standing in the middle of your circle, hold your crystal and begin programming it with the images of your overall natural magic wellness goals. Be clear in your mind as to what they are, because this reflects in the energy that is imparted into the crystal. The clearer your image, the more directed your energy is toward your expectations. This stirs up the natural magic energies, gathers them together in your mind, and directs them toward your goals.

3. Holding the crystal in your right hand up over your head, imagine bringing the elemental powers into your crystal and in turn your quest for wellness by saying:

   Elemental powers of Earth, Air, Fire, Water, and Spirit
   Impart your energies into the structure of this crystal
   So that they become One with my quest for wellness
   Giving me the strength of Earth
   The persistence of Wind
   The assertiveness of Fire

The fluidity of Water
And the divine connection of Spirit.

4. In your mind's eye, visualize the energy of the elemental powers moving into the crystal and becoming One with your overall natural magic wellness goals. After doing so, begin moving the image and energy in the crystal outward until it fills you and your natural sacred space. From there move it farther outward even still, into the cosmos and Oneness.

    When you're done, thank the elemental powers and be sure your candle and smudge stick are fully extinguished. Carry the crystal with you to remind you of your wellness quest.

From now on your wellness quest will be aided by the powers of the elements. Invoke them any time you need them by repeating the ritual.

Natural Magic Blessing for Wellness

Great Goddess and God, give my quest for wellness your blessings and goodwill each and every day.

Natural Magic Exercises for Wellness

The objectives of the following natural magic exercise are to focus on an image, noticing when your mind begins to stray, and to use a cue or focal point to bring your awareness back to the image.

Begin by finding an image to focus on. Mandalas (sacred symbols used in meditation) are very good for this exercise because they have a circular design and the images are conducive to meditation. As a whole, this exercise works better when you have an image that has some type of center point from which the image spreads.

Place the image before you. Now move your focus to the center point of the image. Take a few deep breaths and turn your complete attention to the image center. Observe every detail while merging with the image.

Once you have merged with the center of the image, begin moving your awareness slowly outward. Be aware of your focus. Any time you find your mind wandering, consciously bring your awareness gently back to the center of the image. It becomes your cue or focal point for bringing your focus back into your merge with the image.

With practice you can focus longer and longer without wavering. This exercise can also make you aware of the tremendous amount of chatter that goes on in your mind on a continual basis. This chatter can constantly disrupt your focus, so the idea is to turn the topic of the chatter toward your focus. This is often much easier than turning off the mind chatter completely.

In this second natural magic exercise you create a collage of the images you have for your natural magic wellness goals, and use the collage as a focal point for staying on track in your quest for these goals. Get a blank piece of light blue construction paper and begin placing images of your overall wellness goals on it. If you draw or paint, you can create your images as you perceive them in your mind. You can also collect pictures from magazines that represent the images of your goals. Optimally, each goal should have an image attributed to it.

You can add music to your collage by playing a specific selection while you are creating it. You also play that selection whenever you work with your collage or concentrate on it. If you like, you can add the lyrics or notes of the music to the collage to reinforce the power of the music. You can add scent to your collage, too, by applying essential oils to the four corners or edges of the collage, or by anointing yourself with a scented oil such as sandalwood when you work on the collage and whenever you concentrate on it. The music and scent act as triggering devices for your body, mind, and spirit.

When you are done, you should have a collage of all your overall wellness goals. Use the collage as a way of keeping focused on your goals and quest by placing it in either your kitchen or exercise room. Look at it whenever you need to be reminded of where you want to be in terms of wellness.

Enrichment

Monetary wealth, knowledge, and spiritual enlightenment are the three aspects that create the whole of enrichment. When identifying your natural magic goals, be sure to include all three aspects.

Personal satisfaction and empowerment come when there is an integration of the physical, mental, and energetic. Body, mind, and spirit work naturally in unison. This integration is also what brings your life into balance, making it more fulfilling and harmonious.

Natural Magic Affirmation for Enrichment

Write the following affirmation in your Natural Magic Empowerment Journal. Then repeat it aloud three times:

Today and every day I am on a quest for physical, mental, and spiritual enrichment. Each day I move closer to my goals for empowerment.

Write the affirmation on a small note card. Carry the note card in your wallet or purse; take it out several times during your daily routine, and read the affirmation aloud.

Abraham Lincoln was on the right track when he knew that when you say something aloud, you use two or more senses. Besides using sight, you use speech and whatever else you wish to include. The experience begins to be multisensory. This is what connects you more deeply to Oneness.

Natural Magic Meditation for Enrichment

Relax in your natural magic sacred space by taking a few deep breaths. Slowly inhale, filling your lungs with the elemental power of Air. Hold your breath while counting to three. Sense how the energy seems to still, moving neither in nor out. Now exhale your breath with the intention of releasing any negative energy that has built up in your being. Again, breathe in, filling your being with the elemental power of Air.

Now pause for a moment, and while counting to three, sense the energy in your body neutralizing. Exhale and breathe out any negative energy. Only the positive energy remains, which revitalizes your being all the way from the cellular and physical level, through the mental levels, to the spiritual levels that connect you with the divine energies of creation.

As you take the next deep breath, it fills you full of the life force. As you still your breath to the count of three, you give it direction by using your imagination and focus. Breathing out, imagine that you are carried on the wings of the wind to a magical place where dreams come true.

You find that you have arrived at a place that is flat, without features, and colorless. It is like an untouched canvas, waiting for you to transform it into a picture of natural paradise. What that image becomes is up to you; in your hand you hold a device that can manifest elemental energy into physical matter.

You realize that you can create and make this space, this untouched canvas, anything you want. All you have to do is imagine what you want, then focus on the image while saying, "Elemental powers of Earth, Air, Fire, Water, and Spirit, I call on you to create the image in my mind and transfer it into reality." The device then creates the image into physical reality by transforming your thoughts into elemental energy.

You have access to an unlimited array of catalogues and programs to help you in deciding and creating your image of a natural paradise. Imagine using all the resources available to help you in gaining as much information as possible when conceptualizing paradise. Infuse your own creativity into the process by taking the images and making them more to your liking.

Imagine imprinting the landscape with your impressions of paradise as a place that works on every level from the physical to the divine. Be aware of what works for you in terms of your natural abilities and what you like to do. Incorporate this all into your images of your personal paradise. Focus each image into your device to manifest it into your space.

Using your imaginary device, turn the elemental energy into your personal perception of paradise. Stone sculptures, windmills, solariums, waterscapes, gardens, forests, ocean beaches, mountain valleys, and vast deserts are among the many possibilities. If you could live in a natural paradise, what would it be? Focus on the answer, and the device will make it so. The important thing is to have a clear conception of what it is that you want. The more focused your thoughts, the more focused the results. Getting what you want is often a matter of knowing exactly what it is you truly want.

Once you have a perception of what you want, you need to fine-tune your image of paradise so that it works in a real, practical sense. Imagine the device in your hand creating your optimum conception of enrichment and bringing the image into alignment so that it empowers the various aspects of your life. Sense the empty spaces around you being filled with the images focused in your mind. Color your world in a way that expresses and fulfills who you are as a creative and evolving person, in touch with the many levels of natural energy.

With the images of your personal paradise filling your mind's eye, begin moving your awareness back into your body. Take a deep breath and imagine a tingling energy that starts at the top of your head and moves down through your body till your toes tingle. Using the palms of your hands, begin massaging the various parts of your body. Become aware of the sensation of your hands on your skin. Sense the energy field within and around your body as being cleansed and revitalized.

While the images are still fresh in your mind, write down in your Natural Magic Empowerment Journal any impressions you may have had in the meditation regarding your quest for enrichment.

Natural Magic Ritual for Enrichment

The purpose of the following ritual is to bring divine energies into the physical, mental, and spiritual aspects of your goals for enrichment. You will need a clear quartz crystal point, a bowl of the earth, an incense burner with a smudge stick, a beeswax candle and holder, a cup of well or spring water, a silver coin, a book of knowledge (one that teaches you something), and your Oneness creation. Follow these steps:

1. Bring the elemental powers into your sacred space by doing the three steps of the natural magic ritual for relationships in Chapter 1. Merge with the essence of each element as you move through the directions. The stronger your merge, the more elemental power you bring into your sacred space.

2. Select a divine power to aid you in identifying and attaining your goals for physical enrichment. Standing in the middle of the circle, hold the coin in your right hand and imagine these goals as clearly as you can. Once the image is clear, then say:

   Great, gracious, and mighty [name of divine power]
   Assist me in my quest for physical enrichment
   This coin is a symbol of our alliance.

   Select a divine power to help you with your goals for mental enrichment. Hold the book of knowledge that you selected in your hands and imagine your overall goals for mental enrichment. When the image becomes clear, say:

   Great, gracious, and mighty [name of divine power]
   Assist me in my quest for knowledge and wisdom
   This book is a symbol of our connection.

   Select a divine power to help with your goals for spiritual enrichment. Hold your Oneness creation in both your hands, and imagine your goals for spiritual enrichment. When you feel comfortable with the image, say:

Great, gracious, and mighty [name of divine power]
Assist me in my quest for enlightenment
This circle is a symbol of our spiritual bond.

3. Place the coin, book, and circle on the ground before you so that they form a triangle. In your mind's eye visualize a strand of golden light connecting them all into one. While doing this, say:

Gracious and helpful elemental powers of Oneness
Please help to make the many parts of my self whole again
Please inform and enrich my body, mind, and spirit
And imbue me with your knowledge and energies.

Finish by thanking the elemental powers and divine energies for their help in your quest for enrichment. Always make sure your candle and smudge stick are completely extinguished before leaving your sacred space.

Natural Magic Blessing for Enrichment

Divine energies of Oneness, merge your power with my natural magic goals for enrichment. Let me be wealthy, wise, and enlightened.

Natural Magic Exercises for Enrichment

The objective of the following natural magic exercise is to learn to focus and merge using the senses of touch, smell, and taste. Begin by peeling an orange or other piece of fruit with a distinct aroma. With your eyes shut, take the orange into your hands and using the tips of your fingers go over and sense what each part feels like. Focus on the sensations coming into your fingers before going deeper and merging with them. Using touch and the feelings you experience, become One with the orange.

Next put the orange up to your nose and let the aroma fill your nose and lungs. Each time you inhale, notice all the subtleties and layers of the smell. With oranges there's a tangy citrus smell blended with a wonderful floral bouquet. Focus on every aspect of the aroma and then take the experience even deeper, where you merge with the smell and become One with the orange.

Last, bite into the orange and let your taste buds succumb to its juices. Experience the polarities between the acidic and sweet tastes as they tantalize your palate. With every bite, your savor the flavors that seem to intensely activate your sense of taste. Your mouth is alive with the sensation of orange. Through your taste buds, focus on this sensation, and then merge with it and become One with the orange.

In this second natural magic exercise, you create a collage of images that you aspire to in terms of your natural magic quest for enrichment, and also create a focal point to keep your focus directed toward your enrichment goals. Get a sheet of blank gold-colored construction paper. Create or collect images that represent your overall goals for enrichment. Distribute them on the construction paper so they convey your expectations in terms of your overall enrichment goals.

Afterward, hang the collage where you can frequently see it and be reminded of your quest for enrichment every day. Any time you begin having moments of doubt, refer to your enrichment collage. This will help you to regain your focus and direction as to what you want in terms of enrichment.

Chapter Three

Creating Your Natural Magic Plan

In his book *The Hitchhiker's Guide to the Galaxy*, Douglas Adams poses the question about the meaning of life, the universe, and everything else. He delegates the immense task of computing the answer to this question to the greatest of all computers. The computer replies that it will take a lot of thought. After seven million years of thought, the computer comes up with the answer: 42. The answer, of course, means nothing to the people in the story receiving it, and so they ask for clarification. The computer tells them that they have to know exactly what the question is. They repeat once again that they want to know the meaning of life, the universe, and everything.

The greatest of all computers finally admits that it's not up to the task, but suggests they try an even more advanced computer. This new computer uses organic life as part of its operational matrix, and its name is "Earth."

Admittedly, Adams pokes fun at everything, but at the same time he makes some very profound observations that also apply to natural magic:

- When asking a question, be crystal clear and as specific as possible about what you are asking. This applies to both questions and expectations.

- You don't need giant computers to determine the answer to life, the universe, and everything. The meaning of life and the secrets of the universe are at your fingertips, right here on Earth.

- Remember that the answers you receive may not make sense to you at the time you receive them; but they may make a lot of sense to you a few hours, days, weeks, months, or years later.

- Sometimes you need to use new methods and draw upon new resources to find the answers to your questions.

In natural magic, you will discover that life, the universe, and everything are part of the same whole known as Oneness. Within this Oneness is a consistency of energy, vibration, pattern, and form. This consistency is what I refer to as the *divine design*. It is reflected here on Earth as well as throughout the universe.

The Divine Design

In terms of organic computers, the human mind is one of the best computers around. It uses basic sensory devices that include sight, sound, taste, odor, and feel. Beyond that, it receives more subtle cues and information from the energy fields emanating from the body, mind, and spirit.

If the earth is a computer and the human is a computer, in a perfect world we would link the human computer with the earth computer so that they could work together harmoniously. In this way, the human would be connected to an immense natural database, a resource in which all information and experience is available at all times.

All this points to the importance of the senses. Through your senses you become aware of everything around you and navigate through the world. Each moment you sensually experience life within your body, mind, and spirit, and outside of your body, mind, and spirit. Through this experience you build a database of experiences.

Your senses are also your doorway into the secrets of the universe and the divine design. Accordingly, fine-tuning and using all of your senses—even the subtle energetic ones—becomes essential when communing with and drawing upon the natural energies of the earth.

The best way to fine-tune your senses is to go out in nature and experience it with all your being. For example, gently pick a leaf off a bay tree, crumble it up, and put your fingertips up to your nose and inhale. The aroma not only fills your sense of smell, but also engages your other senses and sends a sensation energetically throughout the body.

Another idea is to pick a ripe apple off an apple tree (or bring one with you when you go outdoors), and slowly bite into it. Taste and feel the juices as they delight every part of your being. Feel the apple in your hand, and notice how it becomes lighter as you eat it. Notice its color, texture, and shape.

When in nature, you notice not only the diversity of things, but also the similarities. Although flowers bloom in a seemingly endless variety of shapes and colors, upon closer examination you will notice that certain basic shapes and colors blend together to create the diversity. Many flowers exhibit radial symmetry and rounded petals, such as Shasta daisies, sunflowers, bachelor buttons, and chrysanthemums. Even flowers such as roses, which seem to have a different shape, exhibit radial symmetry that you can see in a close examination.

The concept that certain basic forms and patterns are universal throughout nature takes nothing away from our experience of the splendor and wonder of nature. Rather it adds to our understanding of the divine design of Oneness. What this design supposes is that there are reoccurring natural forms and patterns. The continued reoccurrence of these forms and patterns is far beyond mere chance and coincidence. These natural forms and patterns exist not only on Earth, but everywhere in the Universe and ultimately throughout Oneness.

Out of the infinite possibilities, certain numbers continually come up in day-to-day life. An example is the number 12. There are 12 months in a year, 12 inches in a foot, and 12 notes (C, C#, D, D#, E, F, F#, G, G#, A, A#, B) in Western music.

In addition, out of the infinite number of shapes, certain configurations continually prevail. For example, the circle and sphere occur everywhere in the world of flowers. This suggests that certain designs naturally occur more than others. These become archetypal in nature, and as such reoccur within the different layers of physical and energetic reality.

Put into being at the time of creation, these repetitive patterns and forms represent a link into the energies of creation that can provide insights into life, the universe, and everything. These basic designs combine to create Oneness. Interestingly, everything can be perceived in terms of these few archetypal forms and patterns. The next step is to understand them as they appear and as part of Oneness.

Universal Forms and Patterns in Nature

We began examining universal forms and patterns in nature with the section on sacred geometry in Chapter 1. In that section, the point, circle, and sphere were described as well as how these forms exists throughout Oneness and the energetic implications in terms of natural magic. I would now like to add three more forms: the circle/sphere divided in half, the triangle, and the spiral.

Circle/Sphere Divided in Half

The circle (sphere in its three-dimensional form) signifies wholeness. When you draw a line through a circle to make two halves, it then signifies the dual polarities of nature. These dual polarities include female/male, positive/negative, hot/cold, and light/dark. This duality goes all the way down to the atomic level, and is demonstrated on the energetic level in the alternating and direct current in electricity.

The half-moon mirrors the circle divided in half twice every lunar cycle, waxing and waning. In living beings, this form symbolizes the action of cells dividing, which is an essential ingredient in the evolution and maintenance of life. The division of one into two is how life arose and became the infinite variety that now exists.

Triangle

The triangle represents the trinity. Energetically it is expressed as positive/neutral/negative. Spiritually it is expressed as maid/mother/crone and son/father/wise man. The trinity represents the three phases of life.

Naturally, the shape is found in the formation of minerals, such as clear quartz, fluorite, and calcite. It can also be seen in the tops of mountains. The triangle is found in other shapes, such as the rectangle (two triangles put together), pentagrams, and the Star of David.

Metaphysically the triangle with its upward point, symbolizes the human quest to ascend to the higher spiritual realms. In the same context, it also symbolizes the divine light beginning as a point in the cosmos and spreading across the earth. The Egyptian pyramids, constructed out of series of triangles, are physical expressions of this spiritual ascension.

Spiral

The spiral is the symbol of infinity and Oneness. It represents an expanded sense of awareness. Geometrically the spiral is rounded in such a way as to be in proportion with the "golden ratio." In nature, this pattern can be seen in the construction of a nautilus shell and in the proportions of the human body. In terms of architecture, Frank Lloyd Wright used the concept when he designed the Guggenheim Museum in New York City.

Energetically, the spiral represents the eternal quest. As such, it denotes forward movement and growth that is in harmony and balance with the natural energies of the elements and polarities. In natural magic, the spiral has the effect of moving energy, also called *chi,* in a constant flow so that you continually move forward in your personal quest.

The Golden Ratio

Also known by the Greek letter *Phi,* the golden ratio can be found in the Great Pyramid at Giza in Egypt and in the works of Plato and Pythagoras. It is also found in the Greek Acropolis near Athens and in Leonardo da Vinci's masterpiece *The Last Supper.*

Phi is the relationship in nature between two parts of a whole. This relationship is expressed by the ratio of the whole to the larger portion, being the same as the ratio of the larger portion to the smaller portion. It creates a harmonic progression that moves forward in a way resembling generations of people; that is, each new generation grows larger than the previous generation by an exponential ratio that approximates Phi. Each generation is connected to the ones that preceded it. Accordingly, it can be viewed as a link to ancestral energies.

The golden ratio was first calculated by Leonardo Pisano Febonacci. He came up with a series of numbers, later known as the Febonacci series, based on the number of breeding pairs of rabbits through successive generations. The series followed this sequence of numbers—1, 1, 2, 3, 5, 8, 13, 21, 34, etc. Each new number comes from adding the previous two numbers together. What is important here is not the numbers themselves, but the ratio between each number in the series. The ratio between 3 and 5 is the same as the ratio between 5 and 8, which is the same as the ratio between 8 and 13. Mathematically taken out to three decimal points, the golden ratio, or Phi, is 1.618. Like Pi (3.14 ...), it is an irrational number that can be infinitely calculated.

As a ratio, Phi can be expressed in terms of number, length, area, volume, and on an abstract level, beauty and consciousness. This ratio naturally occurs in the relationship of each finger on the human hand, the pattern of seeds on a sunflower, and in the nautilus shell, among others. The nautilus shell exemplifies this ratio in three ways: the spiral design, the sides of a rectangle drawn around the shell have a ratio of Phi, and each successive chamber has a volume about 1.618 times larger than the one before it.

The continued reoccurrence of the golden ratio within nature once again points to the concept of a divine design. But unlike archetypal forms and patterns that deal with the individual things, the golden ratio represents a universal relationship between things and the whole. This universal relationship signifies the divine or spiritual relationship.

The Nature of Planning

You can use the concepts of the golden ratio and divine design when creating your natural magic plan for relationships, wellness, and enrichment. As goals gave focus to your quest, planning gives design and direction to it. Once you decide on a destination, you must map out how you want to get there. You can often take any one of a variety of routes to get to the same place. But ultimately, as with everything, this variety has to do in many ways with variations on a theme.

Within the divine design exists a universality of goals and plans for attaining them. These universal goals include a close and empowering family, good health, and a comfortable home. Finding someone who loves and cares for you, and whom you love and care for, is a good start to a plan for having a close family. Eating healthy foods and exercising more is a universal plan for health, and finding a livelihood that pays well, building good credit and job skills, and incurring a mortgage are all ways to help you create a comfortable home.

Creating your natural magic plan involves tailoring one of these universal plans so that it fits your situation. When doing this, you have to take into account both intrinsic and extrinsic energies. *Intrinsic energies* are the energies that come from within you. They include your abilities, tendencies, and habits. *Extrinsic energies* are the outside conditions that affect your plan. Keep in mind that the more ideal your inner (mental and spiritual) and outer (physical) environment, the greater chance you have of carrying out your plan and reaching your optimum goal.

A good plan needs to create a harmonic balance between both intrinsic and extrinsic energies. Work toward your strengths in terms of natural and learned abilities. Take into account your personal habits and tendencies. If you have a tendency to oversleep in the mornings, avoid making plans to be somewhere early every morning. If you work well with a structured schedule, work out a schedule where you work at different aspects of your plan at certain times during the day. As a rule of thumb and as a way to minimize your frustration and stress, avoid situations with which you have problems. Focus instead on the things you do well and that harmonize with your natural tendencies.

To be successful, a plan must also account for extrinsic energies. If you want to be a writer but live in an environment where there are constant interruptions, you either have to learn to write with the interruptions or find a space where you can write undisturbed. The solution to extrinsic energies in this case is done by intrinsically changing how you work, or by extrinsically changing where you work. The solution can also be a combination of the two.

For your plan to be successful, you must set realistic timeframes for things to happen. Even if you have to revise your timetable later on, initially it is important for giving forward movement to your plan. You are bringing the dimensions of time and space together when you make a plan to be in a certain spot at a particular time, such as planning to be in a comfortable home in three years.

Your Natural Magic Plan

Now that you have an overview regarding the nature of planning, you are ready to create and draw up the specific steps of your natural magic plan. Creating your natural magic plan involves mapping out how to make your goals happen. This plan has to do with the whole of your goals and where they will take you. From there, separate plans relate to the attainment of each of your individual goals.

Let's say your main goal and plan is to build your earth-friendly dream home out in nature. Your individual goals and main overall plan are:

- Finding and buying a piece of property
- Getting utilities and permits
- Building the house
- Living in your new home

The way to formulate your separate plans is by laying out the steps needed to complete each goal. In the case of finding and buying a piece of property, you might consult the want ads in the newspaper, enlist the help of a real estate broker, ask friends and family members if they know of any land available that would be suitable, and secure financing.

Begin by laying out the sheets of paper that list your natural magic goals for relationships (see Chapter 2). Your goals are already divided into long-term, midterm, and short-term categories. Your long-term goal(s) is the same as your overall goal(s). Optimally your midterm and short-term goals are a plan for reaching your long-term goal(s).

Now all you have to do is begin outlining the steps in a plan for achieving your midterm and short-term goals. Some of your midterm plans may be covered in your short-term goals. It is like a triangle/pyramid in that everything moves up to a central point, and if the goals and plans are set properly, they structurally complement each other. In terms of the golden ratio, they are in harmony and balance and move the overall pattern forward.

On a blank page in your Natural Magic Empowerment Journal, write your goal and then list the steps that you need to take to attain each of your short-term goals for relationships. If your goal is to spend more time with your primary partner, for example, list the steps that will make that happen. Next to each step, pencil in a timeframe of when you would like to implement that step of your plan. Be realistic regarding your dates of completion. Give yourself an ample amount of time, or even a little more time than you anticipated, to do the task you have outlined in your plan.

Once you have finished laying out the plans for your relationship goals, review the pages detailing your natural magic wellness goals, and begin listing the steps to the plans that will make these goals a reality. If you want to start a diet, list the things you need to do to make that happen. Include when you would like your diet to begin and approximately how many pounds or how much body fat you would like to shed. On the next blank page of your journal, write your goal and then under it list the steps of your plan for actually attaining that specific goal. Be sure to list the date that you hope to attain it by.

When you have completed writing the plans for your wellness goals, spread out the pages of your enrichment goals. On a separate sheet of paper list the goal. Under the goal, outline the steps you need to take to attain each goal. Next to each step of your natural magic plan, write in a date of expected completion. Start by listing the plans for your short-term goals, and then move onward and list the steps for making your midterm and long-term goals a reality. Keep in mind that planning is an evolving process that is continually happening as you achieve one goal and move on to the next.

Earth Energies

Now that you have outlined your natural magic plans, it is time to begin working with the earth energies to propel you on your quest toward success. When making and implementing your natural magic plans, you need to work with the energies inherent in the earth.

The practice of working with the earth's natural energies is called *geomancy*. The practice of using the golden ratio and divine design is part of geomancy. In his article, "Geomancy," included in the anthology,

The Power of Place and Human Environments, Richard Feather Anderson writes, "Geomancy may be described as an ancient, holistic, integrated system of natural science and philosophy, used to keep human activity in harmony with natural patterns: from seasonal cycles to processes that maintain the balance of nature, to the geometrical proportions found in the way all organisms grow."

Geomancy melds modern scientific knowledge about things such as archetypes and the golden ratio with the ancient spiritual practices of being in balance and harmony with the earth energies. These spiritual practices drew upon the energies inherent on and in the earth. These energies are known by a variety of names, but some of the most common are Earth spirits, elementals, nature devas, and faeries. These are energies that you can call upon to help you manifest your natural magic empowerment goals for relationships, wellness, and enrichment.

Struggling with these Earth energies, such as building your home on a faery trod or shar, can bring many problems. A faery trod is a natural pathway on which the faeries travel. A shar is an area of disharmonious energy that can cause ill health and misfortune. It's best for your health and state of mind to stay away from these areas that are sacred to the faeries. On the other hand, working in harmony with these energies can mentally, physically, and spiritually enrich your life.

A modern example of people working together with these Earth energies to achieve enrichment is found in Findhorn, Scotland, where a group of people came together to live in harmony with the land. They wanted to grow a garden, but the soil was rocky and devoid of nutrients. In addition, there wasn't sufficient sunlight to sustain a garden.

In order to overcome these obstacles, the people of Findhorn began working with the nature devas. They believed that the devas held the archetypal pattern for each plant species. Magical and amazing as it may seem, they found that these devas could actually direct energy toward bringing the plant into physical form, as well as help it to flourish.

The first deva that communicated its help to those at Findhorn was the pea deva. The deva psychically explained everything from how far apart they like to be planted to how they dislike being transplanted. Soon after, the people of Findhorn had mastered communication between humans and devas and were talking to the devas for each plant species. The Findhorn garden was so fantastically productive that one cabbage weighed 42 pounds, and one broccoli head was so large that it took six people four months to eat it!

Their experiences with the devas taught the people that Findhorn was more than the physical enrichment of growing giant vegetables, it was also a symbol of cooperation between the plant and human worlds. What the gardeners at Findhorn came to realize is that human and natural energies are part of the same life-force, working and creating together. At this point, the experience became spiritually enriching as well as mentally and physically enriching.

Working with Nature Devas and Faeries

You, too, can commune with the nature devas and faeries. As with Findhorn, the experience can enrich your body, mind, and spirit. Always remember to make every effort to create natural magic plans that are in balance and harmony with these energies, and take a few moments to pause and be thankful when they offer to help.

Appearing like a fleeting image just beyond your vision, nature devas and faeries are magical energies that are connected to nature and reside in a variety of natural settings. In essence they are the energetic embodiment of the natural magic that resides in and on the earth, waiting to be accessed. When you begin connecting with these Earth energies, you move into a new awareness, one where amazing things become possible in an environment of cooperation rather than competition.

Nature devas and faeries are basically different names for the same thing. They are magical beings who derive their sacred power directly from the earth. This power comes both in the form of elemental energies as well as the energy residing in the land from countless generations of plants, animals, and human beings living on it and giving their energy to it.

Everything is energy. This energy is dynamic and continually interacting with other energies. As with everything, energy moves in archetypal patterns defined by waves and fields. As these patterns of energy interact, they are influenced by the elements.

Harmony is the process of blending different elements together while at the same time decreasing their conflict. This elemental harmony and balance is an essential part of natural magic.

Nature devas and faeries are connected to and draw their power from one or more elemental energies. Because of this relationship, the places where you are most likely to find them is in their natural elemental setting: wooded glens, small creeks, old-growth forests, green meadows, marshlands, river valleys, caves, canyons, mesas, and other natural settings. You might find undines, merrows, and water sprites around creeks, waterfalls, and ponds. You are more likely to find dryads, elves, oakmen, and Sidhe Draoi in settings that are more heavily wooded, such as forest groves. For a complete listing of the different types of nature devas and faeries and their individual habits, please refer to my book, *Faery Magick* (see Appendix C).

The best times for encountering faery energy is early in the morning as the sun is coming up or at dusk when the sun is setting. These are the two times during the day when the division between light and dark becomes blurred and when the veil between this world and the faery world is at its thinnest.

Most important, whether you want to encounter a particular faery or you want to experience faery energy in a general sense, you need to go out in nature to the places where this energy resides. Faery energies thrive in the plants, the rocks, and the earth outdoors. This is their natural habitat and the easiest place to commune with them.

Another way of encountering faery energy is to find or create a faery ring, which acts as an energetic gateway for communing with the faeries. In nature, faery rings appear naturally where mushrooms, grasses, or rocks are organized in a circular pattern.

These natural rings are places where the faeries celebrate and dance, and also appear to humankind. Be careful not to be drawn into the circle or you might find yourself spending some time in the world of the faery. Don't enter the land of the faery, just look into the ring or doorway from time to time to better understand their powers and draw upon their positive energies. If you do find yourself in the world of the faery, don't take anything from that realm. Don't ever eat or drink anything a faery offers you. Avoid making any promises to a faery that you can't keep, and avoid lying to or cheating a faery or acting deceptive. Work with the faery energy, but don't let it overwhelm and control you. To do so often results in your poor health and misfortune. There should be a harmony and balance to the relationship. The second exercise in the following section gives you instructions for creating your own faery ring.

Relationships

Because most of us belong to a family, we want and need to be loved and cared for by that family. Unfortunately, in our imperfect world, this isn't always the case. One way you can shed a little light in your corner of the world is to choose to have a better relationship with a member of your family.

Almost everyone desires long-lasting relationships that are fulfilling on every level of human existence. This fulfillment normally involves at least a certain amount of love and caring. In loving relationships, you want to be wanted and needed just as the person you are in the relationship with wants to be wanted and needed. You want to feel as though you belong together in the relationship, whether as a part of a family, in a primary relationship, friendship, or business partnership. Although it's abstract, love and caring will always play significant roles in the development and planning of empowering relationships.

One of the reasons there is a universality of natural forms and patterns is because many forms and patterns are related to one another, just as people in a family are related to one another. In terms of science, they are classified as belonging to one genetic family or another. Again, this points to an overall divine design of Oneness.

Natural Magic Affirmation for Relationships

Say the following affirmation aloud several times before writing it in your Natural Magic Empowerment Journal:

Today and every day I follow my natural magic plan and work toward making my relationships the way I envision them.

Write the affirmation on a note card and place it in a highly visible location in your bedroom where you will often see it (for example, on your bedroom bureau mirror or on a bedside table). Each time you say the affirmation, imagine its meaning and energy flowing into your being until it is part of you.

Natural Magic Meditation for Relationships

This meditation is best done in a reclined position. Begin by inhaling deeply while very slowly counting to three. Now with your lungs full of air, still your breath and again slowly count to three. Imagine the tension in your body rising higher with each number you count. Finally, release your breath to the count of three while sensing all this tension that was rising up being swept away by your exhale. Do this breathing exercise twice more, each time pulsing the tension out of your body. Let your shoulders drop as you imagine a great weight being lifted from them.

Sense a point of energy located just below your ribcage in vertical alignment with your navel. You can find it by taking your hand and moving down the dip in the middle of your ribcage. When the bone stops, you have reached the spot. Let your awareness flow to this point. Sense the energy increasing until two streams are created; one that moves in a line of light down the middle of your body, and a second stream of energy that moves in a line of light upward and downward out of the point of energy. The streams of energy overlap at your midline.

Now in your mind's eye, imagine the light moving up and down your body bringing your being into balance and alignment. Imagine the light moving in and out of your body connecting you with your surroundings, with the earth and sky.

With your intention, connect with a line of light the part of the first line that is at your feet with the part of the second line that extends upward. Next connect with a line of light the part of the first line that is at your head with the part of the second line that extends upward. You now have two triangles of light that when put together, make one large triangle of light. Like a beacon shining down from the sky, bask in its glow that makes you feel warm and tingly all over.

Again in your mind's eye, extend a line of light from the part of the first line at your feet to the part of the second line that moves downward. Afterward, extend a line of light from the part of the first line at your head to the part of the second line moving downward. Now you have two triangles of light below you as well as above you. And again these two triangles below fit together in one large triangle, meaning you have a large triangle above and a large triangle below. When you put the two large triangles together, they form a large diamond of light, beaming down from the sky and up from the earth. All this light intersects and connects into the original point of energy.

Next, imagine four spirals of golden light sprouting up and filling each of the smaller triangles of light. The triangles begin expanding and moving ever outward into infinity. Again you feel a sensation of being warm all over. This is an indication that you have connected and are ready to tap into Oneness.

Tapped into the cosmic database and source of all creation, you can now access any information that you need to construct your natural magic plan for relationships. You have an open channel to every archetype; you can create anything you want using the divine designs included in each. Add the elements, and the divine plans spring to life, creating worlds from their energies. Now choose a plan that helps you create and manifest your natural magic goal.

Sense the golden spirals of light energizing every part of your being, from your physical body and individual cells to your mental activity and spiritual self. Sense an awareness that moves from the whole to the individual parts and back again.

Begin following the spirals back into the whole of your physical body. From there, move into the various parts of your body by becoming consciously aware of your feet, legs, stomach, arms, hands, neck, and head. Slowly rub your hands together until you feel as though you have returned to your body.

Before doing anything else and while the impressions of the meditation are fresh in your mind, write your meditation experience down and any information you gathered while meditating that will help you in your plan in your Natural Magic Empowerment Journal. Be sure to integrate the helpful aspects of the mediation in your natural magic plan for more positive relationships.

Natural Magic Ritual for Relationships

The purpose of the following ritual is to bring the elemental polarities together as One and to direct this energy toward your natural magic plan for relationships. You will need a clear quartz crystal point, a bowl of the earth, an incense burner with a smudge stick, a beeswax candle and holder, and a cup of well or spring water. Follow these steps:

1. Bring the elemental powers into your sacred circle by doing the three steps of the natural magic ritual for relationships in Chapter 1. Invite the divine energies of Oneness in by standing in the middle of the circle and saying:

   Divine energies of Oneness
   Please bless my sacred space with your presence.

2. Move to the north point of your circle, and take your crystal from the altar. Facing inward an ample distance from your altar, draw an energetic line of light from the north point to the south point of your circle. Following this line of light, walk to the south point while saying:

Powers of Earth and Fire
Join together in divine union
From two become One.

Move to the east point of your circle, and draw an energetic line of light with your crystal that extends in a straight line to the west point. Following this line of light, walk to the west point while saying:

Powers of Air and Water
Join together in divine union
From two become One.

3. Stand in the middle of the circle and hold your crystal upward, over your head. Bring the elements together as One by saying:

Earth and Fire
Air and Water
Spiral together
And become One.

Holding the crystal with both of your hands, place it at the spot on your body described in the meditation, moving down the middle of your ribcage to where the bone stops. In your mind, envision one of your natural magic goals and plans for relationships. Be clear with the image as you say:

Elemental powers that be
Combine with the divine design
So that my plan and pattern
Will help me attain my goal.

Merge and move the elemental energy toward your natural magic goals and plans for relationships. Do this for several minutes.

When you are done, thank the elements and divine energies of Oneness for their help and make sure that the smudge stick and candle are fully extinguished.

Natural Magic Blessing for Relationships

Divine energies of Oneness, please help me to discover the way to long-lasting, close, and caring relationships. Thank you for your help and blessings.

Natural Magic Exercises for Relationships

In the following natural magic exercise you plant a Peace Rose as a way to connect with the rose devas and to honor your natural magic plans for relationships. Begin by obtaining a Peace Rose that you can plant in either the ground or a pot. You can purchase bare-root rose bushes that are dormant in the winter months, or you can purchase a rose bush that is more developed in the spring and summer months. I have chosen the Peace Rose because it represents goodwill and compassion, but if you prefer, you can select another type of special rose that represents love and goodwill to you.

The unique story of the Peace Rose began in 1935 when a French hybridizer named Francis Meilland took 50 of his prized seedlings and propagated them. By 1939, he came up with one particular variety that had extraordinarily beautiful flowers. As World War II was rapidly consuming France, he opted to distribute three bud eyes to different parts of the world. The one sent to the United States was on the last plane out before the Nazi occupation began. After the war, the United Nations chose this flower and named it the Peace Rose, to symbolize the goodwill and peace they were celebrating.

After obtaining your Peace Rose, sit down with it in your natural sacred space. Merge with it as a means of contacting the rose deva. The best way to do this is to become aware of every aspect and detail of the rose. Smell its fragrance. Touch it, and feel its velvety softness. Gaze at its outward beauty.

Once you have sat and merged with the rose for a while, ask for the rose deva's help in choosing what is best for your Peace Rose in terms of location, soil, sunlight, and care. Afterward plant your Peace Rose, and ask for the blessings of the rose deva and Oneness. Check in and commune with the rose deva from time to time for any further instructions. As with any long-term relationship, your Peace Rose will thrive with the proper care and attention.

In this second natural magic exercise, you create a faery ring as a way of bringing the energy of the faery into your natural sacred space. Begin by drawing a circle on the ground where you want your faery ring to be. Next, select enough stones to line the parameter of your circle. The stones should touch one another and outline the entire circle.

After you set the stones in the ring, connect them by using the clear quartz crystal from your altar. Take the crystal and draw a clockwise (sunwise) circle of white light that connects all the stones in the ring. White is the color of the spirit and is frequently used in energetic healing. If you prefer golden or green, these colors also work well. When connecting the stones, it helps to imagine a continuous thread of white light flowing from the crystal tip.

Connecting the stones in your faery ring with light activates the faery circle, and opens the door to communicating with the faery energy. Spend time merging with this energy, and bringing it forward into your natural magic plans for more positive, caring relationships.

Wellness

Creating a harmonic balance is essential in any plan for wellness. This harmonic balance takes place with your physical body, in your mind, and within your energetic spirit. When you are balanced within yourself as well as with the outside natural energies, you create the optimum conditions for healing and good health.

Natural Magic Affirmation for Wellness

Say the following affirmation aloud, and then write it down in your Natural Magic Empowerment Journal:

Today and every day, I do everything I can to bring about my optimum state of wellness.

Write the affirmation on a small note card. Each day for nine days, go outdoors for a few minutes during the day and say this affirmation aloud. When you read aloud, you use two senses, your sight and sound. In this way, you give wings to your affirming message.

Natural Magic Meditation for Wellness

Sit or recline comfortably where you will not be disturbed. Close your eyes, and begin by taking a deep breath, holding it, and exhaling. Do this three times and pause for a few moments.

Now take another deep breath. As you do, slow your breathing, still your breath a little longer, and then exhale slower than before. Do this three times and then pause for a few moments.

Next, inhale at an even slower rate than before. Feel everything slowing down as you still your breath. Things become even slower as you exhale. Do this three times, becoming slower and slower until the last time you exhale, you feel all of your tension flowing out of you on your exhale. Now you are ready to be recharged.

In your mind's eye, imagine small golden spirals of light floating around. You pull them to you and eat them like energetic candy. They give off a burst of light that gives you the energy to move forward in your planned patterns for wellness. Sense all of the aspects of your being becoming more and more healthy by the moment. As your image becomes healthier and the energy becomes stronger and more intense, you realize that you can manifest whatever you want. It's all a matter of your intention and expectation, how well you plan, and how you direct the natural energies within you and surrounding you toward what you need and want.

Now sense a warm, golden light that surrounds you in a giant diamond configuration. Feel its golden rays imparting their natural healing benefits. The more you harmonize and balance yourself with the healing golden light, the better you feel in terms of your health and overall vitality. Imagine a light that connects all your different parts together as one whole organism. This makes you whole and healthy.

Perceive yourself as a magical, brilliant golden spider. When you are in one place and wish to be in another, you merely cast your web out to where you want to be, and then walk the web from one point to another. At this point you cast other strands out, and before long you have a golden web of light that is a natural wonder both in terms of aesthetics and practicality. With each strand you continue to draw lines of energy and traverse them as you move toward your goals for wellness.

The golden web connects and makes a whole web, and you sense your connection to the divine. This awareness opens doorways that give way to even more doorways that lead to infinity and Oneness. It is what gave birth to the circle of life and the polarities of energy. Nothing is ever destroyed; instead it changes and is reborn. This is part of the divine design.

As you travel the golden web of light in your mind's eye, imagine establishing a plan to get you where you want to go. Imagine that you are moving along the path set out in your natural plan for wellness. As you move closer, you become more harmonically balanced with the natural energies of the earth. Imagine yourself achieving your natural magic goal and plan for wellness.

Slowly begin coming back to your body. Take several deep breaths, and bring your awareness to the various parts of your physical body. Rub your hands, arms, legs, and feet to bring your awareness back to your body and the present place and time.

Before doing anything else, write down in your Natural Magic Empowerment Journal any impressions and insights you gathered during the meditation.

Natural Magic Ritual for Wellness

The purpose of the following ritual is to set up an elemental star or pentacle as a way of directing natural energies toward your natural magic goals and plans for wellness. You will need a clear quartz crystal point, a bowl of the earth, an incense burner with a smudge stick, a beeswax candle and holder, and a cup of well or spring water. Follow these steps:

1. Bring the elemental powers into your sacred circle by doing the three steps of the natural magic ritual for relationships in Chapter 1. Invite the divine energies of Oneness in by standing in the middle of the circle and saying:

   Divine energies of Oneness
   Please bless my sacred space with your presence.

2. Go to the north point, and with your crystal raised upward in your receptive hand (your left hand if you are right-handed), call out:

   Energies of Earth
   You are my flesh
   You are me
   You give me the foundation to move forward.

   Go to the east point, and with your crystal in your receptive hand and raised upward, call out:

Energies of Air
You are my Spirit
You are my goals
You give me the creativity to move forward.

Go to the south point, and with your crystal in hand, call out:

Energies of Fire
You are my life
You are my plans
You give me the drive to move forward.

Go to the west point, and with your crystal in hand, call out:

Energies of Water
You are my actions
You are my quest
You give me the means to move forward.

3. Move to the center of your circle, and merge with Oneness to bring in the energies of natural magic. Hold your crystal in your power hand and point it at the north point. Get an image in your mind of who you are as a person. As you do, draw an energetic five-pointed star or pentacle of white light in the air at the north point with the tip of the crystal.

   Move the point of your crystal around the circle to the east point. Imagine your goals for wellness. As you do, draw an energetic five-pointed star of white light in the air at the east point of your circle with the crystal.

   Move the point around to the south point, and imagine your natural magic plans for wellness. Again, use the crystal tip to draw an energetic star in the air at the south point.

   Move the point of the crystal around to the west point and imagine yourself on your personal quest. Use the crystal to draw an energetic star in the air at the west point of your circle.

   Hold the crystal point up in the middle of circle. Draw an energetic star of white light below you on the ground, and above you over your head. Now take a few minutes and merge with each element of your pattern—Earth, Air, Fire, Water, and Spirit. Finish by calling out:

Energies of Oneness
Earth, Air, Fire, Water, and Spirit
You are my balance
You are my success
You give me everything I need.
Thank you, helpful powers.

When you are finished with the ritual, be sure the candle and smudge stick are fully extinguished before leaving your sacred space.

Natural Magic Blessing for Wellness

Thank you elemental energies for your help in my natural magic quest. Please continue to show me the way to optimum wellness and bless my positive efforts.

Natural Magic Exercises for Wellness

In the following natural magic exercise, you plant an herb and flower garden as a way to connect with the herb and flower devas, and to honor your natural magic plans for wellness.

Begin by selecting a location for the garden and the herbs and flowers you want to include in it (see Appendix B). The location can be a small section of land or a pot that you can move indoors to enjoy the herbs in the winter.

Before starting the planting process, sit down, recline, or stand comfortably in your natural sacred space and commune with the herb and flower devas of each of the herbs and flowers you are going to plant. Ask for help and instructions on how to make the optimum herb and flower garden. When planting, use this information to increase the productivity of your garden. Your herb garden can aid your quest for wellness as well as providing a living symbol of your plans and design for wellness.

In this second natural magic exercise you research the optimum environment for the success of your plan for wellness. On a blank page in your Natural Magic Empowerment Journal, list the type of environment that would be most conducive to you actualizing your wellness plans and goals. Because this is a dream environment, let your imagination run wild when listing the conditions that could help you in your personal quest.

Next list the ways you can make your present environment more like your dream environment. Be as specific as possible. Go down your list, one item at a time, and begin actually making as many of the changes you listed as you can in the next few days, weeks, or months. As you make these positive changes, your health will positively transform as you continue on your quest to wellness.

Enrichment

Whenever one of your natural magic plans comes to fruition, it's time to express your gratitude to the earth energies who helped you. With physical enrichment comes spiritual enrichment—as long as you are in harmonic balance with the natural energies that continually move your awareness forward.

Riches can be found in many forms and in many guises. As you progress through life, your ideas and expectations of what enrichment is will most definitely change. The usual transition is from physical to spiritual enrichment, although in the final mix, they are one and the same.

Natural Magic Affirmation for Enrichment

Say the following affirming phrase aloud several times before writing it down in your Natural Magic Empowerment Journal:

Today and every day, I move forward on my quest to work with the Earth energies and focus on my natural magic plan for enrichment success.

Write the affirmation on a note card, and post it somewhere in your work space. Keep track of your plans, crossing out each step as you take it, moving you ever closer to attaining your natural magic enrichment goals.

Natural Magic Meditation for Enrichment

Recline or sit comfortably in a place you will remain undisturbed. Take several deep breaths. Let each breath fill your lungs. Hold it for a few moments, and then exhale, releasing any stagnant energy or tension that might be weighing upon you. Each breath makes you feel lighter and more relaxed.

With your physical eyes closed, open your third eye, located in the middle of your forehead. Take one of your fingers and lightly stroke the area with small clockwise circles. Sense your third eye begin to lightly tingle. As you stop rubbing it, you become aware of it opening even wider.

Looking through your third eye, your perception of yourself and everything around you energetically expands. Your awareness includes not only the physical image, but also the subtle energy fields that emanate from everything, both animate and inanimate. Like viewing yourself through a cosmic mirror, you see the many layers of your being, from the physical to the energetic, and how these layers connect with the many layers and energies of Oneness.

As you move through the layers, you come to a giant tree whose leaves continually change shape and color. You marvel as a point of light becomes a circle, which then splits and becomes two spheres, which each split to form four flowers with round, yellow centers surrounded by eight white petals.

Although the shapes and sequence of changes seem at first infinite, upon closer observation, you begin seeing recurrent patterns. You watch the leaves, noticing that the diversity is indeed infinite while at the same time exhibiting basic patterns and a divine design.

Reaching out, you touch one of the leaves; it quickly moves through a series of transformations that look like snapshots flowing by. These snapshots shape-shift into snapshots of your life and how you want it to be. You quickly realize you can have whatever you want, and in the process the tree gives you a synopsis of how to make it happen. It's as if from the branches of the tree come the fruits of your expectations and efforts.

Understanding the universal patterns before you, you learn to navigate in terms of your environment. Some environments are more conducive to enrichment, whereas others have a tendency to suck you into their despair. The idea in natural magic is to stay harmonically balanced physically, mentally, and spiritually. You realize that as with the golden ratio, your quest for enrichment continually moves you forward.

Now take another deep breath in and out, and bring your awareness back to your physical body. Rub your hands together for a few moments and then slowly open your eyes. Focus for a few moments on the present time and place, then write in your Natural Magic Empowerment Journal any impressions and insights you experienced while meditating.

Natural Magic Ritual for Enrichment

The purpose of the following ritual is to call in the faery energies and get them to help in your natural magic plan for enrichment. You will need a clear quartz crystal point, a bowl of the earth, an incense burner with a smudge stick, a beeswax candle and holder, and a cup of well or spring water. Follow these steps:

1. Bring the elemental powers into your sacred circle by doing the three steps of the natural magic ritual for relationships in Chapter 1. Invite the divine energies of Oneness in by standing in the middle of the circle and saying:

   Divine energies of Oneness
   Please bless my sacred space with your presence.

2. Begin by going to the north point and calling in the faery energies and nature devas:

   Faeries of Earth, please give me the stability to make the best possible choices.

   Next go to the east point and call in the faery energies and nature devas:

   Faeries of Air, please give me the wings to soar high above and see the larger picture.

   Go to the south point and call in the faery energies and nature devas:

   Faeries of Fire, please give me the ambition to continue on my quest.

   Now go to the west point and call in the faery energies and nature devas:

   Faeries of Water, please give me the fluidity to meet any challenge.

3. Taking your crystal from your altar, move to the center of your circle. Use your crystal to draw an energetic line of light around the circle beginning at the north point. Then raise the crystal aloft, and say:

Natural magic energies
Please direct your helpful elemental power
Toward my goals and plans for enrichment.

Merge with the faery energy, and direct it toward your goals and plans for a few minutes.

When you are done, thank the elemental energies, Oneness, and the faery energy for their help. Make sure any burning embers from your candle and smudge are fully extinguished before you leave your sacred space.

Natural Magic Blessing for Enrichment

I welcome any help that I might receive from the energies of the earth. With their blessings, I keep moving forward and on course toward my natural magic goals for enrichment.

Natural Magic Exercises for Enrichment

In the following natural magic exercise, you plant a tree and watch it grow. The tree's lifetime parallels your own.

Begin by obtaining a small tree that you can plant. Be sure to choose a tree that will do well in your climate; a little research might be necessary (or ask your local nursery where you purchase the tree).

Once you have selected your tree, sit with it for several minutes and merge with its essence. Communicate with the tree deva to learn the needs of your tree.

Using the instructions you received from the tree deva as well as the practical directions that come with the tree, plant your tree in either the ground or pot. The tree represents and embodies your natural magic goal and plan for enrichment.

In this second natural magic exercise, you create a chain that signifies your natural magic plan for enrichment.

Begin by selecting a natural magic goal and plan for enrichment that you want to work toward. Cut a strip of colored paper for each step in the plan. Make the first strip 1 inch long, the second 2 inches long, the third 3 inches long, the forth 5 inches long, the fifth 8 inches long, the sixth 13 inches long, and so forth until you have a strip for every step of your natural magic plan for enrichment.

On each piece of paper write its corresponding step in your plan. Glue the ends of all the strips, except the smallest 1-inch strip, into separate circles. Once the glue dries, link each glued circular strip to the previous one to make a chain. Glue the 1-inch strip to the chain. When the glue dries, tack or tape the circular chain by the 1-inch strip to a spot that is highly visible in your work space where you will often see it.

The chain represents the sequence of your goals and how each step is in balanced ratio to both every other step and the whole. When balanced, energy flows uninhibited toward the achievement of archetypal form and pattern. Keep in mind that environmental factors can either impede or accentuate how this flow progresses in terms of physical reality.

Chapter Four

Choosing Empowerment Tools for Natural Magic

The naturalist John Muir spent the first part of his life working hard, but when he injured his right eye in a freak accident, it caused him to go blind for several months. At that time, he vowed that when he regained his sight, he would spend the rest of his life seeing and experiencing the wonders of nature.

After recovering his sight, Muir set out on foot into the wilderness with a sleeping bag, a supply of bread and tea, a knife, and his journal with pencils for writing about his experiences. On the front of his journal he wrote, "John Muir, Planet Earth, Universe."

In the beauty of nature he experienced a Oneness with divine creation, particularly when his travels brought him to California and the Sierra Nevada Mountains. He would walk through the mountains for long periods, entering the "eternal now," where each day never ended but blended into the next. In the Sierras he found himself dissolving and becoming One with the landscape.

To John Muir, mountains were fountains. They were natural places where divine energy spews out of the earth. In one particular experience, he climbed to the top of Cathedral Rock in Yosemite National Park in California. Atop this giant monolith, he described the sensation of doors opening and revealing the "transcendent" realm.

When describing his experiences in the Sierras, Muir wrote, "The whole body seems to feel beauty when exposed to it as it feels the campfire or sunshine, entering not by the eyes alone, but equally through all one's flesh like a radiant heat, making a passionate ecstatic pleasure-glow not explainable. One's body then seems homogeneous throughout, sound as a crystal."

Muir's experience contrasted that of one of his first traveling companions, whom he referred to as his Sancho Panza. While Muir was having a profound sensual and spiritual experience walking through nature, his companion thought the wonders of Yosemite to be nothing more than a bunch of rocks and trees and nothing to get excited about. This shows that it's possible for one person to have a divine experience, while another person basically has no experience whatsoever.

Having a spiritual experience in nature and being aware of the divinity all around you is an essential aspect to both natural magic and life. Nature needs to be experienced with all of your senses and with every part of your being—physically, mentally, and spiritually.

Connecting and becoming One with the energy of the earth is your main tool for natural magic. As with John Muir, you can live off the land for physical sustenance, learn about all the plants and animals in your world for mental sustenance, and experience the wonders of nature for spiritual sustenance. In this sense every aspect of nature is a tool for personal growth, waiting to help you move along on your natural magic quest.

Natural Magic Tools

Within the realm of this connecting and becoming One with the energy of the earth, many techniques and tools exist for accessing and utilizing natural energy. Obviously, going outside and experiencing nature is the first step in this process. Beyond that there are many natural magic tools you can use to enhance your relationships, wellness, and enrichment.

Your natural magic tools work on two basic levels. First, they connect you with the energies of divine creation and natural magic. Second, they help you to move your natural magic plans forward toward their eventual completion. In this sense, tools are not necessarily physical objects, but more of an extension of yourself. As such, they are portals into worlds, dimensions, and states of awareness that transcend your present boundaries.

In a practical sense, tools help you to get where you are going and can come in many forms. In a universal sense of the word, everything is a tool on some level, as long as you know how to use it. Within natural magic this means that everything in nature is a tool both connecting you to divine creation and to moving your natural magic quest forward to completion. Every flower you smell and tree you touch moves you closer to your quest.

In magic you use tools to connect with divine energies and invite them into your sacred space. Because tools are used to accomplish a task, they offer a means to an end—which is often not an end at all, but a transition to the next level. Within natural magic this means that you tap into and harmonize with the energies of the earth. These energies can then be utilized to improve your relationships, health, and enrichment.

One of your greatest tools is your Natural Magic Empowerment Journal. It provides you with a means to keep you focus on your goals and plans and a way of tracking your experiences and progress as you move along your chosen path.

Every technique taught in this book is a tool for helping you on your natural magic quest for your goals in life. Once you have a goal and a plan, sit down and determine the tools you will need to help you in your plan. If your enrichment goal is an Earth-friendly home, for example, after getting your plans together, you would begin gathering the building materials and tools you would need for the project.

In terms of natural magic these tools come in an infinite variety of forms. Some of these covered so far include meditations, rituals, affirmations, prayers, natural magic exercises, working with nature devas and faeries, sacred geometry, and the natural magic quest, as well as focus, power spots, elemental energies, and connecting with the divine. The idea with tools is to use the ones that work for you, and combine them in order to achieve the desired effect.

The following sections increase your knowledge and usage of natural magic tools. When working with herbs and plants, flower essences and oils, and stones, use the ones that work best for you. Also use these tools in conjunction with the other natural tools you have learned. Besides these, herbs, flower essences, and stones are often used with other tools and techniques such as homeopathy, acupuncture, bodywork, and hands-on healing.

Herbs and Plants

Herbal medicine has evolved over a period of thousands of years. Modern medicine based many of its drugs and medications on herbal cures because of the chemicals and compounds found in the herbs. Even still, pharmaceutical companies have found it hard to duplicate some of the compounds due to their natural complexity

Hippocrates said, "Let your food be your medicine and your medicine be your food." Household spices not only make foods tastes better, but also aid in dietary ways. They often promote appetite and digestion. Herbs come in many forms, but as a rule, the fresher the better. The following is a short list of household herbs and plants. Consult Appendix C for a list of books that give a more extensive explanation and listing of natural magic herbs.

- **Basil.** Good for gas and stomach pains, colds and flu, constipation, vomiting, calms headaches and menstrual cramps, attracts prosperity and fertility, a holy plant in India.

- **Chamomile flower.** Use for colic, upset stomachs, ulcers, fever, antibacterial, menstrual cramps, insomnia, oil is used on swellings, bruises, and rashes, in a bath for hemorrhoids and other inflammations, calming effect.

- **Coriander seed.** Strengthens urinary system, bladder infections, stomach problems including gas and indigestion, stimulates appetite.

- **Cranberry.** Diuretic and urinary antiseptic used for kidney and bladder infections.

- **Garlic.** Cure and prevention for intestinal worms, sore throat, prevents and treats infections, lowers blood cholesterol, normalizes blood pressure, good for liver and gall bladder, colds, flu, chronic bronchitis.

- **Ginger.** Remedy for colds, fevers, flu, calms stomach, activation and circulation of vitality, alleviates nausea.

- **Marjoram.** Painkiller, helps cure toothaches, spasm, colic, upset stomach, swollen joints and rheumatism, headaches, use in baths to clear lungs and bronchial tubes.

- **Onion.** Expectorant, helps in digestion, alleviates cold and flu symptoms, antiseptic, antispasmodic.

- **Peppermint.** Remedy for nausea, indigestion, and heartburn, diarrhea, cramps, headache, stimulates memory, aids in sleep and dreams, colds, flu, congestion, enlivens vital energy when used in a bath.

- **Rosemary.** Stimulates liver and digestion, increases circulation and slightly raises blood pressure, promotes appetite, used depression and weak nerves.

- **Thyme.** Excellent lung cleanser, natural antiseptic, expectorant for whooping cough, headaches and hangovers, stimulates circulation and digestion, psychic strength.

Flowers and Essential Oils

Flowers and essential oils are a mainstay of vibrational medicine. Based on Albert Einstein's idea that everything is matter, the form of health involves using the properties of flowers and other plants as a basis for healing the various aspects of your overall being. In particular, flower essences have been shown to help people handle the harsh impact of Western medications. Aromatherapy, bodywork, and therapeutic baths are some of the techniques that utilize essential oils.

The essences themselves are derived from the flowers, leaves, bark, and roots of plants. Each essence has unique properties that can facilitate positive change within your physical, mental, and spiritual being.

Essences can be used separately or in combinations. When applied in any way to the skin, they are diluted with a carrier or base oil, such as olive, almond, sunflower, or safflower oil. Essential oils are very concentrated and should always be diluted before using them.

When using essential oils or any natural magic tool and technique, remember that your physical body and personal needs are unique to you. What works for someone else may not work or even be healthy for your body. This is why it is important to be cautious when using an essential oil you haven't tried before. You might find you have an allergic reaction to certain oils and scents. The best thing to do is to try a little bit first on a small patch of your skin to gauge your body's reaction. Follow your intuition and what your body tells you.

For a list of essences and their effect, please consult Appendix B.

Stones

Because of color and mineral content, each stone emits a vibrant energy. When you come into contact with this energetic field, it affects your being on both a physical and energetic level. The effect can be positive and healing.

As you learned with your clear quartz crystal that you use in the rituals, stones can also be cleansed of energy and programmed or charged with energy. You should always clean any stone that you haven't used before or that someone else has handled.

When programming a stone, you should align your expectation with the natural properties of the stone. If you are the only person who comes in contact with a stone, you can build on the energy in the stone by recharging the programming each time you work with it.

For a list of stones and their energetic properties, please consult Appendix A.

Relationships

Relationship tools include books on almost every aspect of relationships, communication skills, personal habits, self-awareness of how others perceive you, aromatherapy, the sharing of food, caring, loving, giving physically, mentally, and spiritually, building cooperation rather than competition, and improving your personal appearance.

Beyond your relationships with other people, this also includes your relationship with the earth. These tools include planting a garden, walks in nature, using herbs, flower essences, crystals, and gemstones.

Anything that puts you in touch with the subtle energies of nature is a natural magic tool.

Natural Magic Affirmation for Relationships

Say the following affirmation aloud several times before writing it in your Natural Magic Empowerment Journal:

Today and every day I will expand my awareness so that I can perceive every aspect of nature as being a tool for accessing the energies of natural magic. These energies move me forward in my natural magic quest for relationships.

Write the affirmation on a small note card that you place somewhere in your bedroom where it is easily visible. Each time you say it to yourself, let its meaning come into your being until it is part of you.

Natural Magic Meditation for Relationships

Relax by getting in a comfortable position and taking a few deep breaths. Slowly inhale, filling your lungs full of air. While holding your breath for a few moments, visualize all the stress and tension in your body coming together into a swirling ball. As you exhale, sense the swirling ball being blown from your body.

Drop your shoulders and relax for a moment before taking another breath. Again imagine the tension and stress in your body forming a swirling ball and being released through your exhale. Do this breathing exercise as many times as you need to make the stress level in your body diminish to the point where you feel completely relaxed.

Imagine you are a dewdrop spread out on the broad leaf of a maple tree. A ray of sunshine streams down through you and on the other side is an array of colors that form a rainbow. The many colors form a pathway across the sky. The colors are brilliantly vivid to the extent of being florescent.

Your awareness moves like a bird, following the course of the rainbow as it moves through the heavens. Effortlessly, you soar higher and higher in pursuit of the treasure at the rainbow's end. What you find is that as one rainbow ends, another begins in such a way that there is definition between the end of one and the beginning of the next. No matter whether you look backward or forward, the stream of light and color is continuous.

Imagine that you are walking up a long winding path up the side of a mountain. At certain points in your journey, you can catch glimpses into the distance of places a long way away. They are what keep you moving onward and upward.

Along your way, you encounter a variety or flowers, herbs, and stones. You learn through experience that each flower, herb, and stone is a tool for connecting to the energies of the earth and natural magic. You discover that you can experience nature and everything around you on every level from the cellular to the divine. From the smallest particle to the largest pattern, everything is One.

Reaching the top of the mountain, your senses tingle with excitement and joy. You sense a doorway opening up before you, and walking through it, you enter the world of the divine. The places that have long seemed so far away, now appear everywhere around you. The colors, shapes, sounds, smells, and exquisite natural beauty of the earth is suddenly crystal clear from your vantage point high atop the mountain peak.

Mountains are fountains of divine energy, and you feel yourself drinking and bathing in this divinity that now surrounds you. The sensation is akin to being nurtured and held by your divine Mother and Father. You are overwhelmed with a feeling of finally being home. You are at peace with yourself and your world. You understand that everything eventually comes full circle and returns to where it began, which is not an end, but a new dawning within the timeless forms and patterns of nature.

Take a deep breath and begin to feel yourself coming back to your physical body. Tune in to each of your senses and become aware of your surroundings. Rub the various parts of your body with your hands, such as your arms, stomach, throat, and top of your head.

Spend a few moments relaxing before doing anything else. Then write down in your Natural Magic Empowerment Journal any impressions and ideas you had during the meditation.

Natural Magic Ritual for Relationships

The purpose of the following ritual is to create a magical grid that you can use to direct energy toward better relationships. You will need a clear quartz crystal point, a bowl of the earth, an incense burner with a smudge stick, a beeswax candle and holder, a cup of well or spring water, four pieces of rose quartz, and some rose oil. Follow these steps:

1. Apply the rose oil to the outside of the candle. Next, bring the elemental powers into your sacred circle by doing the three steps of the natural magic ritual for relationships in Chapter 1. Invite the divine energies of Oneness into your ritual by standing in the middle of the circle and saying:

   Divine energies of Oneness
   Please bless my sacred space with your presence.

2. Using the pulse breath technique you used to cleanse your clear quartz crystal (see Chapter 1), clear your four pieces of rose quartz of any unwanted energy.

   Program each of the pieces of rose quartz with your natural magic goal for relationships. After programming them, rub a drop of rose oil on each of them, and ask for the blessings of your favorite Goddess of love. I have used Aphrodite, but if your prefer, you can insert the name of your favorite love Goddess:

   Mighty Aphrodite, Goddess of love and relationships
   Bless these stones with your divine light.

   Go to each of the four directions, starting with the north point, and place one of the pieces of rose quartz there. Before setting the stone in place at the specific directional point, rub the stone in between your hands for a few minutes until it warms up, and then say:

   [North] Elemental powers of Earth
   Empower this stone with your energy.

   [East] Elemental powers of Air
   Empower this stone with your energy.

   [South] Elemental powers of Fire
   Empower this stone with your energy.

   [West] Elemental powers of Water
   Empower this stone with your energy.

3. Stand in the middle of the circle with your clear quartz crystal in your hand. Point the crystal at the piece of rose quartz toward the north point. Imagine a white light being generated by your clear quartz crystal and moving into the rose quartz. Begin moving the point of your crystal gradually from the stone at the north point to the stone at the east point, drawing a connecting line between the two with the white light coming out of your crystal.

Move from the stone in the east point to the one in the south point, then to the stone in the west point, and finally back to the stone in the north point. Basically you have redrawn your circle, but in this case you have connected the stones together energetically with white light into a radiant crystal grid.

Because all of the stones are programmed with your natural magic goal for relationships, the grid is well suited for promoting energy to that end. When you sit in the grid, it generates energy for love and relationships and vitalizes you with this energy. This grid provides a great place for doing your meditations and blessings for relationships.

Before leaving the area after the ritual, be sure to fully extinguish your candle and smudge stick. Thank the elements and the Goddess of love that blessed your stones.

Natural Magic Blessing for Relationships

Blessed Lady, Great Goddess of love, today and every day fill me with your divine light so that I might always know the meaning of love and the many tools available for attaining it.

Natural Magic Exercises for Relationships

In the following natural magic exercise you make a potion for love. Begin by mixing equal parts of papaya juice, peach juice, and white grape juice. Add three drops of vanilla, and then stir the potion with a wooden spoon until it is well mixed. As you do this, say:

Goddess of love
Bless and fill this potion
With your divine light
So it will help me in my quest.

As you drink the potion, imagine all of your goals and dreams coming to fruition just the way you want them to in terms of your natural magic goals and plans for relationships. Traditionally, fruit was thought to be the food of the gods and considered to have a direct link to the divine.

In the second natural magic exercise, you select a flower and learn everything you can about it. This includes its form, plant family, color, fragrance, chemical structure, medicinal uses, mythology, elemental connections, natural cycles, and environmental requirements. The idea is to see and understand every aspect of the flower.

Once you know everything about it, this flower becomes a tool for you to connect with the realm of natural magic. At a certain point, you become One with the flower. In a two-way cycle, you become the flower and it becomes you. This is a mutually cooperative flow that benefits both you and the flower.

Once you learn all about a flower, plant it in your garden and become One with it. When it completes its cycle, gather the seeds and continue the cycle of Oneness.

Wellness

The World Health Organization defines wellness as being more than the absence of illness. Being healthy involves the active state of physical, emotional, mental, and social well-being. Tools you can use to achieve that well-being include diet, exercise, harmonious personal space, leisure, relaxation, vitamins and herbs, as well as homeopathy, massage, books, workshops, counseling, meditation, ritual, affirmation, and prayer.

Natural Magic Affirmation for Wellness

Say the following affirmation aloud three times before writing it into your Natural Magic Empowerment Journal:

Today and every day I recognize the tools of natural magic are everywhere around and easily found. Each one of them helps me on my natural magic quest for wellness.

Write the affirmation on a small note card. Place the card someplace near your altar or journal so that you see it every time you are around your tools.

Natural Magic Meditation for Wellness

Relax by getting in a comfortable position and taking several deep breaths. Close your eyes and slowly inhale, filling your lungs with air. As they expand, sense a healing energy that spreads throughout your body. Next, slowly exhale while imagining all the stress and tension in your body being released with your breath. Do this breathing exercise several times until you feel your body reaching a state of relaxed vitality.

Imagine that you are under a waterfall of blue light. The light splashes down from your head to your toes, bathing you in its cool soothing blueness. You sense all the negativity in your body, mind, and spirit being washed away in the light. Focus on any part of your body that might need extra attention, and the blue light will go in and flush the negative energy out of that area. Sense every part of your being vibrating in harmony with the light.

Now take another deep breath in and out and in your mind's eye, imagine you are floating in a meadow of green light. The light caresses you from all angles, soothing you in its greenness. You feel a surge of healthy energy moving throughout your being. The places where negativity used to be are replaced by healthy and rapidly growing patterns that move you toward your natural magic goal for wellness.

The green light is like a bean stalk. Wherever a seed is planted, it sprouts up and grows into a thriving vine of your own design. You sense your body, mind, and spirit vibrating and becoming One with the green light. You are aware that anything is possible with the proper seed, soil, water, and light. From there, all it needs is your care to become whatever you want it to be.

Now take another deep breath and imagine you are ascending in a ray of golden light. The light permeates every cell of your physical being and every particle of your energetic being. All of your healthy patterns are being nourished as they bask in the light. A golden vitality spreads throughout your body, mind, and spirit, and you feel invigorated in your quest for wellness. You have a burning desire to fly higher and higher until you reach your goal of perfect health. You use every natural magic tool that you can to make this happen. As you breathe in and out, you become aware that you are golden.

You are a child of Earth, and when your body dies it will return to Earth. Your body, mind, and spirit is infinitely entwined with the body, mind, and spirit of Earth. You are reborn many times into many bodies that progress on your path to a intimate connection with the divine. Within this connection, you realize your own divine nature. The further you ascend, the more everything becomes One.

Sense your awareness slowly moving back into your body. Briskly rub the palms of your hands together for a minute, and then use your hands to rub your arms and top of your head, bringing sensation and perception back into the "now." Take a few moments to relax and enjoy the sensation of coming back into your body. Then take a few minutes to reflect upon your experiences in the meditation. Afterward, write any insights and impressions you experienced during the meditation in your Natural Magic Empowerment Journal.

Natural Magic Ritual for Wellness

The purpose of the following ritual is to create a magical healing grid that promotes wellness. You will need a clear quartz crystal point, a bowl of the earth, an incense burner with a smudge stick, a beeswax candle and holder, a cup of well or spring water, a piece of bloodstone, a piece of citrine, a piece of amethyst, and a piece of fluorite. Follow these steps:

1. Bring the elemental powers into your sacred circle by doing the three steps of the natural magic ritual for relationships in Chapter 1. Invite the divine energies of Oneness in by standing in the middle of the circle and saying:

   Divine energies of Oneness
   Please bless my sacred space with your presence.

2. Clear each of the stones of any energy that may be present in them by using the pulse breath technique you used to energetically cleanse your clear quartz crystal. After cleaning each stone, then program it.

   Beginning with the piece of bloodstone, program it with the physical aspects of your natural magic goal for wellness. Energetically, bloodstone is good for circulation, vitality, and strength.

   Program the piece of citrine with the mental aspects of your goal for wellness. Energetically, citrine is good for clarity, concentration, and memory.

   Program the amethyst with the spiritual aspects of your goal for wellness. Energetically, amethyst is good for spiritual development, divine connection, and divination.

Program the fluorite with your overall natural magic goal for wellness that balances body, mind, and spirit. Energetically, fluorite is good for harmony, balance, and altered states of awareness.

Move to the north point of your circle and place the piece of bloodstone at the point. As you do, say:

Elemental powers of Earth
Empower this stone with your energy.

Move to the east point and place the piece of citrine on it. As you do, say:

Elemental powers of Air
Empower this stone with your energy.

Move to the south point and place the piece of amethyst on it. As you do, say:

Elemental powers of Fire
Empower this stone with your energy.

Move to the west point and place the piece of fluorite on it. As you do, say:

Elemental powers of Water
Empower this stone with your energy.

3. Move to the middle of the circle. Pointing your crystal at the piece of bloodstone in the north, imagine a beam of white light coming out of your crystal and moving into the bloodstone. Next, move the white light around the circle by going from the stone in the north point to the citrine in the east, the amethyst in the south, the fluorite in the west, and finally back to the bloodstone in the north.

Further empower your natural magic healing grid by inviting in your favorite Goddess or God of healing. I use the Goddess Isis. Insert a different healing goddess if you wish:

Isis, Great Goddess of healing
Bless my healing grid with your divine energy.

Before leaving the area after the ritual, be sure to fully extinguish your candle and smudge stick. Thank the elements and the Goddess or God of healing.

Natural Magic Blessing for Wellness

Today and every day, may the divine light of Oneness bless, heal, and protect my well-being.

Natural Magic Exercises for Wellness

In the following natural magic exercise you plant an herb garden. Begin by selecting a spot for your herb garden. The size of your garden is up to you to decide. It can be an area in your yard, a window box, or a flowerpot. Be sure to use organic soil with worm castings and no chemical additives.

Select what types of herbs that you want to plant in your garden. Using the list under "Herbs and Plants" in this chapter, choose herbs that will help you attain your wellness goal. Stick with herbs and spices that you use in cooking, such as basil, coriander (cilantro), marjoram, onions (seed or bulb), and garlic (bulb). Some herbs such as rosemary can become large bushes so choose according to your space available.

Once you have chosen what seeds you want to plant, bless them before planting them. Hold a batch of seeds in your hands while saying:

Divine Mother, please bless these seeds with your natural magic.

Plant the seeds in the soil and water your herb garden. Ask the nature devas for their help in caring for your herbs. Certain plants such as basil can be regularly topped, meaning that you clip the top of the plant, which has the effect of creating more leaves because two tops grow out of where there used to be only one. Remember, using fresh herbs and spices in your foods will magically enhance them.

In this second natural magic exercise, you take a healing herbal bath. Begin by gathering a vial of lavender essential oil and your clear quartz crystal. Fill the bathtub with warm water. Add 10 to 20 drops of the essential oil in your bath water, and with your crystal in hand, enter the bath and begin letting its natural healing energy take effect.

Lie back and imagine you are an artist who does remote viewing. Before you sits a blank canvas and to your side is a palette of paint. Imagine your crystal is a brush, and you are painting a picture of who you want to be in terms of your natural magic goal for wellness. When you're done painting the picture, energetically move the impression into your crystal.

Relax and enjoy the healing effects of the lavender. It is great for relieving headaches, tension, and promoting sleep. Lavender also has a very pleasing aroma that can add to your well-being.

Enrichment

Because enrichment is such a multilayered experience, many tools are available to help you in this area. For some people such as John Muir, going out and being with the beauty of nature was a divinely enriching experience, whereas you may have more tangible goals that you seek. Select the tools that will most help you on your natural magic quest for enrichment. Blend the techniques and tools together that work for you to help improve your well-being and lifestyle.

Natural Magic Affirmation for Enrichment

Say the following affirmation aloud three times before writing it in your Natural Magic Empowerment Journal:

Today and every day I am enriched with the knowledge that everything is a tool for helping me to become more aware that Oneness is both within me and all around me.

Write the affirmation on a small note card. Carry the card with you and refer to it from time to time, particularly when you are in a natural setting.

Natural Magic Meditation for Enrichment

Assume a comfortable position, close your eyes, and begin taking a few deep breaths. As you draw in your breath, imagine you are expanding in all directions. Hold your breath and imagine you are building energy. Exhale and at the same time release the energy toward your natural magic goals for enrichment. Do this exercise three times, each time directing the energy toward your enrichment.

In your mind's eye, imagine you are a point of light that starts out as a speck that through time becomes a larger and larger beacon. As you become larger, you go from being a point to being a circle. You have moved from being a one-dimensional person to being two-dimensional. In this form, you have pattern, but no depth.

Progressing in your adventure, you become a sphere that rotates around divine light. Reflecting all colors of the rainbow, it is the light that gives all living things life. The color gives things character. The aroma gives it depth. All things connect together in the circle of life. Discovery is a matter of peeling the many layers.

You have many tools at your disposal for this purpose, but your main tool is your imagination and ever-changing perception. The layers are often like veils. When they are lifted, suddenly everything becomes apparently clear. The experience expands the energetic field around you in conjunction with your overall awareness, continually stretching out and growing toward that divine light.

Imagine becoming pure unmanifested energy and moving beyond the realm of time and space. Arced before you is a series of colored strands of light that move out into infinity. The colored strands are tools for helping you to manifest into whatever you desire to be.

After consideration, you select a strand of light that is the deep blue color of lapis lazuli. Entering into the light, there is soft, pleasing music all around you along with a sweet fragrance. Your senses come alive and you feel yourself beginning to take form. Following the light, you sense yourself slowly manifesting and shifting into the shape that you want to become. The music, the fragrance, and the colored light all affect your shape-shifting experience.

With practice you learn to use sounds, aromas, and colors to achieve whatever effect you desire. The more you follow the light, the more defined your shape becomes until you finally become the life entity you want to be, living in the place you want to live.

Even though you have taken physical form, you are still very much aware of your energetic self. The physical shell is something you have manifested, and thus is something you can change and make whatever you want it to be.

Take some time to come back into your body. Take a few deep breaths and project your awareness back into physical body. Use your fingers to massage your arms and legs. Take a few moments to relax and enjoy the moment. Before doing anything else, write down in your Natural Magic Empowerment Journal any impressions and insights you had during the meditation.

Natural Magic Ritual for Enrichment

The purpose of the following ritual is to create a talisman for enrichment. You will need a clear quartz crystal point, a bowl of the earth, an incense burner with a smudge stick, a beeswax candle and holder, a cup of well or spring water, some jasmine oil, and a piece of malachite. Follow these steps:

1. Rub several drops of jasmine oil onto the candle. Bring the elemental powers into your sacred circle by doing the three steps of the natural magic ritual for relationships in Chapter 1. Invite the divine energies of Oneness in by standing in the middle of the circle and saying:

   Divine energies of Oneness
   Please bless my sacred space with your presence.

2. Clear the piece of malachite by placing in your hand and imagining a clear mountain stream. Pulse your breath and send the image into the malachite, cleansing it of any energetic patterns.

   Cover the piece of malachite with jasmine oil, and then rub it between your hands until it gets warm. As you do this say:

   Divine energies of Oneness
   Empower this stone with enrichment.
   So be it.

3. Put the piece of malachite on your altar in front of the candle. Standing before it, merge with the candle flame and the stone while bringing in the divine energies of Oneness. Focus on the various aspects of your natural magic goals for enrichment. Visualize these aspects becoming part of the stone. The deeper you merge, then the more energy you will set into the stone.

   Sense the enrichment energy moving out all around the malachite. With your expectation, move this field of energy outward until it fills an area approximately 30 feet around the stone.

   Before leaving the area after the ritual, be sure to fully extinguish your candle and smudge stick. Thank the elements and the divine energies of Oneness.

You now have a natural magic talisman for enrichment. You can keep it on your altar, carry it with you wherever you go, or put it on your plans for a new house. The talisman is your tool for connecting and empowering your natural magic goal.

Natural Magic Blessing for Enrichment

Great Goddess, each and every day please bless me and those that I love with your divine gifts of prosperity and enrichment.

Natural Magic Exercises for Enrichment

In the following natural magic exercise you make a natural magic placket for enrichment. You will need a piece of green cloth made of a natural fabric such as cotton. The cloth should be a square that is 8 inches on all sides. You also need some red cotton thread, a sewing needle, eight bay leaves, and something that represents your natural magic goal for enrichment, such as a coin with your birth year on it, a photograph, a copy of a business contract, or a good luck charm.

Begin by folding the cloth crosswise so that it makes a triangle. Using the needle and red thread, stitch up one of the two open sides of the triangle so that only one side is open. While stitching think about the symbolism that the green cloth represents the Goddess and the red thread represents the God. They work together as One.

Place the eight bay leaves in the open end of the triangle. In numerology, 8 is the traditional number of prosperity and enrichment. Also place your symbol for your enrichment goal into the placket. Ask for the blessings of the Goddess and God by saying:

Oh Great Goddess and God
Bless this placket with your divine enrichment.

Finish by sewing up the remaining side, and completing your placket for enrichment. Keep it on your altar a minimum of three months as both a point of focus and energetic helper in your natural magic quest. When you are done with it, you can return the bay leaves to nature and reuse the bag. Keep your enrichment symbol on your altar.

In the second natural magic exercise, you make a material and tool list for each of your natural magic goals for enrichment. Begin by writing your goal down in your Natural Magic Empowerment Journal. Below it, list the steps for your plan. Then below that, list all the materials and tools that you will need to make this happen. Within tools, there are the ones that you absolutely have to have to make it happen, and the ones that are not absolutely necessary, but would make the whole experience a whole lot better. List your necessary tools first and then the tools that would better the experience and result. Then gather those tools you will need for success and use them.

Chapter Five

Aligning Yourself with Your Natural Magic Goals

Author and healer Denise Linn grew up in a small farming community. When she was 17, she was riding her motorbike down a country road with cornfields on both sides. Without warning a car swerved over and rammed the bike. As she struggled to keep from falling over, the car hit the bike again, sending her and the bike crashing to the ground. Struggling to get up, she came face to face with a strange man who was pointing a gun directly at her. She was terrified. She did not know this person. Why did he want to kill her? Without words or emotion, the man pulled the trigger, and as Linn describes it, "The deafening blast changed my life forever."

Linn was in a coma for several months but eventually recovered. In this tragic, near-death experience she came to understand that life is precious. In her book, *Sacred Space* (see Appendix C), Linn writes about how a golden light completely enveloped her. Within the light was harmonious music and divine love. All dimensional boundaries faded away, and she perceived everything as connected. Before the experience she perceived everything as separate and that when the body died, so did the person. After the experience, she perceived everything in terms of spirit and energy. Energy never dies, but rather becomes transformed, and as such is eternal.

From that day on, Linn began to notice how everything from the flowers, trees, and songs of birds were part of divine creation. Her experience led her to seek out spiritual teachers and healing techniques from a diversity of traditions that included Cherokee, Hawaiian, Aborigine, African, and Zen Buddhism. From these teachings, she began working with healing the spaces in houses, and this evolved into her practice of Interior Realignment.

The basis of Interior Realignment is that every room or space has energies that influence anyone who comes into the space. When this energy is of a healing and positive nature, you immediately sense this and the effect is beneficial. When this energy is negative in any way, you sense this negativity and the effect is unsettling.

Whether the energy of a room or house is positive or negative has a profound effect on what you do in the room. If the room is your workspace, its positive energy can help you to be successful in your endeavors, while negative energy can hinder your efforts. This points to the importance of creating a positive space in every room of your house.

In terms of natural magic, creating a positive and healing space is essential to the success of your natural magic goals. The following sections give you an overview of sacred space and how you can use these ideas and techniques to create a positive environment for your well-being. Basically by creating a positive space for living and working, you are bringing yourself in alignment with your natural magic goals.

What Factors Influence Your Sacred Space

Everything is made up of energy. One of the intrinsic characteristics of energy is that it is dynamic and always in motion. Molecules, atoms, and particles all move in universal patterns that determine their physical nature. Polarities are what keep energy in motion because it is constantly fluctuating between the poles, searching for a balance. This harmonic balance is the key when working with the many different energies in order to align your sacred space and home in positive ways.

Your sacred space and home are also made up of energy. Everything in your sacred space as well as in your home emits an energetic field. This field includes the structure itself in terms of its location and the materials that went into making it, the items that occupy the various spaces in your dwelling, and the people, animals, and spirits that come into the space. All of these energies interact to create the ambience and energetic field.

If you live in a home that is made of wood, the energy is much different—and often preferable—than if it's made of adobe, metal, or rock. The structure is often comprised of a combination of materials that influence the energy of your domicile. I once lived in an apartment that was made of concrete and steel. In one way it exuded strength and protection, but in another way, it felt confining and oppressive, like a bunker.

Location also plays an influencing role in the overall energy of your sacred space and home, particularly in terms of the elements. The land that your sacred space and home are situated on as well as the land that surrounds those spaces has an immediate effect on their energy fields. Living on what used to be a battlefield, dumping ground, or graveyard has a vastly different energy than living on what used to be a beautiful garden or a sacred gathering place for celebrations.

Besides the land, the wind, the sun, and rainfall patterns interact with the energy of the land and your dwelling and sacred space. For example, living in a place where the breeze moves through the trees and birds are always singing can be calming and stimulate your creative nature, whereas a place that is constantly besieged by a fierce wind can leave you and the surrounding landscape beaten, weathered, and worn. Living in a sunny location can be stimulating and warming to your home and spirit, whereas living in a location that is unbearably hot can leave you tired, grumpy, and miserable. Living in a place that has medium rainfall can have a calming effect on your emotions and helps everything to grow, whereas living someplace where the rain never stops and is continually pounding on everything can leave you emotionally drained and depressed.

Although some areas might be more affected than others, the energy fields emitted by the structure affects the whole energy of your home. In contrast, the energy fields of the items or things that occupy the various rooms of your home have a more immediate effect on the particular space they occupy. For example, appliances, such as a refrigerator and stove, affect the energy of the kitchen; your bed and bureau affect the energy in your bedroom; and your couch and chairs affect the energy in your living room.

The energy field of an item or thing is determined by its placement in the room, the materials from which it is made, and the energetic patterns of whoever made it and whoever has come into contact with it. Basic psychometry suggests that people's feelings, thoughts, and personality imprint their physical objects and surroundings. This imprinting is not limited to people, but also includes animals and spirits.

In terms of sacred space this means that all occupants of a home imprint the space with their energy, extending to the land and before the home was built. When someone enters your space, they leave a residue of their energy even after they have left. This is one reason why it's important to regularly cleanse your space.

Your home, like your sacred space, is a mirror of you and your energy in the same way that your physical appearance reflects who you are. Rather being separate, your home is an extension of who you are. You influence the energy of your home. In turn, its energy influences your energy.

Cleansing and Charging the Energy of Your Home

Energy is supple and can be changed and refined. Your home provides an environment that optimally should be conducive to your well-being. A positive environment can help you in the quest for your natural magic goals. Fortunately, you can improve or change the energy in your home and sacred space by using various simple, yet remarkably effective, cleansing and charging techniques.

As with crystals, homes also need to be purged of unwanted energies before they can be charged with an energetic pattern. Before beginning both the cleansing and charging processes, you need to be clear as to your expectations and intentions. In other words, specifically what kind of space are you trying to create and for what reasons?

Here are some cleansing techniques:

- **Cleaning.** Clutter reflects disorganization, and in a practical sense, makes things difficult to find when you need them. If you're always looking for things, you need to begin organizing the spaces in your home so that items are easily located. Also physically cleaning the dirt, mold, and grime from your home helps to energetically cleanse it. For instance, the windows of your home are your eyes to the outside world, and when they are dirty, your vision becomes muddied and blurred. In addition, the scent of your home needs to be pleasing for it to be a harmonious living environment.

- **Rituals.** Rituals invoke divine energy and can be used in conjunction with blessings and prayers. You can also use your ritual tools, such as candles, smudge, salt, and water in the cleansing and purification process.

- **Salt.** This is one of the oldest and best methods for cleansing your space of stagnant energy patterns. The crystals of salt absorb and neutralize any energetic patterns that they come into contact with. I recommend using sea salt and pure water mixed together and sprinkled on the four directions of your sacred space or home in a clockwise pattern. If you like, you can dip a sprig of greenery in the salt water and wave it slightly to sprinkle the mixture. Avoid sprinkling salt water on anything that it may damage such as furniture, clothing, silk flowers, or house plants.

- **Smudge.** Smudge sticks are a traditional Native American technique that utilizes the cleansing properties of certain herbs, such as cedar, sage, lavender, and sweet grass, as well as resins such as copal. When lit, the smoke cleanses the energy of a room as well as any unpleasant odors. For best results, smudge your sacred space and home every day.

- **Drums.** Another traditional Native American technique, pounding on drums enlivens the energy of a space and naturally clears out any negative energy. The rhythm, tone, and cadence of the drum create an altered state of consciousness especially conducive to ritual, mediation, and prayer.

- **Bells and tones.** This is an Eastern technique that uses sound to purify the energy in a space. In addition to regular bells, you can use Tibetan Prayer Bells, also known as Ting Shaw Bells, and Tibetan Bowls to cleanse an area. Bamboo flutes, music, and wind chimes can also be used to cleanse the space. Or you can use your voice and tone an "Om," or sing or hum a beautiful song to create positive energy in your sacred space and home.

After you have cleansed the energy of your home, you need to charge it with the energy you desire. The idea is to charge the energy so that it is conducive and in alignment with your natural magic goals.

Here are some charging techniques:

- **Sunlight and moonlight.** This offers a natural method for charging a space with energy. You can use this technique in conjunction with other techniques. Flood the area with sunlight or moonlight depending upon the desirous energy: Sunlight fills your space with active, fire energy; moonlight fills your space with receptive, water energy.

- **Rituals and prayers.** As with cleansing, this technique invokes divine energy and uses expectation and intention to charge an area with specific energy.

- **Crystals and stones.** Crystals and stones can be programmed with any energy that you can imagine. Once they are programmed, you can use them to change and charge the energy of a space.

- **Living flowers and plants.** Flowers and plants enliven the energy of a room and give it a natural and healthy feel. Remember to keep the flowers and plants in your home and sacred space healthy as they reflect the energy in the space.

- **Pictures and art objects.** Putting pictures and art objects that portray and exude happy and positive emotions in your home and sacred space are excellent ways for charging the energy.

- **Clapping.** Clapping is one the best ways of setting an energetic charge so that it stays in place. Clapping can also be used to deliberately move your state of awareness in an instant.

Relationships

Use the ideas and techniques of sacred space to align yourself and your home with your natural magic goals for relationships. Before starting the meditation, ritual, and exercises, go over your natural magic goals for relationships as you wrote them out in your Natural Magic Empowerment Journal. Having a clear understanding of what you want is essential when bringing the energy of your home and sacred space into alignment with your natural magic goals for relationships.

Natural Magic Affirmation for Relationships

Say the following affirmation aloud several times before writing it in your Natural Magic Empowerment Journal:

Today and every day, I am aligning my thoughts and actions with my true desires for creating and enjoying more positive, harmonious relationships.

Write the affirmation in large letters on a clean sheet of paper. Put the paper in a place such as a bedside table or bathroom mirror, where you will see it and can easily read it when you go to sleep and when you wake up each day.

Natural Magic Meditation for Relationships

Get comfortable and begin to relax by breathing deeply. Slowly inhale, taking in as much air as it takes to fully expand your stomach and lungs. Hold your breath for a few seconds, and imagine a nurturing light filling every aspect of your being. As you exhale, envision heavy weights of stress being lifted off your neck, shoulders, and back. Drop your shoulders, and sense your essence becoming lighter. Continue taking deep breaths in and out for a few minutes until you feel in a state of relaxed vitality and filled with light.

Imagine the light filling your body and expanding outward until it forms a ring of light rays around your body. Envision the light becoming a deep cobalt blue color with an outer ring of silver. Use your expectation and intention to spread out the energetic light field around your body. In your mind's eye, imagine the light growing from one inch, to one foot, and then to one yard around your body. Each time it expands, your energy increases and becomes more vibrant.

Next, begin focusing on your natural magic goals for relationships. Picture a couple of your primary goals and those special relationships, and how you would like them to become more positive and harmonious.

Once you have a clear image of each goal in your mind's eye, transfer the image to the energetic light field within and surrounding your body. Bring the image and light together so that they are harmonically balanced and in alignment with one another.

Sense the light becoming stronger and expanding out even further around your body. As it expands, take a ray of light and move it all the way out until it connects with one of the relationships in your natural magic goals. If the relationship is with another person, connect your energetic light field with the other person's energy. While doing this, picture in your mind the dimensions of the relationship as it currently exists. Use your expectation and light to clear away any stagnant energy that may have accumulated in the relationship.

After cleansing the relationship of all unwanted energy, begin energizing it and bringing the energy of the relationship in alignment with your natural magic goal. Change the color of the light from blue to golden, and fill the relationship with this golden light. Imagine the relationship growing healthy and strong from this energetic interaction.

When you are done cleansing and energizing this relationship, move on to the next relationship in your natural magic goals and do the same thing with it. Continue with the process until all the relationships in your natural goals for relationship have been cleansed of all inert energy. Bring each one into alignment with your goal for the relationship and charge it with the golden light.

Take a few moments to come back into your body. Wiggle your toes and fingers and stretch your arms and legs. You feel relaxed, energized, and glowing from the light. Take this feeling with you wherever you go.

Before doing anything else, write any insights and impressions that you had as a result of cleansing and charging your relationships in your Natural Magic Empowerment Journal.

Natural Magic Ritual for Relationships

The purpose of the following ritual is to cleanse and revitalize your relationship with the earth and nature. You will need a clear quartz crystal point, a bowl of the earth, a large incense burner or bowl with a smudge stick, a beeswax candle and holder, and a cup of well or spring water. Follow these steps:

1. Bring the elemental powers into your sacred circle by doing the three steps of the natural magic ritual for relationships in

Chapter 1. Afterward, invite the divine energies of Oneness in by standing in the middle of the circle and saying:

Divine energies of Oneness
Please bless my sacred space with your presence.

2. Invite an Earth Goddess or God from the spiritual pantheon of your choice. I have invoked the Celtic Goddess Anu for this purpose. Ask for help from the Goddess or God by saying:

Great Anu, Goddess of the earth
I respectfully request your presence
Bring your divine energy into this space
Give your blessings to this ritual.

3. Light your smudge stick. Beginning at the north point of your circle, walk around the parameter while holding the lit smudge stick in your hand. Catch any falling ash or sparks in the incense burner or fireproof bowl. Fan the smoke so that it spreads out over your circle. As you do so, say:

All negative energies
Be gone from this space
So that it might be cleansed
In the name of the Lady Anu.
Ayea, Ayea, Ayea!

Stand in the middle of the circle and face the north point. In your mind's eye, envision the relationship you would like to have with the earth and nature. Once the image becomes clear in your mind, say:

Oh great and powerful Anu
Energize this sacred space
With your divine energy of Earth.

Clap loudly three times while sending the image of your intended relationship with the earth and nature into your sacred space.

When you are finished, thank the Earth Goddess or God you invited into your space along with the elemental powers and Oneness. Before leaving the area, be sure that the smudge stick and candle are fully extinguished.

Natural Magic Blessing for Relationships

Great Goddess and God, please bless my honest efforts. I ask that you help me to align my life to my to my natural magic goals for relationships.

Natural Magic Exercises for Relationships

In the following natural magic exercise you redecorate your home to be more conducive to positive, harmonious relationships. Begin by lighting a smudge stick and walking with it through all the rooms of your home. Fan the smoke as you walk, making sure that the smoke gets everywhere, particularly in corners and places where energy stagnates. Use a fireproof bowl or large incense burner to catch any dropping ash from the smudge stick.

After cleansing your home with the smudge smoke, take a bell and ring it three times in each room. Literally ring in the energy you want in your relationships. As you walk through each of the rooms and ring the bell, imagine your natural magic goals for relationships and think about how they relate to each of the rooms of your home.

After energizing your space, go back through each room and redecorate them for relationships. For the living room you could drape a soft chair in red, the color of love. In the kitchen you could put pictures on your refrigerator of yourself having a positive interaction with other people, and for your bedroom you can paint it rose-colored and decorate it with statues and paintings that reflect happy relationships. There are many ways to redecorate your home for relationships. Use your intuition and be creative both in your redecorating and relationships.

In this second natural magic exercise you plant a pot of flowers outside your front door so that every time you look or walk out, you see something exquisitely beautiful and inspiring. Begin by selecting a mixture of seeds or flower plants that grow well in your climate and locale. Fill a flowerpot with the best soil you can find. Before planting, bless the soil by saying:

Great Mother of creation
Bless this Earth with your vitality
So that the plants will flower
With your divine love.

Plant everything into the soil and care for its needs. Remember, place the pot outside your front door so every time you look or walk out, you see the pot of flowers. Remember, you will need to care for the flowers at regular intervals. It's important to water the plants regularly, clip off any dead foliage, and keep your garden healthy and vibrant as a reflection of your relationship to nature, yourself, and others.

Wellness

The energy of your home has an immense effect on your wellness. The following wellness meditation, ritual, and exercises give you ideas for improving the health of your home and sacred space. Before embarking on these wellness methods, review your Natural Magic Empowerment Journal to get a clear vision as to your goals for wellness.

Natural Magic Affirmation for Wellness

Say the following affirmation aloud three times before writing it into your Natural Magic Empowerment Journal:

Each and every day, I honestly quest to bring my life into harmonious alignment with my natural magic goals for wellness.

Write the affirmation in large letters on a sheet of clean paper and post the paper where you can easily see and read it when go to sleep and when you wake up.

Natural Magic Meditation for Wellness

Before doing this meditation, take a hot bath. Sprinkle a handful of sea salt and several drops of lavender oil into the water. Lay back in the bath and sense the warm water soothing and healing you as you breathe in. Feel your muscles relax as the stress and tightness moves out of your body as you breathe out. Imagine how in the mediation, you are going to cleanse your body of any stagnant energy and fill it full of dynamic and vital energy.

After your bath, recline or sit comfortably. Take several deep, complete breaths. Each time you inhale, momentarily hold your breath, and exhale, envision the different parts of your body being cleared of any stagnant, unwanted energy. Begin with your feet, and sense them being cleansed from the soles of your feet to your toes and up to your ankles.

Take another deep and complete breath, and move your awareness up to your calves, knees, and thighs, and sense the unwanted energy and any discomfort traveling out of your legs. Next, focus on your waist, stomach, back, and chest. Breathe in energy and breathe out any unwanted, stagnant energy in these areas of your body. Continue moving your awareness into your shoulders and down your arms to your elbows and hands, breathing in energy, and breathing out any unwanted energy or discomfort.

Take another breath in and out and as you exhale, drop your shoulders and release any stress and negative energy in your shoulders and arms. Move your awareness to your neck, face, and head. Breathe in energy and breathe out any unwanted, stagnant energy. Feel the unwanted energy flowing up and out of your crown chakra at the top of your head.

Now in your mind's eye, imagine rays of golden sunlight streaming down and enveloping your entire body. Sense the light invigorating the various parts of your body. Beginning at your feet and moving upward, visualize the warm golden light filling each area with dynamic energy that revitalizes you all the way to the core of your being. Continue doing this for several minutes.

Take another deep and complete breath and imagine your body, mind, and spirit coming alive and harmonizing together as one entity. The whole of your being is filled with healing and loving light. You experience a divine glow that connects you with Goddess, God, and Oneness, and aligns you with the very core of positive, harmonious energy.

Now imagine the sacred flower of life blossoming from within you. Visualize it spreading outward until it softly fills your entire body, mind, and spirit. As the flower grows, it sets in and preserves the dynamic energetic patterns that were brought by the golden light. The flower also strengthens your connection to the divine. This enhances the positive, harmonious energies that continue to vitalize your body, mind, and spirit. You realize that you are One with all things, and all things are One with you.

Bring your focus back into your physical body. Take a deep breath in and out, and move your fingers and toes. Stretch like a cat, slowly open your eyes, and bring your awareness back to the present time and space. Sense the healing energy that vibrates throughout your body. Bask in the feeling for a few moments before arising from the meditation.

Before doing anything else, write down in your Natural Magic Empowerment Journal any impressions and insights that you had while meditating. Also write down what it felt like to be enveloped in the light and aligned with the core of positive, harmonious energy.

Natural Magic Ritual for Wellness

The purpose of the following ritual is to cleanse and revitalize your home to be more conducive to healing and wellness. This ritual is to be done in your home rather than in your natural magic sacred space. You will need a clear quartz crystal point, a bowl of the earth, a large incense burner or bowl with a smudge stick, a beeswax candle and holder, a cup of well or spring water, and a bowl of sea salt. Follow these steps:

1. Bring the elemental powers into your sacred circle by doing the three steps of the natural magic ritual for relationships in Chapter 1. Then clear your crystal and use it to draw an energetic circle of light clockwise, around the outside of your home. Invite the divine energies of Oneness in by standing in the approximate middle of your home and saying:

   Divine energies of Oneness
   Please bless my home with your presence.

2. Take the bowl of sea salt and beginning at the north point, go clockwise around all the rooms of your home and sprinkle pinches of sea salt on the floor as you go. Salt is a strong energetic purifier that has been used by most spiritual traditions for thousands of years. As you walk around the rooms of your home, cleansing with salt, proclaim:

   All evil and negativity
   Be gone now and forever more
   In the name of all that is divine
   Be gone, now and forevermore!

3. Take the cup of well water, hold it between your hands, face the north point, and bless the water by saying:

   By all that is holy, harmonious, and positive
   Bless this water now with your divine power.

   Starting at the north point of your home, walk clockwise around the rooms, and sprinkle a few droplets of water on the floor. As you do so, declare:

   Divine energies of healing and wellness
   Please fill this space with your bright blessings
   So that all those who enter become healthy and well
   Forever and a day.

Clap loudly three times to set the pattern in place. Then thank the energies of Oneness for their help in cleansing and energizing your home for wellness. Before leaving the area, be sure that the smudge stick and candle are fully extinguished.

Natural Magic Blessing for Wellness

Dear Goddess and God, please bless my body and my surroundings with your divine energy so they are in harmonious alignment with my natural magic goals for wellness.

Natural Magic Exercises for Wellness

In the following natural magic exercise you create a wellness place in your home. Begin by choosing a specific spot in your home that feels good to you; for example, a refreshing or relaxing spot where you like to sit or recline. Clear any unwanted energy from the spot by lighting your smudge stick and smudging the area. As you do, say:

All that is unwanted, negative, and unhealthy
Be gone from this place
Now and forever more.
So be it!

Sit somewhere near the center of the space and inhale deeply. As you exhale, softly tone the sound "Om." As you do this, envision your natural magic goals for wellness coming to fruition. Picture your body, mind, and spirit as you would like it to be. Spread this energy throughout the space as you continue to tone "Om."

In terms of creating a healing environment, you can paint the walls green or golden, add a stereo and play soft, healing music, hang pictures that convey a sense of wellness, and add pleasing scents to the space. You can also program crystals and stones, as well as other wellness tools to promote positive, harmonious energy in your wellness spot.

In this second natural magic exercise, you create two amulets, one to protect your home and one to protect your sacred space. Begin by selecting two stones. First create the amulet for your home, then repeat the process with the second stone while in your sacred space to create a protective amulet for your sacred space. Also be sure to place the second stone near the entrance of your sacred space.

Fill a small bowl with sea salt and place the amulet stone for your home in the bowl, covering it with the salt. You only need to do this for about a minute or so to cleanse the stone of any unwanted energies. When you are done, throw away the salt. Do not reuse it.

Next, charge the stone by setting it out in the sunlight for a few days. After that time, place the stone in your power hand (your right hand if you're right-handed and your left hand if you're left-handed). Begin rubbing the stone with your fingers and thumb. As you do this, create an image of protection in your mind's eye. Then, starting at the north point, begin walking clockwise around the rooms of your home. Walk the parameter nine times while continuing to rub the stone and imagining the powerful image of protection. If you have something or someone's energy that you particularly want to protect against, emphasize this energy being safely protected in your image.

Place the stone on a flat surface in front of you, and say the following blessing three times:

Lady of Light, bless this stone with your powers of protection so that only positive, harmonious energies may enter this place.

Clap your hands loudly three times, setting the image of protection into your amulet stone. Place it near the entrance of your home.

Enrichment

Decorating your home and workspace for enrichment is one the ways of charging the energy. When your living and working environment are conducive and in harmonious alignment with your natural magic goals for enrichment, it helps rather than hinders your efforts toward success.

The following meditation, ritual, and exercises give guidelines for cleansing and charging your home and sacred space for enrichment. Before beginning, review your natural magic goals for enrichment in your Natural Magic Empowerment Journal. Remember, this is an evolving process, so don't be afraid to adapt and change your goals to meet your present needs. Keep in mind that you need some continuity to the process, meaning that completely changing your goals every other day hinders rather than helps your empowerment process.

Natural Magic Affirmation for Enrichment

Say the following affirmation aloud three times before writing it into your Natural Magic Empowerment Journal:

Today and every day, I think and act in ways that align me with my natural magic goals for enrichment.

Write the affirmation on two small note cards. Place one card in your work area so that you see it when you are working, and place the other card near your front door so that you see every time you enter or leave the home.

Natural Magic Meditation for Enrichment

Get comfortable and relax. As you breathe deeply, imagine a beam of white light shining through you and spreading a warm feeling that both relaxes and invigorates you. Continue taking deep breaths as the white light spreads out over your body, mind, and spirit. As you breathe in the light, you feel at One with both yourself and the universe.

Now in your mind's eye, imagine you are a great white bird flying high in the sky on a night lit up by a luminous full moon. The moonlight illuminates your way as you soar ever higher. Like a beacon, the light guides you through the darkness to your destination up among the pillowing clouds.

As you touch down, you see before you a giant crystal pyramid. When the moonlight moves through the crystal, it changes the light into a kaleidoscope of color that pours out the other side. Moving up to the face of the crystal pyramid, you peer into it and see clear images of your natural magic goals for enrichment.

A white feather falls softly from your plumage. You pick it up and gently touch it to the side of the crystal pyramid. As you do this, a energetic doorway opens. Stepping into the crystal pyramid, you sense yourself transforming into a being made of pure white light. You move your awareness to where the images of your natural magic goals for enrichment are. You see that the images are also made of light. Moving your awareness into the images themselves, you feel yourself aligning and becoming One with them, until there is no separation between you and your natural magic goals for enrichment.

As you take a deep breath in and out, your energy pours out through the other side of the crystal, you sense yourself shifting into a rainbow of colors. With the shift comes the realization of each of your natural magic goals for enrichment, and how each of them relate to the whole of your life. You become a multifaceted person of many colors. Each color is an aspect of the image that you project to the world.

Gradually bring your awareness back into your body. Stretch your arms and legs, and rub them with your hands. Slowly open your eyes, and as your focus moves back into your body and you become aware of your physical surrounding, remember that you are white light and all the harmonious colors that radiate from it. Before doing anything else, write down in your Natural Magic Empowerment Journal the impressions and insights that you had during and as a result of the meditation.

Natural Magic Ritual for Enrichment

The purpose of the following ritual is to move the dynamic energies of enrichment into your natural magic sacred space and your life. You will need a clear quartz crystal point, a bowl of the earth, an incense burner with a smudge stick, a beeswax candle and holder, and a cup of well or spring water. Follow these steps:

1. Rub a few drops of lavender oil on the candle and on your wrists and ankles. Wipe any remaining oil from your hands. Bring the elemental powers into your sacred circle by doing the three steps of the natural magic ritual for relationships in Chapter 1. Invite the divine energies of Oneness in by standing in the middle of the circle and saying:

   Divine energies of Oneness
   Please bless my sacred space with your presence.

2. Carefully hold the candle holder with lit candle in your hands. Then face each of the four directions, starting with the north, and say:

   By all that is holy and divine
   Please cleanse this sacred space
   Of all unwanted, negative energies.
   Ayea, Ayea, Ayea!

3. Return the candle to your altar, and pick up the crystal in your hands. Move to the center of circle, and spend a moment getting

a clear image of your natural magic goal for enrichment in your mind's eye. Hold the crystal high in the air in your right hand, and say:

Divine powers of enrichment
Please charge this sacred space
With your positive, harmonious energy.
So be it!

Thank the elements and Oneness for their help in your ritual. Before leaving the area, be sure your candle and smudge stick are completely extinguished.

Natural Magic Blessing for Enrichment

Dear Goddess and God, please bless my home and sacred space with your divine, enriching light each and every day.

Natural Magic Exercises for Enrichment

In the following natural magic exercise you transform your workspace into a place for enrichment. Begin by energetically cleansing your space by walking through your space while beating on a drum. The sound of the drum gets energy moving, and in particular vibrates unwanted, negative energy out of the space. Be sure to cleanse all the corners because this is where energy tends to stagnate. As you beat on the drum, say:

All evil spirits and foul energies
In the name of all that is divine and holy
Be gone from this place
Be gone, now and forevermore.

Once you have cleansed the space, walk around the room and determine how you can improve the energy of the space so that it is more conducive to enrichment. Ways of doing this include organizing and cleaning the clutter, particularly on and around your work area, putting flowers, crystals, or a bamboo plant on or next to your desk or work area, placing pictures around the room that display prosperity, and putting books that to you signify prosperity so that you see them while you are working.

Use your intuition in this enrichment transformation process. If in doubt about something, try it anyway and notice how it feels energetically and how this energy influences you when you are working. Keep it there if it works and remove it if it doesn't. It's a good idea to try things one at a time because it's easier to gauge their individual, and then collective, effect on the energy of the space.

In this second natural magic exercise, you charge a glass of water with the energy of your goal for enrichment. Begin by taking a clear quartz crystal and first cleaning it physically with water and salt, and then energetically cleaning it using your expectation and breath. Do this by holding the stone in your hands, closing your eyes, and envisioning a single point of bright white light against a dark background. Take a deep breath and pulse your breath outward through your nose and imagine planting the image of the single point of bright white light into the stone itself. If you prefer, you can imagine a ray of light coming from your third eye (located in the middle of your forehead) and beaming the image into the stone. Or you can imagine bright white light with the image imprinted in it flowing through your arms and out your fingertips into the stone. Repeat this process a total of three times to clean the stone.

Next, charge the crystal by envisioning in your mind's eye one of your natural magic goals for enrichment. With your breath, pulse the image of the goal and its successful fruition into the crystal. Again, repeat this process a total of three times.

Take a glass of well or spring water and carefully put the crystal into it. Cover the glass and let it sit in sunlight or moonlight for at least three hours. Remove the crystal and bless the water by saying:

Divine ones, please bless this water with your divine, enriching energy.

As you drink the water, imagine it filling and harmoniously aligning you with your natural magic goal for enrichment. Drink it and be it!

Chapter Six

Enacting Your Natural Magic Plan

The ancient tale of Liu Pang compares to the modern stories of *Harry Potter* and *The Lord of the Rings*. Coming from a peasant background, Liu Pang became a leader of an army that sought to depose the Ch'in Dynasty, known for their atrocities on scholars and the common people. When Liu Pang's parent became sick and passed away, the great rain-maker, shaman, and diviner, Huang-shih Kung, came to Pang's aid and with the ancient knowledge of Feng Shui helped him choose a sacred burial site. Because of the natural power of ancestral energy, this assured Pang's ascension to the emperor's throne.

This set up a final battle between Liu Pang and his rival, the warlord Hsiang Yu, emperor of the Ch'in. Yu had the evil sorcerer, Hui Jen, drain the energy around the burial site of Liu Pang's ancestor. In a battle of wizards and magic, the Taoist Huang-shih Kung prevailed, and subsequently Emperor Liu Pang founded the Han Dynasty, known for being more benevolent to the people than its predecessor.

Through ancestral energy and power of Feng Shui, this tale illustrates the magical relationship that Chinese geomancers have traditionally had with nature. They perceive nature and Earth as being a living, breathing entity. Every phenomenon in nature has breath, making the breath of nature one of the foremost concepts in Chinese spirituality. This breath enters every stem, fiber, and particle, and as a result, gives everything movement and life. Between the expanding breath and the reverting breath, all of nature can be explained in terms of this energy. It is perceived on one hand as the polarities of female (yin) and male (yang). On the other hand, these two breaths of nature are not two separate breaths, but when balanced, one breath. This is akin to the idea of the Goddess and God, who separately represent the divine polarities of female and male, but together their sacred union produces Oneness.

The Basics of Feng Shui

Feng Shui (pronounced "fung schway") literally means "wind water." Primarily Feng Shui deals with your relationship with nature and how this relationship can be brought into balance and harmony. Within Feng Shui, vital energy fills everything in nature, including mountains and rivers. The pathways of energy in mountains are called dragon veins, while those in waterways are called water dragons. The three building blocks of Feng Shui are the compass; the pa-k'ua/bagua (eight directions); and the theory of change as outlined in the I-Ching.

The flow of chi (pronounced "chee") energy from one entity to another is the basis of Feng Shui. The spirit or chi of a space affects your well-being. This translates to everything in your surroundings, down to the smallest details of furnishing and décor, has the ability to either help or hinder your goals and plans in life. The basic components of Feng Shui are yin and yang, the five elements, and the eight directions.

More than being terms describing the female and male polarity, yin and yang are complementary rather than competitive concepts that refer to the relative differences between all natural phenomena. Night, cold, peaceful, and north are yin energies, whereas day, heat, active, and south are yang energies. Yin and yang attract each other and the relationship is continually changing as the energy fluctuates back and forth. Nothing is totally yin or yang, but instead contains both, with an inclination toward one or the other. As Richard Craze states in his book, *Feng Shui*: "The yin of the north was combined with the yang of the south to create spring and the east, while the yang was combined with the yin to create fall and the west." (For details on this and other books on Feng Shui, see Appendix C.)

In terms of your home, office, or even your body, yin and yang are all about balance. If you have too much of one, you need to balance it with the other. The east and south portions of your house are the yang side, and the west and north portions are the yin side. Activities that are more yang, such as work, rituals, and enacting your natural magic plans, are best suited for the yang side, whereas yin activities such as sleep, meditation, and relaxing are best done on the yin side.

The five elements of Feng Shui are Fire, Water, Wood, Metal, and Earth. All matter is comprised of combinations of these five elements. As with the energies of yin and yang, the idea in Feng Shui is to keep the elements in balance. Each element has a supporting, destroying, and draining element. The destroying element comes into play when the supporting element is weak. Here are some specifics of each element:

- **Fire.** A dynamic element that promotes passion, warmth, excitement, and expression. Too much fire can exhaust you and make you over-confident and self-absorbed. The elemental color is red. Fire supports the Earth element, destroys the Metal element, and drains the Wood element. Fire's shapes are triangles.

- **Water.** A calming element that promotes sensitivity, flexibility, creativeness, and depth. Too much water in your life can make you easily hurt or indecisive. The elemental color is black, sometimes blue. Water supports the Wood element, destroys the Fire element, and drains the Metal element. Water's shapes are curvy and wavy lines.

- **Wood.** A growing element that promotes confidence, vitality, understanding, and relationships. Too much wood can make you boring and impenetrable. The elemental color is green. Wood supports the Fire element, destroys the Earth element, and drains the Water element. Wood's shapes are rectangles.

- **Metal.** An enriching element that promotes solidity, leadership, and organization. Too much metal can make you unkind to others and obsessed with wealth. The elemental colors are silver, gold, and white. Metal supports the Water element, destroys the Wood element, and drains the Earth element. Metals shapes are rounded on one side and square on the other, like an archway.

- **Earth.** A magically steady element that promotes foundations, security, comfort, and caution. Too much Earth in your life can make you stubborn and overextended. The elemental colors are brown and yellow. Earth supports the Metal element, destroys the Water element, and drains the Fire element. Earth's shapes are trapezoids.

In Feng Shui they take the four traditional directions of north, east, south, and west, and expand them to eight by adding northeast, southeast, southwest, and northeast. When you do this, you wind up with an eight-sided shape known as the bagua. Each direction represents a different area of your life. Starting at the top of the bagua and going clockwise, the areas are:

- North—Career
- Northeast—Knowledge and self-cultivation
- East—Family and health
- Southeast—Wealth
- South—Fame
- Southwest—Marriage
- West—Children
- Northwest—Helpful people and travel

When applying this information to your home or a room, it is customary to call the place where the main entrance is located north, and to go from there around the octagon. One of the easiest ways to do this is to draw out a basic floor plan of your house or room and to overlay the octagonal bagua on top of it.

Understanding Chi

In her book *Feng Shui*, Sarah Rossbach writes, "Chi is the vital force that breathes life into the animals and vegetation, inflates the Earth to form mountains, and carries water through the Earth's ducts." Without chi nothing would exist. Its essence is what transforms the unmanifested into the manifested. It is the energies of creation in their pure and primordial form.

Chi, the universal energy of life, flows between spirit and matter. Its basic characteristics include:

- Works in circular motions rather than straight lines.
- Flows along the "lung mei" or dragon's veins.
- Always moves between yin and yang.
- Tries to find a balance between polarities.
- When it flows well, your life is enhanced.
- When it is disrupted, it can wreak havoc in your life.

Chi is like a glass of water. When you first pour it, the water is pure, fresh, and full of vital energy. When you drink the water, it imparts that vitality to you. What if instead of drinking it, you let the glass of water set for a couple of days? It starts to look and smell terrible, and turns into something you wouldn't want to put in your body.

Likewise, when chi is flowing, it is fresh and vital, but when it stagnates, it becomes stale and toxic, which is not something you would want to have in your environment. Feng Shui is about using the principles of yin and yang, the five elements, and the eight directions to increase the flow of chi in your house and in your life.

When chi stagnates and doesn't flow at all or flows badly, it is called "sha," which creates a "shar." Chi flowing in balance brings good health and fortune, when it becomes sha, it brings bad health and misfortune. Things that create sha in your home include poorly lit areas, clutter, unused spaces, harsh or clashing color schemes, furniture in straight lines, dark and unused corridors, anything harsh or ugly, dying or unhealthy plants, and empty corners.

Practical Feng Shui Solutions

The problem-solving approach is often the most productive. Focus on correcting specific problems rather than making blanket or drastic changes. The idea is to implement one solution at a time and assess the result before going to another solution.

Feng Shui is not the answer to all of your problems, but one of the many natural magic tools at your disposal. Feng Shui is most effective when you can relate a problem to something around your home, and make the necessary changes. The idea is to optimize the chi in your home so that it brings the corresponding areas of your life into balance. Here are some ways to enhance the chi in your home and life:

- **Sounds.** Wind chimes, bells, music, and the sound of water can generate and move chi throughout your home.
- **Bright objects.** Crystals, mirrors, and lights can bring chi into a house and get it to flow in places such as corners. Place a mirror halfway down a long corridor to stop the chi from racing through.
- **Color.** The color red generates and activates the chi in a room. Different colors in the various areas of your home can stimulate chi for particular things, such as relationships, wellness, and enrichment. Harmonious and gentle colors soothe and calm disruptive sha.
- **Electrical objects.** Radios, stereos, and fans generate and move the flow of chi around an area. Electrical devices also settle unpredictable sha.
- **Living objects.** Plants, flowers, birds, cats, dogs, and fish in aquariums generate chi. Aquariums are particularly good generators because of the water element and the movement of the fish. Also fish tanks are a way to attract money into your space.
- **Moving objects.** Things like mobiles, fountains, and windmills can generate chi and activate lingering sha energy so that it flows back into balance.
- **Heavy objects.** Stones, statues, and other heavy objects anchor the chi to a particular area in terms of the eight directions or bagua.

Relationships

When enacting your natural magic plans for relationships, the idea is to get the chi working for you rather than against you. Any area of your home where you interact with other people, such as your living room, dining room, and bedroom, are places to stimulate the chi for action.

Before beginning the meditation, ritual, and exercises in this section, review your natural magic plans for relationships as you outlined them in Chapter 3.

Natural Magic Affirmation for Relationships

Say the following affirmation aloud several times before writing it in your Natural Magic Empowerment Journal:

Today and every day I am actively working on my natural magic plans for relationships.

Write the affirmation on a small note card. Place the card near your bed so that you see it before you go to sleep and when you wake up.

Natural Magic Meditation for Relationships

After getting in a comfortable position, begin taking several deep breaths. Slowly inhale and sense the movement of the air as it fills your lungs. As you hold your breath, the air swirls throughout your physical, mental, and spiritual being. While exhaling, feel all the stagnant energy moving out of all the aspects of your being. Again take in a deep breath and sense its vital energy entering your being. Hold your breath for a moment and feel the energy expand until it envelopes your entire being. With your exhale, move out any negative energy that may have built up. Each time you do this breathing exercise, slow down the process and relax with it. Take as many deep breaths as you need to reach a state of relaxed awareness. Your energy is vital, and you feel relaxed and at peace with yourself and everything around you.

Imagine you are a sailboat floating on a sea of tranquility. The wind in your sails gently glides you along. The water and the wind cooperate together to keep you afloat and in motion. With practice, you learn to position your sails in such a way as to move in any direction that you desire. You are in complete harmony with the direction of your life and the water and wind that move you to where you want to go.

Sense yourself shape-shifting into a sleeping black tortoise. You have a giant, hard shell that is your place of slumber and security. You are like a sleeper in the earth, waiting to be awakened so that you can once again move your energy outward in alignment with your natural magic quest.

Sense yourself shape-shifting into a red phoenix. Feel your energy move from the sleeping stage to one that is lively and full of vitality. You are reborn to once again rise up out of the ashes to become alive with desire and purpose.

Spread your wings and soar into the heavens. Become One with the sky. The fire and light of the Sun moves you ever forward on your quest.

Sense yourself becoming a white tiger. You are agile, daring, and unpredictable to everyone but yourself. You are the future that you envision with your natural magic goals and plans. You are strength and determination. You are like a flood that no one can stop. You align yourself and move forward with every degree of your self. Your focus and energy is unwavering as you move closer to your goal.

Sense yourself shape-shifting into a green dragon. You feel nurturing and full of good fortune. You know where you are going, and have every confidence that you will reach your goal. You breathe fire and fly through the sky on your natural magic quest. You are the wind and the water as they come together as One. You are dynamic, connected to the world around you, and aware that all things have consciousness. This consciousness is what interweaves and binds everything into some semblance of the whole. You are your natural magic goal for relationships, and your goal is you.

Gradually bring yourself back into your body. Take time to move from the meditation to the waking world. Before doing anything else, write down in your Natural Magic Empowerment Journal any impressions and insights you might have had during the meditation.

Natural Magic Ritual for Relationships

The purpose of the following ritual is to give energy and life to your natural magic plans for relationships. You will need a clear quartz crystal point, a bowl of the earth, an incense burner with a smudge stick, a beeswax candle and holder, a cup of well or spring water, and a piece of jade. Follow these steps:

1. Bring the elemental powers into your sacred circle by doing the three steps of the natural magic ritual for relationships in Chapter 1. Energetically cleanse the piece of jade with the smoke from your smudge stick, and then invite the divine energies of Oneness into your space by standing in the middle of the circle and saying:

   Divine energies of Oneness
   Please bless my sacred space with your presence.

2. Go to the north point and awaken the sleeping energies by saying the following mantra:

   OM, MA, NI, PAD, ME, HUM

   Go to the east point and give the energies creation and manifestation by repeating the mantra:

   OM, MA, NI, PAD, ME, HUM

   Go to the south point and give the energies life energy and vitality by repeating the mantra:

   OM, MA, NI, PAD, ME, HUM

   Go to the west point and give the energies the strength to move into the future by repeating the mantra:

   OM, MA, NI, PAD, ME, HUM

3. With the piece of jade in your right hand, move into the center of your sacred space. Facing the north point, begin turning in a slow circle with the intention of bringing all of the energies together as One. When you again face the north point, repeat the mantra:

   OM, MA, NI, PAD, ME, HUM

   Hold the piece of jade, a symbol of good-fortune, up in your right hand, and say:

   Lady of good fortune
   Give my quest your blessings.

   While envisioning in your mind's eye enacting your natural magic plans for relationships, shout out:

   Ayea! Ayea! Ayea!

   Thank the elements and Oneness for their help. Before leaving the area, be sure the candle and smudge stick are completely extinguished.

Natural Magic Blessing for Relationships

Divine powers of Oneness, please bless me with the strength and wisdom to enact my natural magic plans for relationships.

Natural Magic Exercises for Relationships

In the following natural magic exercise, you assess the chi in the relationship areas of your house. Begin by taking a compass, and stand in front of the main entrance to your house with your back to the door. Take the compass and turn it until the north arrow is pointed at you, south is away from you, east is to the left of you, and west is to the right of you. The other four points—northeast, southeast, southwest, and northwest—are located between these points.

According to the eight directions of the bagua, the areas of your house that deal with relationships are east (family/health), southwest (marriage), west (children), northwest (helpful people/travel). East is the left side of your house, west is the right side, southwest is to the left of the west point, and northwest is to the right of the west point.

Go to each of these directions, and use your intuition to assess the chi in the area. If there is a window, what does it look out upon, and if there is a door outside, where does it go. If your house is rectangular, the east and west points are walls, and the southwest and northwest points are corners. Take note of what objects are in each of these areas of your house. Open yourself up to the chi in each of these areas, and how they relate to the relationships in your life. When you are done, write down in your Natural Magic Empowerment Journal your assessment of the chi in each of these areas.

In this second natural magic exercise, you decorate the relationship areas of your house so that the chi flows better. Begin by making a list of any problems you might be having in terms of family, marriage (your primary partner), children, and helpful people. If you having problems with your primary partner, for example, go to the marriage area of your house (the southwest corner of your bagua), and see what you can do to generate chi and get rid of any sha energy. Placing a plant, fountain, or mobile in the area are good ways to generate chi.

Living rooms and bedrooms are natural areas of relationships. As with your house, you can take these rooms in your house, and beginning at the entryway, you can draw the octagonal bagua around the room. As with your house, the relationships areas are east, west, southwest, and northwest. The colors red, pink, and white promote chi for relationships. The color white is for children. White, gray, and black generates chi energy for helpful people, and green for family and health. Also reds and oranges are yang colors and blues and greens are yin colors. The idea is to balance the energies in an area.

Wellness

Enacting your natural magic plans for wellness involves living in an environment that is conducive to your health. Your home is often your primary environment, and thus should be a primary area of focus. Rooms in your house that naturally deal with wellness include your kitchen, dining room, bedroom (sleeping), and bathroom. Use the techniques introduced in Feng Shui to enhance these areas so that the chi energy flows in balance.

Before beginning the meditation, ritual, and exercises in this section, review your natural magic plans for wellness. Take those first steps of your plan, and begin your quest for wellness.

Natural Magic Affirmation for Wellness

Say the following affirmation aloud several times before writing it in your Natural Magic Empowerment Journal:

Today I am taking the first steps of my natural magic plan for wellness.

Write the affirmation on a small note card. Post the card on your refrigerator and keep it there until you finish the first steps.

Natural Magic Meditation for Wellness

Begin by standing up and stretching your arms and legs by standing on your tip toes and reaching for the sky. Get in a comfortable position, and relax by taking seven deep breaths. With the first breath, sense your body inhaling energy through your first chakra, located between your thighs. With the second breath, sense your body inhaling energy through your second chakra located at your navel. With the third breath, feel your third chakra, located in your stomach area, fill up with energy. With the fourth breath, move up to your heart area, location of your fourth chakra, and breathe in and fill it full of energy. With the fifth breath, expand the energy in your fifth chakra, located in your throat area. With the sixth breath, inhale energy into your third eye, located midway just above your eyebrows, home of your sixth chakra. With the seventh breath, breathe in through your seventh chakra located at the top of your head. As you do this, expand your awareness so that it connects to the divine. Feel yourself connecting to Oneness.

Take another deep breath and imagine drawing a energetic line of light that connects all your chakras together, moving from your first chakra up to your seventh and back again. Sense the chi in your body moving from the bottoms of your feet up to the top of your head and back again in a constant circular flow. With each breath you take, you are like the waves of an energetic ocean, continually moving in and expanding, moving out and reverting. You are in harmony with yourself as a complete and whole human being.

Take another deep breath and imagine you are a six-petaled flower, beginning your journey to florescence. Each petal is one of the six breaths of nature—cold, heat, dryness, moisture, wind, and fire. You are the earth, which carries your roots. You are the air, which is your breath. You are the fire that fills your spirit with life. You are the water that fills your veins and carries you on a river to the future. You are the self you are in this life, trying the best you can to move forward. You are Oneness, just as it is you.

Take another deep breath and imagine you are beginning to take the first steps in your natural magic plans for wellness. Blessed by the Goddess and God, you begin your quest. The light shines on you, and a zillion spirits cheer your send off. You are like a tidal wave, rising toward your destination. You are like an avalanche, and no one can stop you.

Take another deep breath and imagine you are pure light. Feel the love within and all around you harmonize into energies of peace and wellness. Each chakra and energetic field within you vibrates with the energy of wellness. You can become whoever you want to be with your expectations and actions. Now is the time to bring your expectations into the realm of action.

Take another deep breath and bring your awareness back into your body. Feel your chakras buzzing with energy. After returning to your body, stand up and stretch your muscles. Before doing anything else, write down in your Natural Magic Empowerment Journal any insights and impressions that you are having.

Natural Magic Ritual for Wellness

The purpose of the following ritual is to move the eight types of chi energy toward enacting your natural magic plans for wellness. You will need a clear quartz crystal point, a bowl of the earth, an incense burner with a smudge stick, a beeswax candle and holder, and a cup of well or spring water. Follow these steps:

1. Bring the elemental powers into your sacred circle by doing the three steps of the natural magic ritual for relationships in Chapter 1. Afterward, invite the divine energies of Oneness in by standing in the middle of the circle and saying:

   Divine energies of Oneness
   Please bless my sacred space with your presence.

2. This ritual uses eight points rather than the usual four. Take the bell and move to the north point of your circle. The north represents conception with a nurturing chi. To move this chi into your space and toward your plan, ring the bell three times, and say:

   OM, MA, NI, PAD, ME, HUM

   Move to the northeast point, halfway between the north and east points. The northeast represents a flourishing chi. To move this chi into your space and toward your plan, ring the bell three times, and say:

   OM, MA, NI, PAD, ME, HUM

   Go to the east point, which represents a stimulating chi that helps you move forward in your life. To move this chi into your space and toward your plan, ring the bell three times, and say:

   OM, MA, NI, PAD, ME, HUM

   Go to the southeast point, half way between the east and south points. Southeast represents a creative chi. To move this chi into your sacred space and toward your natural magic plans for wellness, ring the bell three times, and say:

   OM, MA, NI, PAD, ME, HUM

   Go to the south point, representing a vigorous chi that fills your plan full of life and vitality. To move this chi into your sacred space and toward your plan, ring the bell three times, and say:

   OM, MA, NI, PAD, ME, HUM

   Go to the southwest point, located between the south and west points. The southwest point represents a soothing chi that acts as a healing force. To move this chi into your space and toward your plan, ring the bell three times, and say:

   OM, MA, NI, PAD, ME, HUM

Move to the west point of your circle, which represents a calming chi that brings your entire being into a sense of relaxed awareness. To move this chi into your space and toward your plan, ring the bell three times, and say:

OM, MA, NI, PAD, ME, HUM

Go to the northwest point, located halfway between the west and north points. The northwest point represents an expansive chi that helps you to enact your natural magic plans for wellness. To move this chi into your sacred space and toward your plan, ring the bell three times, and say:

OM, MA, NI, PAD, ME, HUM

3. Move to the center of the circle, and in your mind's eye envision all the chi energies coming together as One and being directed toward your natural magic plans for wellness. Once you have a clear image, ring the bell three times, and say:

OM, MA, NI, PAD, ME, HUM
Divine energies of Oneness
Bring harmony and balance
To the eight types of chi
And move them into my natural magic plan for wellness.
Ayea! Ayea! Ayea!

Thank the elements and Oneness. Before leaving your ritual area, be sure that the smudge stick and candle are completely extinguished.

Natural Magic Blessing for Wellness

Great Goddess and God, as I begin my quest for wellness, please bless my natural magic plan with your divine energy and guidance.

Natural Magic Exercises for Wellness

In the following natural magic exercise, you redecorate your home so the chi energy promotes wellness. Begin by going through your kitchen, dining room, bedroom, and bathroom while assessing the flow of chi energy in each of these rooms. In the dining room, you can use soft shapes and colors to promote a calm eating atmosphere. In the kitchen, you can place a mirror over your stove to reflect and move the chi and you can place positive and uplifting pictures on your refrigerator to generate helpful chi energy. In the bathroom, you can use soft colors and a picture or mirror behind the toilet to generate and move the chi. Toilets represent places where the chi can literally get flushed away (another good reason for keeping the lid down!).

If your bedroom is in the eastern part of the house and has a window or doorway where the morning sun comes in, you have a lot of yang energy coming in at you. It is an active energy that is not conducive to sleep. You need to temper the energy with colors such as blue, green, and soft pastels. You want shapes that curve and are soft rather than hard. In terms of directions, place your bed on the north or west. Adding this yin energy will also help you generate a more gentle and loving energy in the room.

In this second natural magic exercise, you remove the clutter so that the chi energy flows better, promoting the wellness of your house, and in turn, you. Begin by locating an area of your house that feels cluttered, such as a room, closet, or cupboard. Clutter is not necessarily messy, but more of an accumulation of items that you no longer use. This hoarding of material objects that have passed their time of usefulness represents an inclination to hang onto the past and not move forward. This forward movement and energy is essential when embarking on your quest for wellness and enacting your natural magic plan.

The first thing to do is remove everything from the area. Once you have everything out, you can start going through things, determining what to keep and what to toss. (If an item is in good condition, consider giving it to someone else who could use it, or donating it to charity. Nursing home and libraries often appreciate books and magazines, and animal shelters gratefully accept donations of worn but clean blankets and towels.) When deciding what to get rid of, start with things that have a negative energy of some type associated with them. These items should definitely go. The things in your house should optimally give you positive thoughts and energy. Next go through and determine items that you no longer use, and remove as much of them as you can from the area. These are the items that can sometimes keep you from moving forward.

After deciding what you want to keep, plan how you want the remaining things to go back into the area. Things do not always have to be neat and organized, but they should be arranged in such a way that works for you. There's nothing more aggravating and stressful than to search for something you can't find because it's not where it's supposed to be.

Enrichment

The enrichment of areas of your home includes the study/library, office, garage, and outside yard. Your house as a whole is also representative of your enrichment, whether it's a palace, temple, or simple sanctuary. Enrichment is different for everyone as evidenced by the multitudes of designs, structures, and furnishings. When decorating your home, choose not only things that reflect who you are, but also things that make you feel good so that when you walk into your house, you are immediately met by a positive feeling of peace and contentment.

Before beginning the meditation, ritual, and exercises in this section, go to your Natural Magic Empowerment Journal and review your plans for enrichment. In particular, scope out the first step in the plan, and how you're going to take that step.

Natural Magic Affirmation for Enrichment

Say the following affirmation aloud three times before writing it into your Natural Magic Empowerment Journal:

Today, I actively begin my natural magic quest for enrichment by taking the first step in my plan.

Write the affirmation on a small note card. Place the card in your work area and leave it there until you complete the first step in your plan for wellness.

Natural Magic Meditation for Enrichment

Get comfortable, and begin taking several deep breaths. As you inhale, envision your natural magic plans for enrichment in your mind's eye. As you hold your breath, gather energy and chi, and when you exhale, direct the energy toward action and the enactment of your natural magic plans for enrichment.

Each time you take a breath, sense the chi coming into your body, build the energy, and release it toward your natural magic plan. Continue taking deep breaths until you feel relaxed and at One with your plans for enrichment.

Imagine your body is a giant electro-magnet, drawing in energy and light from all around it. Everything is energy, and the energy is everywhere around you. Sense your body pulling in this energy. Feel it filling your inner being with light. Draw in the energy until every part of you tingles and vibrates with anticipation.

Focus on the center of your palms, the bottom of your feet, and the top of your head. Sense the energy inside of you becoming balanced and in harmony with the polarities of natural magic. Feel the energy inside you swirl in your feet, legs, pelvic area, stomach, back, chest, arms, hands, neck, face, head, and crown. Envision a strand of white light connecting all of the parts together into one whole.

Imagine that the energy that you accumulated in your body is expanding outward, being directed by your expectation and intention. Sense a flow of light surrounding your body, and shooting out rays in every direction. Direct the energy toward your natural magic plan for enrichment. Visualize the plan beginning to form, and moving toward its destination—your natural magic goal for enrichment.

Picture yourself taking the first step to your plan. Go through everything that is involved in taking the step—whether it's choosing house plans or training for a promotion or new career. Visualize yourself doing all the things necessary to complete the first step. See yourself being successful in your efforts.

Gradually begin moving your awareness back to your body. Stretch your arms and legs and take a few deep breaths. Take your time getting up, waiting until your awareness has fully returned to your body. Before doing anything else, write in your Natural Magic Empowerment Journal any impressions and insights you might have as a result of the meditation.

Natural Magic Ritual for Enrichment

The purpose of the following ritual is to walk the nine palaces and move this energy toward enacting your natural magic plans for enrichment. You will need a clear quartz crystal point, a bowl of the earth, an incense burner with a smudge stick, a beeswax candle and holder, a cup of well or spring water, a bell, and eight rocks (these can be from your yard). Follow these steps:

1. Bring the elemental powers into your sacred circle by doing the three steps of the natural magic ritual for relationships in Chapter 1. Afterward, invite the divine energies of Oneness in by standing in the middle of the circle and saying:

   Divine energies of Oneness
   Please bless my sacred space with your presence.

2. Place each one of the eight rocks on the eight directions—north, northeast, east, southeast, south, southwest, west, and northwest. As you set each rock down, ring the bell over it three times.

   Go to the north point, and chant:

   OM, MA, NI, PAD, ME, HUM

   Next go to the southwest point, and chant:

   OM, MA, NI, PAD, ME, HUM

   Go to the east point, and chant:

   OM, MA, NI, PAD, ME, HUM

   Go to the southeast point, and chant:

   OM, MA, NI, PAD, ME, HUM

   Go to the center of the circle, and chant:

   OM, MA, NI, PAD, ME, HUM

   Go to the northwest point, and chant:

   OM, MA, NI, PAD, ME, HUM

   Go to the west point, and chant:

   OM, MA, NI, PAD, ME, HUM

   Go to the northeast point, and chant:

   OM, MA, NI, PAD, ME, HUM

   Go to the south point, and chant:

   OM, MA, NI, PAD, ME, HUM

3. Move back into the center of the circle, and begin bringing all the energies of the nine palaces together as One. Sense the chi energy building as you chant the name of a Goddess or God of enrichment nine times. After the ninth time, shout:

   Ayea! Ayea! Ayea!

   With your expectation and intention, move the energy toward your natural magic plans for enrichment.

   Thank the elements, Oneness, and the Goddess or God you invoked in the ritual. Before leaving the area, be sure that your candle and smudge stick are completely extinguished.

Natural Magic Blessing for Enrichment

Divine energies of Oneness, please bless me with your wisdom and help me take the first step on my natural magic quest for enrichment.

Natural Magic Exercises for Enrichment

In the following natural magic exercise you enhance the chi energy in your home for enrichment. Begin by taking a compass, and standing with your back to your front entrance. Turn the compass till north is point at you. The area of your house that relate to enrichment include the north (career), northeast (knowledge/self cultivation), southeast (wealth), and south (fame). Go to each of these areas and use your intuition to assess the chi energy in relation to their impact on your enrichment.

In your Natural Magic Empowerment Journal, make a list of any problems you may have in terms of enrichment. Relate the problems back to career, knowledge, wealth, and fame. Go to the area where you feel you have the most amount of problems, and move or add something to generate and enhance the chi energy. Try one thing at a time, and assess its impact on your life. Ultimately you are the one who decides by your experience, what works for you and what doesn't.

In this second natural magic exercise, you enhance the chi energy in your office or workspace for enrichment and the enactment of your plan. Begin by placing your desk so that you can see the entrance to the room. If this is not possible, place a mirror on the wall in front of your desk so that you see a reflection of the entrance. The entrance the place where things come into your space, and it's better to face them than to have your back to them.

Colors such as red and orange stimulate the chi energy of a room, and blues and greens calm the energy of a room. Do not attempt to make the energy too stimulating or too calming. The idea is to achieve a balance so that you are stimulated to work, but not worn and stressed out over the experience. Fountains, healthy plants such as lucky bamboo plants, and fish tanks are excellent for offices because they generate chi and promote growth. Fish tanks in particular are a sign of money, which is why so many Chinese restaurants have them.

Chapter Seven

Building Natural Magic
Relationships

In the movie *The Man With Two Brains,* Steve Martin plays
a brain surgeon whose first wife has passed away. Through
circumstances, a woman, who is only after his money, hood-
winks him. Before marrying the woman, he consults the
portrait of his deceased wife by asking, "Rebecca, if there's
anything wrong with my feelings for Delores, just give me a
sign."

Suddenly a voice begins screaming, "No!" the portrait
starts spinning around, the house begins shaking, the wall
behind the portrait cracks, and everything in the house
begins flying. After all this happens, Steve Martin's character
responds by saying, "Just any kind of sign, I'll keep on the
lookout for it."

This scene from the movie is a comic view of the idea that
spirits and nature are often trying to help, but you have to be
aware of the signs and what they are trying to tell you. In
Steve Martin's case the signs are obvious, but he chooses not

to acknowledge them, and does what he wants to do, even though the consequences turn out to be disastrous.

More often in life, the signs from spirits and nature are much more subtle. What you need to do is build relationships with helpful entities that include the earth and nature, divine energies, animal allies, spirit guides and ancestral energy, and helpful people. By doing so, you become more in tune with the signs around you and learn to take appropriate action.

Encountering something in life, particularly when it keeps happening, usually causes you to think about and explore its relation to you. Why has this thing come into your space at this time? The trick is to decipher the meaningless from the meaningful and to pay attention to the signs that show you something significant about your life.

Now that you have begun your natural magic quest, the time has come to build relationships that help you in this endeavor. It's hard to do everything by yourself, so the more help you get from nature and helpful spirits, the better. Nature's allies can come in many forms, from the physical to spiritual. The idea is to cultivate these relationships and to be aware of the signs, information, and physical help that they provide.

Your Relationship with Earth and Nature

I was peacefully lying on the beach in Honolulu, Hawaii, enjoying the warm sun and the sound of the surf. Suddenly I felt something on my arm, and when I looked over, I saw that a black feather had landed on it. At first I tried to ignore it, but something kept nagging at me energetically. I sat up, and for a moment tried to figure out what it was. Looking out at the water, I saw my husband swimming, and then in a flash it hit me. I remembered that he had the key to the rental car in the pocket of his swim trunks. I called out to him to check his pocket, and sure enough, the key was somewhere in the Pacific Ocean. Everything turned out all right because we were able to retrieve another key from the rental company, but the experience taught me to be aware of the natural signs around me.

The art of receiving signs and communication from birds is known as augury. One of the oldest forms of divination, it is depicted in cave drawings that date back to prehistoric times. Cultures throughout the world have watched the patterns of birds, and regarded their presence and the bestowing of a feather as a divine sign from nature. Many stories exist that tell the tale of someone who is guided by the call, flight, and feather of a bird to a successful quest.

Other natural signs that have been traditionally used as oracles include flowers, trees, and Earth itself. Shamans and priestesses have long honored Earth and nature and looked to it for guidance and help. They sought to learn from the natural patterns and to develop relationships that were in harmony and balance with these patterns.

In modern times, nature has been portrayed as something that needs to be struggled with and controlled. Writers and big-game hunters such as Earnest Hemingway and Frank Buck gave the impression that humans were supposed to compete with and conquer nature in a one-sided relationship that they regarded as a sport. Using technology to annihilate species of animals and turn the earth into an asphalt jungle has nothing to do with sport and everything to do with extinction—nature's *and* humankind's, because we are ultimately tied together into one on the planet Earth.

Regarding Earth and nature, it is time to build relationships that are cooperative rather than competitive. Trying to conquer and control everything in nature is a huge consumption of energy. Its aim is futile. Nature always comes back, often with a fury. As with the traditions of shamans and priestesses, the idea is to build relationships with Earth and nature that are in harmony with the natural progression of things.

Divine Relationships

A young peasant girl named Joan had a divine vision that motivated her to successfully lead an army into battle against a conquering foe. A psychic named Edgar Cayce used his divine connection to diagnose people's ailments and give them natural cures. His success rate was high, and he is still regarded as one of the great psychics of modern times. In particular, Cayce said he accessed a divine database called the Akashic Record.

Similar to psychologist Carl Jung's "collective unconscious," the Akashic Record is an energetic imprinting of everything that ever happens. All matter leaves an energetic trail that can at some point of awareness, be traced back through the web of its origin. This means that there is a record of all that has ever happened physically, mentally, and spiritually because it all left an energetic imprint that still exists, no matter how long ago it happened.

What this means is that there is an immense database created by the energetic patterns of everyone, past, present, and future. The past has happened, the present is happening, and the future is yet to happen, and thus can be changed. It is a divine database where the knowledge of the ages can be accessed in a flash. At your disposal is a resource that is more valuable than any jewel or precious metal.

As you move along your natural magic quest, you can answer the questions that continually crop up along the way by querying this energetic database. Building strong relationships with divine energies in the form of Goddesses and Gods is one of the best and quickest ways to access this divine database. Honor and connect with these divine energies, and they will continually help in all of your quests. This is a relationship that will span out into infinity and multiple lifetimes. It helps you not only in your quest in this lifetime, but also in your overall quest, moving into every lifetime.

Spirit Guides and Ancestral Energy

The ancient Celts buried the bodies of those who had passed away in sacred groves where they believed the spirit and power of their ancestors would become part of the land. This ancestral energy could then called upon at any time by anyone who knew how to awaken its secret power. The mythology of King Arthur and the knights of the round table embodies this concept in the form of the "sleeping king," whose power waits to be awakened and utilized by those who are deemed worthy by their actions and know how to tap into it.

Chinese spiritual traditions, such as Feng Shui, believe that when the physical body dies, the spirit lives on. Because of this, the chi of "good" and "bad" spirits is all around us. Spirit guides and ancestral energy are generally helpful spirits that bring positive energy into our lives.

Each of us has one or two primary spirit guides. Spirit guides cannot take away your problems, but they can guide you to helpful sources and people that facilitate solutions to your problems. Spirit guides can also help protect you from negative energy being directed at you by people and spirits that wish you harm. With the help of your spirit guides, you can raise your harmonic and energy level to a higher level, making it much more difficult for someone to deter or knock you off track. Because of this, spirit guides are invaluable in terms of your natural magic quest.

Animal Allies

When I moved to the country, one of the first things I did was get two dogs. About three years afterward, I was out watering the flower garden with my four-year-old son, when suddenly the dogs started barking near where my son was playing. The dogs took positions, one on each side of my son, and pushed him toward me. The dogs kept barking and barking. I stopped what I was doing and moved closer to the dogs. I grabbed my son, and noticed a loud noise started coming from a spot close to where he and the dogs had been. Moving a little closer to the noise, I realized that the dogs were barking at a 5-foot rattlesnake, rattling its tail in the grass. This experience showed me firsthand the importance of having animals, our dogs, as allies.

Animal allies have many names including totems, power animals, animal guides, familiars, pet companions, and spirit animals. They come in physical and spirit form, and as such can help you in a number of ways both physically and energetically.

I have a Siamese cat with whom I have strong energetic bond. Whenever I feel emotionally distraught, she always comes over to me and wants to know what's wrong. She will rub up against me, lick my nose, meow, paw at me, crawl into my lap, and do whatever she can to change the energy. Even more interesting is when I'm not feeling well, she will come sit on the area where I have the pain. She seems to instinctually know where to sit, and what I have found is that when she sits on that spot for a while, I feel better physically and energetically.

Each animal has different qualities and abilities. By communing with your animal ally, you gain access to those qualities and abilities. There is no universal meaning that exists for all animal allies. Animal lists are interesting to look at and may be helpful to refer to, but keep in mind that these lists only represent one person or tradition's interpretation.

Different cultures assign different meanings to different animals. It's important to trust your intuition and personal feelings to find the meaning of your animal ally.

When looking for animal allies, begin by exploring a specific animal's characteristics in nature. Your animal allies can sometimes change over time. Ways to know your animal allies is to be aware of an animal you feel drawn to that comes repeatedly in meditation, dreams, or continually keeps showing up in your life. You will tend to share qualities with your animal ally. Because of this, one of the questions you might ask yourself is, what animal do you feel like right now? Please refer to the suggested readings in Appendix C for more in-depth information regarding animal allies and how to discover them.

Relationships

You need to build relationships that can help you in your empowerment process. Some of the things that can help this process is surrounding yourself with positive people who have goals that are compatible with yours. Get rid of the negative people who hinder you and don't feel good to be around. A key indicator is when you get done interacting with a person, how do you feel? You should on the whole feel empowered and full of energy rather than irritated and drained. In the following meditation, you will learn how to contact and communicate with the spirit of your animal ally.

Before beginning the meditation, ritual, and exercises in this section, review your natural magic plans for relationships as you outlined them in Chapter 3.

Natural Magic Affirmation for Relationships

Say the following affirmation aloud three times before writing it in your Natural Magic Empowerment Journal:

Today and every day, I am building positive relationships with my animal and spirit allies that will help me attain my natural magic goals for relationships.

Write the affirmation on a small note card. Put the card in the corner of your bathroom mirror so that you see it every morning as you are getting ready for the day.

Natural Magic Meditation for Relationships

Begin by getting comfortable. Close your eyes and take several deep breaths. Slowly draw in your breath, filling your lungs with air. As you hold your breath for a few seconds, sense the air energizing your body, mind, and spirit. With your exhale, push all of the stagnant energy out of your being. Each time you take a breath, you feel a cleansing sensation that fills you with vital and flowing energy, while ridding you of any unwanted negative energy. Keep taking deep breaths until you feel cleansed and fully charged with energy.

Now in your mind's eye, imagine walking through a beautiful green meadow on a warm spring day. Birds are singing and wildflowers are in bloom, splashing a bouquet of color across the meadow. As you breathe in, you discover the air is fresh and sweet with the fragrance of the flowers. A gentle breeze strokes your skin, and you feel a smile beginning at your mouth and spreading across your being, until you are also smiling from within.

You travel through the meadow to the side of a mountain that reaches high into the sky. At the base of the mountain is the opening to a large cave. Moving through the cave opening, you enter a large cavern that is lined with crystals and stones that glow with a soft iridescent light. As you survey the interior of the cave, the light changes colors and hues. The energy in the place is balanced between an invigorating wave and serene calmness. You intuitively sense a sacredness about the cave that invites you into its protective womb, making you feel completely at home.

Finding a place in the center of the sacred cave, you sit down and begin meditating. Take a deep breath and sense your spirit moving through an energetic doorway to another world. It is a world where spirits gather to connect and communicate with each other. You have come to connect and communicate with the spirit of your animal totem.

Through the shadows of light and dark of the cave, you see a magnificent tree standing in the corner, its branches spreading out in all directions. You move along the branches of the tree that seems to stretch out into infinity. As you search, you feel a tugging that pulls you like a magnet. It begins faintly, but becomes stronger as move closer to the source. You encounter a fork in your path, and you move left. When a second fork appears, you move left once again. The tugging becomes stronger and stronger as you continue moving along the energetic pathway. Before you is a third fork, at which juncture you move off to the right, and come face to face with the spirit of your power animal.

Like the opposite poles of a magnet, your spirits join in an energetic union that merges your spirit and your power animal's spirit as One. When this connection happens, communication becomes instantaneous. It's a sense of knowing that transcends both thoughts and words. You sense energetic impulses moving faster than the speed of light, spiraling through your Oneness of spirit. At this point, your ally imparts a simple message for you, and only for you. You acknowledge the message and thank your animal ally.

As you take another deep, complete breath, you move back through the tree, and then through the energetic doorway into your sacred cave. As you do this, you take all the information imparted by your animal ally with you. You reflect on the sensation of being One with your power animal and what that felt like in terms of your animal nature. For a few moments, you energetically shape-shift into your power animal, and sense the world from this perception. When you shape-shift, you again become One with the spirit of your animal totem. It is your animal ally, there to help you whenever you ask for help.

Now take another breath in and out, and begin bringing your awareness back into your body. Stretch your arms and legs, and feel energy filling every part of your being. Take a moment to reflect on what it felt like to be One with your power animal. Before doing anything else, write down in your Natural Magic Empowerment Journal the simple message your animal ally imparted, plus any impressions and insights you had as a result of the experience.

Natural Magic Ritual for Relationships

The purpose of the following ritual is to honor and give thanks to your animal allies. You will need a clear quartz crystal point, a bowl of the earth, an incense burner with a smudge stick, a beeswax candle and holder, a cup of well or spring water, and a piece of malachite. Follow these steps:

1. Bring the elemental powers into your sacred circle by doing the three steps of the natural magic ritual for relationships in Chapter 1. Invite the divine energies of Oneness into your space by standing in the middle of the circle and saying:

   Divine energies of Oneness
   Please bless my sacred space with your presence.

2. Cleanse the piece of malachite by bathing it in the smudge smoke for at least a minute, and letting the smoke fully surround it. Next,

program the stone by holding it in your right hand while visualizing in your mind's eye all the characteristics of your animal ally. Pulse your breath out of your nose while envisioning the characteristics being imparted into the stone. One of the natural qualities of malachite is animal communication.

3. Go to the middle of your circle with the piece of malachite in your right hand. Invite the spirit of your animal allies into your circle by saying:

Essential spirit of cats [you can use whatever animal you like here instead of cats]
Please bless this sacred space with your presence.

Honor and give thanks to your animal allies by holding the piece of malachite up in your hand and saying:

Essential spirit of cats
Thank you for the help you give me
In return I send to you
The divine love of the Goddess
And divine peace of the God.
So be it!

Thank the energies of the elements and Oneness. Before leaving the area, be sure your candle and smudge stick are fully extinguished. When you are done, place the piece of malachite on your altar as a continual divine connection to your animal allies.

Natural Magic Blessing for Relationships

Great Goddess, protector of animals, thank you for helping me to build empowering relationships with my animal allies.

Natural Magic Exercises for Relationships

In the following natural magic exercise you become your animal ally for a day. If you have more than one animal ally, select the one you want to be for the day. You can repeat this exercise for each ally you have if you like.

Begin by listing in your Natural Magic Empowerment Journal all the characteristics of your animal ally. If you're not sure, consult an informational resource such as an encyclopedia, or if your ally is something in your immediate environment, observe its characteristics. Review these characteristics before you start your day.

Rather than trying to act like the animal itself, you are incorporating the animal's characteristics into your way of doing things. If your animal ally is a cat, for example, you are trying to be more aware of smells and sounds, moving with more grace, and being flexible enough to land on your feet. This exercise makes you more aware of your animal ally's characteristics and how you can incorporate them into your life and natural magic quest for relationships. It also strengthens your bond with your animal ally.

In this second natural magic exercise, you observe a person for the first time. Begin by selecting someone you want to observe. If the person is agreeable to it, you can do the exercise together. Begin by closing your eyes, taking a deep breath, and clearing your mind. Now open your eyes and begin looking at the person. The idea is to observe the person without judging what you are observing. Observe their face: What is the person's expression, how is the person's face shaped, what is the color of their eyes, contour of their cheeks, any wrinkles or freckles, color of their hair, and shape of their lips and ears?

Next observe the other parts of the person's body. Take notice of how they move, how they talk, and how they interact with the world. Again, stay away from judgments, and stick with observations such as shape, color, texture, size, tone, and so forth. With this, determine what animal the person most resembles right now. By doing this exercise, you increase your awareness of the other person as well as your mutual relationship with nature.

Wellness

It's important to build relationships with people who promote, rather than hinder, your natural magic goals for wellness. For the most part, avoid people who don't have your best interests in mind, particularly in terms of your health. Surrounding yourself with people who are health conscious and have wellness goals of their own helps you in your own wellness empowerment process. If you have family members who insist on trying to derail your quest for wellness, you can't cut them out of your life, but you can minimize your interaction with them.

Natural Magic Affirmation for Wellness

Say the following affirmation aloud three times before writing it in your Natural Magic Empowerment Journal:

Today and every day, I choose to have healthy relationships with people that are positive and empower me on my quest for wellness.

Write the affirmation on a small note card. Post the card on your refrigerator so that you see it when you are in your kitchen.

Natural Magic Meditation for Wellness

Begin by sitting or reclining comfortably, and close your eyes. Take several deep breaths. Slowly inhale and fill your lungs with air. As you hold your breath, feel all the tension in your neck and shoulders coalesce into a ball of tense energy. With your exhale, release the ball of tension from your body. Inhale again and as you do so, elevate your shoulders slightly. Hold your breath and focus on the tension coming together into a ball of energy. Exhale and release it with your breath while dropping your shoulders down. Sense all the tension moving out of your body. Do this breathing exercise several more times until you feel a peaceful calm pervade your body, mind, and spirit.

Imagine moving through the meadow to your sacred cave. You stop along the way to smell the flowers and listen to the birds sing. When you reach the opening of the cave, the light emanating from it is a soft blue color. As you enter the cave, it changes to a deep shade of forest green. You feel a healing sensation as you enter the interior of the cool cavern. You walk to the center of the cave and sit down.

Now take another deep breath and in your mind's eye, sense an energetic door opening up before you. Using your imagination, create an energetic double of yourself. Although your double is separate from your physical body, it is still part of your overall energy and spirit, and as such, an extension of your awareness. With your double, you can essentially be in two places at the same time, much the same way that you can do two different things with your right and left hands.

With your awareness in your double's body, you move through the energetic doorway in the spirit realm. Once there, you sense spirit essences hovering

163

quietly around you. Some of the essences have a familiar feel to them and others seem very foreign. You communicate with the familiar ones. In turn, they direct you toward a group of spirit essences that are gathered around in a circle.

Approaching the circle, you are immediately overcome with the knowledge that these are the spirits of your ancestors, guides, and your guardian angel. They welcome you into the circle, and you become One with their energy. Your angel introduces you to your ancestors and you also see relatives whom you knew in your present lifetime, who are now deceased. Connecting with these energetic essences seems to complete a circuit within you that makes you feel essentially whole.

You recognize that some of these spirits have become your spirit guides in your current lifetime. You thank them for their help, and ask for their help in your natural magic quest for wellness. Before leaving the circle, you thank your guardian angel and the spirits of all your ancestors. You sense a halo of light surrounding you as you move back through the doorway to your sacred cave. Your double flows into your primary being and you once again become One.

Take another deep breath, move your awareness out of the cave. Gradually bring your awareness back into your physical body. Wiggle your fingers and toes, stretch your arms and legs, and open your eyes without really focusing on anything in particular. Take a moment to reflect on the experience of traveling to the spirit world and meeting your guardian angel, ancestors, and spirit guides. Before doing anything else, write in your Natural Magic Empowerment Journal the impressions and insights that you had as a result of the meditation.

Natural Magic Ritual for Wellness

The purpose of the following ritual is to honor and bring your spirit guide(s) and ancestral energies into your circle. You will need a clear quartz crystal point, a bowl of the earth, an incense burner with a smudge stick, a beeswax candle and holder, a cup of well or spring water, and a gift for your spirit guide(s) and ancestral energies. (The gift can be as simple or elaborate as you like. Just make sure it's something from nature or that reflects nature.) Follow these steps:

1. Bring the elemental powers into your sacred circle by doing the three steps of the natural magic ritual for relationships in

Chapter 1. Invite the divine energies of Oneness into your space by standing in the middle of the circle and saying:

Divine energies of Oneness
Please bless my sacred space with your presence.

2. Bring the energy of your spirit guide(s) and ancestors into your sacred space by saying:

Spirits who guide me
Ancestors who empower me
Please come into this circle of light
And bless it with your energy.

3. Take your gift and hold it up in the middle of the circle. As you do so, say:

Spirit guides and ancestral energies
I honor you with this gift
For all the help and light you give me
Every day of my life.

Place the gift on your altar as a symbol of your everlasting appreciation. Thank the energies of the elements and Oneness for their help in the ritual. Before leaving the area, be sure your candle and smudge stick are completely extinguished.

Natural Magic Blessing for Wellness

Great God, please bless my spirit guide(s) and the spirits of my ancestors. Thank you for helping me to build empowering relationships with them.

Natural Magic Exercises for Wellness

In the following natural magic exercise you ask your spirit guide a question. Begin by formulating a question either about your guide or about your natural magic quest for wellness. Write the question in your Natural Magic Empowerment Journal. Next, close your eyes and ask your question aloud, addressing it to your spirit guide.

Take a deep breath and clear your mind of all thoughts. Now ask your question once again. Wait for the first thing that comes into your mind. Write it in your Natural Magic Empowerment Journal. If it doesn't make sense, then close your eyes, and ask the question again. Remember, the answer may require some deciphering on your part. Also the answer may be pointing you to another source that can answer your question.

In this second natural magic exercise, you find a peaceful, easy spot in nature where you can go to charge yourself with energy. Begin by selecting a place that you know of or someplace you have heard about that is known for its natural beauty and tranquil setting. You may already have a spot you go that makes you feel good and energizes you when you go there. If not, consult people you know and environmental magazines and park directories for ideas. Go to the place and experience what it is like. Determine if being there calms and empowers you.

Once you have an empowering spot in nature, go to it (physically, if possible; or imagine yourself there) whenever you feel stressed out and drained of energy. Take pictures of this special place so that you hang them on your refrigerator, in your work area, and on your dresser. You can also use the pictures to make a small shrine in your house as a way to relax and charge yourself with positive energy.

Enrichment

When building relationships for enrichment, beware of people who are opportunists. Although they may seem initially helpful, on the whole they have a tendency to be out for themselves, meaning they will sell out you and everything they believe in given the right price. In addition, a relationship with an opportunist always winds up being one-sided. You do all the giving, and they give nothing in return.

Enriching relationships are two-way relationships. They benefit both parties involved. So build relationships with people who empower you, and who you also empower. This is the key to building lasting relationships that will help you in your natural magic quest for enrichment.

Natural Magic Affirmation for Enrichment

Say the following affirmation aloud three times before writing it into your Natural Magic Empowerment Journal:

Today and every day, I choose to become the person I genuinely want to be, and to surround myself with people who positively empower me.

Write the affirmation on a small note card and place the card where you can see while you are working on your natural magic goals for enrichment.

Natural Magic Meditation for Enrichment

Get in a comfortable position, close your eyes, and begin relaxing by taking several deep breaths. Inhale and fill you lungs with air. As you hold your breath for a moment, sense an energy filling your body with light. Exhale and feel all the stagnant and negative energy moving out through your breath. Do this breathing exercise until you feel both relaxed and energized.

Imagine yourself moving through the meadow toward your sacred cave. Take time to feel the warmth of the sunlight, and the cool breeze as it echoes through the grass and surrounding trees. As you approach the opening of the cave, you hear a tone that when you hear it, makes you feel peaceful and at ease with yourself and the world. Entering the cave, you are met with a golden light that is enriching and full of vitality. In your mind's eye, now move to the middle of the cave, and assume a comfortable meditative position.

You take another deep breath and as you exhale an energetic doorway opens before you. You create a spirit double of yourself, and send it through the doorway as an extension of yourself. It is a way of taking your awareness to other places and dimensions without harming your physical body.

Through the doorway, you move into a dimension where you encounter the energies and spirits of the divine. You encounter gods and goddesses, who are linked by strands of light that connect them together. They are like the many faces of one God and one Goddess, who when united, form the whole of Oneness.

You look at the many faces of the divine, and as you do so, you thank them for the help they have given you in the past, and the help they will give you on your natural magic quest for enrichment. You move into the whole of Oneness, and give thanks for the vitality and help you have been given in this lifetime. A golden light fills you full of the power of the divine.

You connect with your divine self—that part of you that harkens back into the source of creation. You feel the empowering energy of the Earth Mother as she fills your being with an overflowing sensation of life at its fullest. You are a vessel filled with light that shines within you and all around you. You have the power to manifest into anyone you want to be, and to attain your deepest and dearest goals.

Now take another deep breath, move your awareness out of the sacred cave. Walk into your double so that you become One again, and then begin moving your awareness back to the present time and place. Open your eyes slowly, and use your hands to rub your arms and legs. Take your time while continuing to ponder your connection to the divine. Before doing anything else, write down in your Natural Magic Empowerment Journal the impressions and insights that you received as a result of the meditation.

Natural Magic Ritual for Enrichment

The purpose of the following ritual is to honor and give thanks for your divine relationships. You will need a clear quartz crystal point, a bowl of the earth, an incense burner with a smudge stick, a beeswax candle and holder, a cup of well or spring water, and an offering of something you have made such as a craft, a song, painting, or a poem. Follow these steps:

1. Bring the elemental powers into your sacred circle by doing the three steps of the natural magic ritual for relationships in Chapter 1. Invite the divine energies of Oneness into your space by standing in the middle of the circle and saying:

   Divine energies of Oneness
   Please bless my sacred space with your presence.

2. From the middle of your space, bring the divine Goddess and God into your circle by saying:

   Great Goddess
   Please bring your sacred light into this circle
   Great God
   Please bring your sacred peace into this circle.

3. Give your offering to the divine. If it is a craft display it, if it is music play it, and if it is a poem recite it. After you are done, say:

   Divine energies
   I offer you my creation
   In thanks for all the help you give me
   It is my way of honoring you
   In all of your many forms.
   Ayea! Ayea! Ayea! Blessed be!

Place the offering on your altar. Thank the energies of the elements and Oneness for their help. Be sure that your candle and smudge stick are fully extinguished before you leave the area.

Natural Magic Blessing for Enrichment

Natural energies of Oneness, please bless my divine relationships that empower and enrich me each and every day.

Natural Magic Exercises for Enrichment

In the following natural magic exercise you assess the people who can help you in your natural magic quest for enrichment, and improve your relationships with these people. Begin by taking your enrichment goals as you wrote them in your Natural Magic Empowerment Journal, and write them out on a separate page, leaving enough room under each one to list helpful people. Under each goal, write down people who can help you to achieve this goal. If your goal is a new house, for example, you might want to list anyone you know who is good at architecture, carpentry, or cabinet making.

The next part of this exercise involves sitting down and determining how you can improve your relationship with each of these helpful people. Building good relationships involves an element of give and take, meaning that if you want something, you should figure out something that you can willingly give in return. Make some notes in your Natural Magic Empowerment Journal.

In this second natural magic exercise you focus on meeting someone new every day. Begin by telling yourself, "Today I am going to meet someone new and empowering." As you go through your day, keep this in mind. Be friendly and positive with the people you meet, particularly in situations that impact your enrichment. Ask people about themselves and their families. Remember and write this information down when you can. I have a friend who keeps notes on her phone sheet of the names of people's spouses, children, pets, and birthdays. Every time she talks to someone she asks about and references their spouses, children, and pets by name. She also sends a card on birthdays. This can be very helpful when building relationships. People like it when you put some effort into remembering the things that are important in their lives, and being thoughtful to others in turn empowers you!

Chapter Eight

Finding Natural Magic
All Around You

Julian Cope, singer/songwriter and composer of such classics as "20 Mothers" and "Floored Genius" and author of the book *The Modern Antiquarian: A Pre-Millennial Odyssey Through Megalithic Britain,* walks the ley lines and visits the sacred sites of Great Britain in pilgrimages that extend over 1,500 miles and 500 sites. He travels on the Neolithic trackways, paths people have been walking for thousands of years. They are the energetic arteries of the earth, flowing with natural magic.

What makes Julian Cope unique as an artist is that while he moves along these ley lines, he is inspired to write his songs. As he described it in an interview for *Magical Blend* magazine, "I don't sit around with a guitar. I walk on the sacred landscape with a Dictaphone and I sing my songs straight out as the spirit moves me. That's an artist's duty—to recognize what flame moves within him, and I recognized a totally different flame."

Basically his inspiration comes from the natural energy of the earth, whose energy he has tuned into as a composer and writer. His experience is a great example of how the energies of natural magic are everywhere, waiting to be tapped and utilized in a multitude of intriguing ways.

Shamanism and Nature

Nature is what sustains humankind. In ancient times, and indeed still today, tribal societies depended on a harmonious relationship with nature in order to survive. These societies relied on priests known as shamans, whose role it was to contact and communicate with the spirits of animals, plants, trees, rocks, and the earth.

Linguistically, the word shaman finds its root in the Tunguso-Manchurian word "saman," meaning, "to know." This knowing refers to a spiritual healer who used his knowledge to access the energies of natural magic for healing, divining, and personal empowerment.

One of the oldest spiritual practices, shamanism dates back to the beginnings of humankind. Its foundation stems from the individual's ongoing relationship with the spirits of nature including the elements, ancestral energies, and the divine aspects. Shamans believe that everything whether it is animate or inanimate has spirit or consciousness. Power comes directly from their interaction with these spirits.

To the shaman, all things have a material form and a living essence. This idea prevails throughout the spiritual practices around the world. In Melanesia and Polynesia this essence or spirit is called "mana." In the Japanese Shinto tradition, it is called "kami," which inhabits all natural things. The Aborigines believe that everything is endowed with a "sacredness," while the ancient Greeks perceived the natural world as an animated being, and everything in it was endowed with the "world soul."

In particular, shamans use a combination of psychotropic plants, drumming, and dancing to achieve an altered state of consciousness. This altered state allows them to move beyond the illusions of human perception to a place of awareness where they work with the spirits of nature to diagnose illnesses and do healings. It is in this altered state of awareness that they are able to access the natural magic that is all around.

The world of the shaman is both mystical and practical. Specifically, a shaman's knowledge extends to the healing properties of various plants. Long before pharmacies and modern medicine, the shaman knew what plant to use for a particular type of ailment. This knowledge was passed down from teacher to student, spanning generations. Much of this knowledge and many of these powerful techniques are still used today in one form or another.

Healing Properties of Plants

Many plants and foods you eat have healing properties. Some of these plants include licorice with its anti-tumor properties, green tea with its ability to lower cholesterol, and all edible berries, which speed up the healing of wounds.

One plant in particular that contains a high degree of healing properties is lavender. It contains substances called "coumarins" which have been scientifically documented in lab studies to have a calming effect on the body. The purple flowers of the lavender bush are usually made into an oil that can be used for a variety of healing purposes that include adult acne, colds and flu, and fatigue.

Lavender is the most gentle and versatile plant oil. Because of its healing gentleness on the skin, lavender essential oil is often used in skincare products for babies, children, and adults. When you use lavender regularly, it increases self-awareness, helps you sleep more soundly, be more emotionally balanced, and helps you focus on a given task.

When you smell lavender, it increases your alpha brain waves and helps you to reduce stress and relax. The helpful qualities of lavender can be accessed by inhaling the heady scent of fresh lavender flowers, or by misting the fragrance from a bottle and inhaling the scent. You can also tap into the natural powers of lavender by applying lavender creams or essential oil (most often diluted with a carrier oil such as grapeseed, olive, or apricot oil) to your skin.

Besides lavender, there are many other plants that have beneficial healing properties to them. For more information on the healing properties of plants, please consult Appendix B.

Tree Magic

In shamanism, there is a concept of the world tree. Also known as the "shaman's tree," the world tree is a great flowering tree containing all knowledge that blooms at the center of the world. Shamans are like birds that fly to the world tree, which like the Akashic Record, is a divine database of information.

Mythologies throughout the world describe the "tree of life" as a tree that is always green, one that is forever flowering and bearing fruit. When someone eats the fruit, they become immortal. The tree of life is also said to be the essence of all trees.

To the Celts, the tree of life was an apple tree, to the Chinese it was a peach tree, and to the Semites it was a date tree. In Scandinavian mythology a gigantic ash tree named Yggdrasil is the cosmic axis that holds each of the nine worlds of creation. Three worlds are below, one of them being the world of the dwarves, three worlds inhabit the middle, one of them being this earthly plane, and three worlds above, one of them being the world of the elves and another being the home of the Gods and Goddesses.

Shamans have long used trees as a contact point into the other world. Druids revered groves of oak tress as sacred, and used the natural energy of the oaks as an axis way to connect to the divine energies of nature. Because trees can grow to be more than a thousand years old, they become sacred storehouses of natural magic. They represent a connection between Earth and the sky, illuminated by the light of the Sun.

Within many spiritual traditions, Earth and Sun represent the masculine and feminine polarities. Together their union creates all that is, both within the manifested and unmanifested realms. This union is manifested in the form of a tree as it finds its roots deep within Earth and its branches spreading upward to the Sun. Also the cycle of deciduous trees, which move from budding, to flowering, to bearing fruit, and then to losing their leaves, is representative of the seasonal cycles and the creative energies of nature.

Every tree you connect and bond with has energy and knowledge to impart to you. That is one reason to revere and protect the trees that are on Earth, rather than cut them down. Rooted in Earth and reaching to the heavens with their branches, trees are natural links to the energy of nature and the cosmos. When you touch a tree and allow yourself to be sensitive to its energy, you can feel this link. It's like touching the source of creation and life and being One with it. This is the essence of empowering your life with natural magic. So go out and hug a tree, right now!

Relationships

Within the empowerment process, you need to reaffirm your natural magic goals. With regards to relationships, this means reviewing your goals and making an assessment of your progress at this point in the process. You live in a dynamic world in which the only thing that is constant is change. This means that sometimes you have to adapt your goals so that they continue to reflect your wants and needs.

The people you have relationships with, like yourself, are in continuous change. Because of this, goals also change. This means you need to be at least somewhat flexible. It doesn't mean you have to completely alter your goals, but it does mean you have to look at people and situations for what they are and adjust your own goals accordingly.

Before beginning the meditation, ritual, and exercises in this section, review your natural magic plans for relationships as you outlined them in Chapter 3.

Natural Magic Affirmation for Relationships

Say the following affirmation aloud three times before writing it in your Natural Magic Empowerment Journal:

Today and every day, I breathe in the loving wisdom of the helpful spirits of nature and Earth.

Write the affirmation on a small note card. Place the card on your altar in your sacred space.

Natural Magic Meditation for Relationships

Begin by running a hot bath and adding 10 to 20 drops of lavender oil to the water. Immerse yourself in the fragrant water for several minutes, and when you are finished, step out and towel yourself off with a soft towel. Then anoint yourself with a couple of drops of pure lavender essential oil on your wrists, ankles, and the top of your head. (It's okay to use lavender oil directly on the skin, or you can dilute it with a carrier oil if you prefer.)

Sit or recline comfortably, and take a few minutes to slowly sip a glass of pure well or spring water while thinking about your natural magic goals for relationships. When you are done drinking the water, close your eyes and begin taking several deep breaths. Each time you inhale, your breath fills you full of energy and your awareness expands. Each time you exhale, it relaxes you, and you feel peaceful and at ease.

In your mind's eye, imagine you are a seed planted in the earth. An embryo encased in a hard covering protects you from the outside world. Sense yourself sending two shoots out that penetrate the casing, giving you your first experiences with the world. One shoot moves downward into the nurturing Earth, and the other moves up toward the vitalizing light.

Earth is your mother in whose womb you are born. As you tap into her energy, she gives you the nourishment that you need to be born and then to sustain life. She can make you healthy and strong because that is her nature. In her body, you plant your roots and begin your ascent into the heavens. Know that the earth supports you in all your endeavors, big or small. As your mother she loves you exactly as you are and for who you are.

The Sun is your father in whose light you are continually growing. You reach up toward his light and expand in his radiance. In the warmth of the Sun, you send your trunk and branches outward and upward. You grow leaves so you can collect even more of his warmth and light. He fills you full of vitality that complements the life given to you by your mother, Earth.

With the help of Mother Earth and Father Sun, your roots, truck, branches, leaves, and fruits continue to grow larger with time. You develop relationships with the birds that come to nest and eat from your branches, and the squirrels that come to hide their food and seek your protection from the dangers that lurk on the ground below.

Your branches become layers of natural worlds that reach to the sky. You are the link between Earth and Sun, Goddess and God. Your spirit spans the ages, empowering all who come into contact with you with the magic of your being. You are the tree of life, whose energy and life force is in all things.

Now begin slowly bringing your awareness back into your physical body and surroundings. Sense how all the parts of your body connect together as you stretch your limbs. Move your hands and feet, and open your eyes, without focusing on one specific thing.

Once your awareness has returned, take a moment to relax and reflect on the sensation of being a tree. Before doing anything else, write in your Natural

Magic Empowerment Journal the impressions or insights that you had as a tree during the meditation.

Natural Magic Ritual for Relationships

The purpose of the following ritual is to draw a sacred circle around a tree and then direct that sacred energy toward your natural magic goals for relationships. You will need a clear quartz crystal point, sandalwood scented oil, and access to a tree. Then follow these steps:

1. Clear your crystal using your expectation and breath, and then program it with the energy of the tree. Starting at the north point, draw a clockwise circle of light around the tree. Invite the divine energies of Oneness into your space by standing at the north point of the circle and saying:

   Divine energies of Oneness
   Please bless this circle with your presence.

2. Place a few drops of sandalwood scented oil (a few drops of sandalwood essential oil blended with a carrier oil, or a premade mixture) on your finger, and draw a small circle on the west side of the tree trunk. Repeat this three times for a total of three circles of scented oil on the tree trunk. As you draw the circles, envision in your mind's eye one of your natural magic goals for relationships. The natural properties of sandalwood oil fill the heart with joy while fostering openness, warmth, and understanding. Imagine these characteristics coming into your relationship goal as the scent of the sandalwood fills your senses.

3. Position both your hands on the trunk of the tree so that they are on either side of the circle you drew on the tree. As you do so, say:

   Blessed and sacred spirit of this tree
   Please share your natural magic with me
   So that my relationships
   Will be strengthened with your energy.

   Thank the energies of Oneness and the spirit of the tree. Before you leave the area, pull up the circle of light by using your crystal and drawing a counterclockwise circle, beginning at the north point.

Natural Magic Blessing for Relationships

Divine spirits of trees, please bless my natural magic goals for relationships with your sacred energy.

Natural Magic Exercises for Relationships

In the following natural magic exercise, you plan a day out in nature with your loved one. Begin by selecting a place in nature that is special for both of you. Pack a lunch of fresh fruits, vegetables, and pure water. When you get there, spend the time together communing together with the spirits of nature. Find a sizable tree where you can both put your hands on its trunk. Ask the spirit of the tree to empower your relationship with its magic by saying:

Sacred tree essence
Whose spirit moves from Earth to sky
Please now empower our relationship
With the magic of your energy.

In the second natural magic exercise, you bless your food with the divine energy of the Goddess and God. Palms down, place your hands over the food and imagine a white light moving from your hands into the food. The light is full of vitality and the divine energy of the Goddess and God. Sense the energy moving down into the food, energizing and blessing it. Give thanks by saying:

Dear Goddess and God
Bless this food you have provided me
Thank you for your divine gift
May it fill me full of your sacred energy.

Wellness

Wellness goals take time and effort to successfully attain. If your goal is to lose weight or eat healthier foods and you find it hard to stay on your diet, the solution is to work at it slowly. It is easier to cut down on things such as soda pop, alcohol, and sweets than it is to eliminate them from your diet all together.

When reaffirming your wellness goals, be realistic as to the timeframe for making your goals a reality. If you are too strict with your expectations, you might find yourself giving up or straying off course.

Unlike relationship goals that generally involve other people, your wellness goals are more personal and involve you and your body. Because of this, it is sometimes easier to remain focused on your natural magic wellness goals. What is most important is to continue making forward movement toward your optimum state of wellness.

Natural Magic Affirmation for Wellness

Say the following affirmation aloud three times before writing it in your Natural Magic Empowerment Journal:

Each and every day, I am healthier in every way as I focus on attaining my natural magic goals for wellness.

Write the affirmation on a small note card. Place the card in your dining room or exercise room so that you can frequently refer to it.

Natural Magic Meditation for Wellness

Begin by rubbing a couple of drops of lavender essential oil on your solar plexus chakra, located in the center of your body between your chest and stomach. Get in a comfortable position and take several deep breaths. Inhale and gradually fill your lungs full of air. As you hold your breath for a couple of seconds, sense your body expanding with energy. Exhale and sense your body relaxing. Continue doing this until you are relaxed, flowing with the energy inside of you and all around you.

Imagine walking on a large pathway that is lined with rose bushes on the right side and blackberry vines on the left. Moving a little to right, you see a Tropicana rose in full bloom, its deep orange-red color is captivating your attention in its radiance. Drifting a little closer, the fragrance of the exquisite rose fills your nostrils with an inspiring floral bouquet like no others. You linger for several moments, savoring the heady scent.

Moving a little to the left, you see that the blackberry vines form a impenetrable thicket. Green, red, and black-colored berries cover the vines like colorful jewels. Carefully stepping closer, you spy a particularly large berry that is the deepest color of red-black that you have ever seen. Bypassing the thorns, you pluck the berry and notice how soft and juicy it feels in your hand. The purple juice colors your fingers as you bite into the berry. Your taste buds are greeted by a sweetness that sends chills of joy up and down your spine, giving the experience a depth that moves into the spiritual.

As you move along the pathway, you reach a fork where the path veers off to the right and left. Though the right path is wider and obviously more traveled, you chose the left path that takes you down a small incline. Reaching the bottom of the incline, you see several pine, cedar, madrone, and fir trees, standing tall against the skyline.

Walking slowly through the trees, you move toward a small creek, nestled in among the woods. Reaching the creek, you step over several large white quartz boulders, and cross to the other side. You follow the path further to a small pool in the creek. The pool is covered by a giant maple with huge green leaves. You sit down at the base of the maple tree, and begin breathing in the energy that vibrates all around you.

You can feel the natural energy in yourself and in everything around you. You breathe in the natural energy and collect it in your being, absorbing all that you can. You sense the energy revitalizing your body, mind, and spirit, making you strong and healthy. The water acts as an ionizer, and the maple tree fills you full of the life force. All the elements and energies come together as One within your being.

Now bring this sensation back with you as you return to your body and present surroundings. Move your toes and fingers and stretch like a cat. Rub your hands together briskly, and sit back and reflect upon your experience for a few minutes. When you are finished, write your impressions and insights into your Natural Magic Empowerment Journal.

Natural Magic Ritual for Wellness

The purpose of the following ritual is to do a healing ceremony using the energy and natural magic of the trees. You will need a clear quartz crystal point, a bowl of the earth, an incense burner with a smudge stick, a beeswax candle and holder, a cup of well or spring water, eucalyptus or cedarwood scented oil (whichever you prefer), a pen, and a piece of paper. Follow these steps:

1. Make sure you dilute your eucalyptus or cedarwood essential oil in a carrier oil as both of these oils can be harsh to your skin. Usually you only need a couple of drops of these essential oils to a vial of oil as they are so potent. Rub a thin film of scented oil over the

candle. Wipe any remaining oil from your hands before lighting the candle.

Bring the elemental powers into your sacred circle by doing the three steps of the natural magic ritual for relationships in Chapter 1. Invite the divine energies of Oneness into your space by standing in the middle of the circle and saying:

Divine energies of Oneness
Please bless my sacred space with your presence.

2. Use the pen to draw a simple outline of your body on the piece of paper. On the image of your body, draw a triangle with a line coming down from the center of its base (looking like a pine tree) on the area where you want to do the healing.

3. Place the picture safely by the candle where it is well illuminated. Next, merge with the Goddess and God of the trees. Take your crystal and program it for healing. Point the tip of the crystal at the spot on the picture that designates the area where you want to do the healing. Use the crystal to draw nine energetic counterclockwise circles around that area on the paper while imagining the problem or illness flowing out of your body.

Pulse cobalt blue light through the crystal three times to clear it. Then use the crystal point to once again draw nine circles around the area depicted on the paper, only this time, draw clockwise circles to charge the area with energy. As you do this, say:

Goddess and God of the trees
Please let your healing energies
Move into this area of my body
So that I may now be well.

Thank the energies of the elements, Oneness, and the Goddess and God of the trees. Before leaving the area, be sure that the candle and smudge stick are completely extinguished.

Natural Magic Blessing for Wellness

Bright Lady and Lord of wellness, please bless me with your natural magic so that I will know your divine healing spirit and be well.

Natural Magic Exercises for Wellness

In the following natural magic exercise, you plant a lavender bush. Begin by selecting a flowerpot or spot outside where you can plant your lavender. Native to the Mediterranean region, lavender (botanical name "lavandula") needs full sun, loose fast-draining soil, with a little water and fertilizer. Most garden centers sell the bushes, ready to be transplanted into your soil.

Once you have planted your lavender bush, hold both of your palms over the plant and bless it by saying three times:

Energies of the lavender deva
Please bless this plant with your divine energy
And also please bless me with your healing energy
May we both grow healthy and strong
Under your ever watchful guidance.
So be it! Blessed be!

In the second natural magic exercise, you make a lavender sachet. Begin by collecting the flowers from your lavender bush. Let them dry completely before putting them in a cloth pouch. The aroma of lavender has a calming effect that is balancing and strengthening. The pouch or sachet can then be added to your dresser drawers, where they give a wonderful and healing aroma to your clothes. You can also put the pouch in your pillowcase to encourage a restful night's sleep.

Enrichment

Enrichment is something that happens on many levels, from the physical to the spiritual. Whereas wellness usually means being in good health, enrichment can often be personal perception and choice. Some people feel they need great wealth in order to attain enrichment, whereas other people desire a happy family life, a satisfying spiritual base, and enough physical wealth to live comfortably.

Because of this disparity in the perception of enrichment, it's important to reaffirm your specific enrichment goals at regular intervals. Over time your needs and perceptions change depending on your experiences. Some people continually want more and more in terms of physical wealth, while other people learn to value health and relationships. The choice is yours to make.

Natural Magic Affirmation for Enrichment

Say the following affirmation aloud three times before writing it into your Natural Magic Empowerment Journal:

Each and every day, I expand and enrich my awareness with the natural magic that is all around me.

Write the affirmation on a small note card. Place the card near your front door so that you see it as you come and go from your home.

Natural Magic Meditation for Enrichment

Begin by applying a few drops of lavender oil on your crown chakra at the top of your head. Rub the oil gently into your scalp. Get in a comfortable position and begin taking several deep breaths. Inhale and imagine you are comfortably laying outside on a warm spring day. Hold your breath for a moment, and allow the spring to enter your being. Exhale and the experience becomes part of you. Sense yourself connecting with the forces of creation and Oneness. Continue breathing deeply, increasing the sensation of bright spring energy with your every breath.

From where you are laying in the warm sun, you hear the faint call of a bird. Attuning your ear to it, the sound becomes louder and louder. Like a beacon, it beckons you to get up and follow it. "Caa! Caa! Caa!" The sound echoes through your being like a call from the Goddess.

Rising to the call, you fly up out your body and begin to follow the calling. Your wings are spread wide so that the wind moves you upward, and by turning slightly, you begin moving where you want to go. Tuning into the sound, you move to where it originates, to a grove of oak trees situated to your southwest.

When you touch down, you are greeted with a sight that is both empowering and magical. Before you is a garden that is like no other you have ever seen except perhaps in your imagination or dreams. Stargazer lilies tower up in a row, surrounded by sweet Williams that come in every color. Beyond that, purple lavender bushes spring up in every direction, bordered by small white, pink, and purple daises. The many colored roses and flowers of every variety form splashes of color here and there, creating a rainbow of color.

The experience of the garden transports you into a magical, altered state of awareness, and you find yourself communicating directly with the spirits of the flowers, plants, trees, rocks, and Earth. You sense an excitement that energetically inspires every cell and particle of your being. By merging, you become One with it all. Your body, mind, and spirit are empowered and enriched on every level of being.

Breathe in deeply and bring this empowered, enriched feeling back with you as you begin returning to your body and present physical surroundings. Stretch your arms and legs, fingers and toes, and gradually bring your awareness fully back into your body. Before doing anything else, write down in your Natural Magic Empowerment Journal the impression and insights you had while meditating.

Natural Magic Ritual for Enrichment

The purpose of the following ritual is to enrich your life by connecting to the tree of life. You will need a clear quartz crystal point, a bowl of the earth, an incense burner with a smudge stick, a beeswax candle and holder, a cup of well or spring water, and a piece of fruit cut in four sections. Follow these steps:

1. Bring the elemental powers into your sacred circle by doing the three steps of the natural magic ritual for relationships in Chapter 1. Invite the divine energies of Oneness into your space by standing in the middle of the circle and saying:

   Divine energies of Oneness,
   Please bless my sacred space with your presence.

2. Beginning with the north point, move to each direction with a different section of the fruit, and say:

   Goddess of Earth
   Bless this piece of fruit
   Thank you for this divine gift
   A symbol of your powers of creation.

   In the east point, say:

   Goddess of Air
   Bless this piece of fruit
   Thank you for this divine gift
   A symbol of your powers of creation.

   In the south point, say:

   Goddess of Fire
   Bless this piece of fruit
   Thank you for this divine gift
   A symbol of your powers of creation.

In the west point, say:

Goddess of Water
Bless this piece of fruit
Thank you for this divine gift
A symbol of your powers of creation.

3. With your crystal in your right hand and the four pieces of fruit in your left, move to the center of the circle, and say:

Thank you divine Lady
For this fruit from the tree of life
Please let its powers fill my spirit
Enriching me with the energies of creation.

Eat each piece of the fruit, savoring every mouthful as a blessing from the Goddess and the tree of life. Save the fruit seeds and plant them in the ground in a sunny place as a way of giving thanks to the Goddess and the tree of life.

When you are finished, thank the energies of the elements, Oneness, and the Goddess. Before leaving the area, make sure your candle and smudge stick are completely extinguished.

Natural Magic Blessing for Enrichment

Divine Lady and Lord, please bless my natural magic goals with the gift of fruition from the tree of life.

Natural Magic Exercises for Enrichment

In the following natural magic exercise, you make a natural magic wand. Begin by finding a suitable stick to use for your wand. It should be about 2 feet long and about ½ to 1 inch thick. Depending on the tree it originated from, you may need to scrape the bark off the stick. Be sure to thank the tree that you take the stick from, being careful not to damage the tree in any way.

Suggestions for decorating your wand include tying or gluing a crystal to the tip, adorning it with colored stones or natural beads, wrapping it with wicker or grape vines, painting it with natural dyes, and carving symbols into it. Your natural magic wand is yours to decorate and use as you see fit. It is especially helpful in rituals as you can tap into the natural magic energies of the tree that the wand originated.

In the second natural magic exercise, you plant a tree. Begin by attaining a seed or seedling and planting it in a flowerpot full of fertile soil. Make sure the tree is suitable to your climate and environmental conditions. After planting, bless the tree by saying:

Goddess and God of creation
Please bless this tree with your divine light
So that may grow tall and mighty
As a vision of the tree of life.

Care for your tree until it is big enough to transplant into the ground. Then plant it in a spot where it can thrive and reach its full potential.

Chapter Nine

Sticking to Your Natural Magic Plan

Renowned actor and writer John Cleese, of *Monty Python's Flying Circus* and *A Fish Called Wanda* fame, wanted to do a comedy series with his wife at the time, actress and writer Connie Booth. When trying to come up with an idea, he remembered an experience that he had at a hotel where the manager was particularly rude to all of the guests. He developed this recollection into the popular British comedy series *Fawlty Towers.*

The network people immediately started trying to talk John Cleese out of doing *Fawlty Towers,* but he persisted in making the shows. The first time the series was viewed, there was a lukewarm response, but when the series was viewed again in reruns, people started to watch and it quickly became a classic. After its success and reviews for originality, John Cleese asked a network marketing person what the hardest thing to sell was, and his response was "something original."

John Cleese's experience reminds us that it is easier to follow in someone else's footsteps than it is to forge your own path. When you set out to conquer new territory, it becomes harder because you have entered what I call the "creative zone." When you enter this zone, you are often ahead of your time, navigating unknown waters with numerous setbacks. At the same time by tapping into the creative zone, you suddenly find that you can enrich your life in a multitude of ways.

The idea is to keep a sense of humor when it comes to attaining your natural magic empowerment goals. Walls and obstacles have a tendency to fall when you forge ahead with sincere effort. With persistence and the steady belief in yourself and your goals, it becomes much easier to see your plans through to fruition. This forms the essence of sticking with your natural magic plan.

Labyrinths

Labyrinths come in various forms and are found in cultures throughout the world. The floor of Chartres Cathedral in France contains a classical medieval 11-circuit labyrinth. Medieval labyrinths divide up into four quadrants and sacred geometry plays heavily in the construction of some of these designs. As with Chartres, older examples occur on the floors of European churches and cathedrals. In England, there are examples of what is known as "turf" or three-dimensional labyrinths, created from the natural landscape. They often envelop a mound or hill, as exemplified by the English site Glastonbury Tor.

The design of labyrinths stems from what is known as a "seed." The labyrinth circuits have to do with how many times the path moves around the center. Unlike mazes, which can have more than one entry and exit and often have dead ends, labyrinths move you through a given path and through the process and can have an illuminating and meditative effect on your body, mind, and spirit.

Labyrinths are symbolic of the quest or path you take in life. A labyrinth spirals and winds around, and in the process of walking or tracing the labyrinth, you confront your shadow self and any inner demons that may harbor there. Within terms of self-mastery, this confrontation is called "the dark night of the soul." By confronting and moving through your fears and self-doubt, you are more readily able to successfully complete your natural magic quest. Life winds you around just as a labyrinth does. By moving through the labyrinth, you learn to adapt to the twists and turns presented to you as you make your way toward attaining your goals.

Labyrinth Designs

One of the most basic seed patterns of labyrinths is a "cross," symbolic of the point where polarities become united into One. The classical three-circuit design, used in Cretan coins from 300 to 70 B.C.E., begins with a cross and four dots that sit midway between the four ends of the cross. As with most labyrinths, you are continually drawing a line from one side of the seed to the other, until you complete the pattern. The first natural magic exercise for wellness, coming up later in this chapter, gives full instructions on creating a three-circuit labyrinth.

The classical seven-circuit labyrinth is created with a seed pattern that is a cross. Within each quadrant of the cross is the top two lines of a triangle. At the base of each triangle is a dot midway between the ends of the two lines. Back and forth, you connect the circular lines together until you have a labyrinth. This design was often used by the ancient Celts and the Native American Tribes, including the Hopi.

A symbol of emergence known as "tapu'at," the Hopi labyrinth is symbol of Mother Earth and her powers of creation. Symbolic of mother and child, it represents spiritual rebirth from one world to another. By entering from the east point of the labyrinth, you begin an inward voyage of discovery. This invokes new beginnings and helps you to learn how to walk in balance with the world.

The other basic seed pattern of labyrinths has a "Y" instead of a cross in the center. The most common examples of the "Y" or "three-pointed" seed pattern are "The Chakra-Vyuha Labyrinth" from India, and "The Baltic or Goddess Labyrinth." For examples of these labyrinths plus diagrams on how to draw them, visit The Labyrinth Society's website, www.labyrinthsociety.org.

Relationships

With regards to relationships, one of the most important things is to believe in yourself and to stay on course. This also means staying positive, even in the face of adversity. Family and friends are essential elements in this process because they are your primary support group.

Although you may not want to burden your family and friends with all of your problems, ideally you can draw upon their help when you need someone to talk to. If this is not the case, then you need to work toward relationships that do provide help when you need it. Relationships should be based on a concept of give and take, so that you are there when your family and friends need you, and they are there when you need them.

Before beginning the meditation, ritual, and exercises in this section, review your natural magic plans for relationships as you outlined them in Chapter 3.

Natural Magic Affirmation for Relationships

Say the following affirmation aloud three times before writing it in your Natural Magic Empowerment Journal:

Each and every day, I stay on course and continue with my natural magic plans for building relationships that are positive and fulfilling.

Write the affirmation on a small note card. Place the card in a conspicuous place where you will see it as you move through your day. Read the affirmation aloud at least eight times a day to remind you to remain on course and to stay positive in your relationships with others.

Natural Magic Meditation for Relationships

Get in a comfortable position and relax by taking several deep breaths. Inhale slowly while imagining a calming energy coming into your body. Hold your breath for a moment while sensing the energy swirling around from your head to your toes. As you exhale, let all the stress and tension in your body flow out with your breath. Inhale again, breathing in that calming energy that feels warm and soothing. Hold your breath for a few moments, letting the energy move to all parts of your body, then breathe out, sending all your stress and tension out of your body. Continue doing this breathing exercise until you feel calm and relaxed.

Now in your mind's eye, imagine a beautiful and radiant shower of golden light falling softly down from the sky, caressing you with the energy of love. The light melts into your being, spreading its joy throughout. You feel a sensation of tranquility and peacefulness that slowly begins lifting you up toward the source of the golden light. The more light and love you take into your being, the higher you float up into the sky.

As you float higher and higher, something catches your eye, and using your breath and awareness, you move over to it. You are drawn to its shiny metallic-red appearance. With your hand outstretched and your heart filled with yearning, you stray away from your light-filled path toward the object of your desire. As you reach it, you run your hand over its smooth shining surface, mesmerized by its facade. For a while it seems satisfying, but then the image begins to tarnish and fade, leaving you in darkness.

Just as your awareness begins to stray, the golden light beckons you back onto your path. Your focus returns and you are once again filled with love and joy. The light fills you full of warmth, and you sense an inner glow within yourself while ascending on your path toward the light.

Several times as you move further into the light, you feel yourself begin to stray off the path, but each time the golden light acts as a beacon, bringing you back into its divine radiance. Your spirit essence resonates with love, joy, and peace. You feel all your relationships becoming positive and empowering.

As you begin moving back into your body, remember that the golden light is always there as a beacon to help you stay on your natural magic empowerment path. This light fills you with love, joy, and peace, and these feelings empower your relationships with renewed energy.

Now take a deep breath and begin moving your toes and fingers. Then stretch your body like a cat, and return your awareness to the present time and place. Before doing anything else, write down in your Natural Magic Empowerment Journal the impressions and insights that you had while floating higher and higher into the golden light.

Natural Magic Ritual for Relationships

The purpose of the following ritual is to walk the sacred path. You will need a clear quartz crystal point, a bowl of the earth, an incense burner with a smudge stick, a beeswax candle and holder, and a cup of well or spring water. Follow these steps:

1. Bring the elemental powers into your sacred circle by doing the three steps of the natural magic ritual for relationships in Chapter 1. Invite the divine energies of Oneness into your space by standing in the middle of the circle and saying:

   Divine energies of Oneness
   Please bless my sacred space with your presence.

2. With your clear quartz crystal in your left hand, begin at the north point of your circle and move across to the south point. Hold your crystal up toward the south point and say:

Fire with Earth
Energize this crystal with your power
Let my ambitions always have foundations
Let your light shine on my path.

Move around your circle clockwise from the south point where you are standing to the west point. Next, cross the circle to the east point. Hold your crystal toward the east point and say:

Wind with Water
Energize this crystal with your power
Let my creativity always be fluid
Let your breath sail me on my path.

Move around your circle clockwise from the east point to the south point, and then cross back to the north point. Hold your crystal toward the north point and say:

Earth with Fire
Energize this crystal with your power
Let my groundedness always keep me steady
Let your stability keep me on my path.

Move around your circle clockwise to the east point, and then cross to the west point. Hold your crystal toward the west point and say:

Water with wind
Energize this crystal with your power
Let my emotions always be true
Let your flexibility help me successfully navigate my path.

3. Move to the center of the circle, and hold your crystal up high while saying:

Earth, Fire, wind, and Water
Energize my natural magic plan for positive relationships
With your elemental powers
Let my spirit share your wisdom,
Let your divinity help me remain
On my natural magic path to empowerment.

Imagine the power in your crystal energizing your natural magic plans for positive and loving relationships. Keep the energy moving toward your pattern for as long as you can. After you are finished, put your crystal on your altar. Pull up the circle, and thank the energies of the elements and Oneness for their help. Before leaving the area, be sure to completely extinguish your candle and smudge stick.

Natural Magic Blessing for Relationships

Dear Goddess and God, please light my way with your divine love so that I remain on the path that is positive and loving.

Natural Magic Exercises for Relationships

In the following natural magic exercise, you give yourself a quick mental pep talk. Self-doubt is within you and manifests itself when you feel overwhelmed and confused about what you are doing, and in this case creating better relationships. What happens is this negative voice starts playing in your mind, going over all your worries and fears. In no time, this voice begins commanding the full attention of your thoughts, heightening your fear and stress level.

When negative self-talk occurs, take time to sit back and remind yourself of the benefits and rewards of sticking with your natural magic plans for relationships. Take out your Natural Magic Empowerment Journal and focus on the positive and empowering aspects of your plans and goals. Repeat your affirmations and blessings for relationships, moving the negative thoughts out of the forefront of your mind and replacing them with positive thoughts. As much as possible, stay focused on the empowering outcome of creating better relationships.

In this second natural magic exercise, you create a love talisman to help you stick with your natural magic plans for relationships. Begin by selecting a stone whose color is pink, purple (lavender), or green, such as rose quartz, amethyst, or aventurine. Clear the stone using either the pulse-breath technique or light a smudge stick and cleanse the stone in its smoke.

Hold the stone in your right hand, and in your mind's eye imagine all the steps in your natural magic plans for empowering relationships. With focused attention, stare at the stone in your hand, and with your breath and touch, pulse these steps of your plans into the stone.

Next, imagine all the positive characteristics and abilities you have to make your plans a success. Again stare down at the stone, and using your focussed attention and breath, pulse the image into the stone. Your talisman is now charged. Carry it with you, and take it out whenever you need a boost of energy and a helpful reminder of your natural magic plans and abilities for relationships.

Wellness

Self-doubt and worrying stem directly from your fears, and can be counter-productive to your natural magic plans for wellness. Worrying creates added stress that has been medically proven to have an unhealthy effect on your body. Metaphysically, what happens is your mind affects what happens both in your body and spirit because energetically they are all connected. This is why it's important to avoid negative thoughts and focus on positive thoughts to stick with your natural magic plans for wellness.

Natural Magic Affirmation for Wellness

Say the following affirmation aloud three times before writing it in your Natural Magic Empowerment Journal:

Today and every day I fill my mind with positive and empowering thoughts, and fill my life with positive and empowering actions that move me toward my natural magic goals for wellness.

Write the affirmation on a small note card. Carry the card with you so that you can take it out and read it to yourself several times a day, especially when you are feeling fearful or worried.

Natural Magic Meditation for Wellness

Get comfortable and begin relaxing by taking several deep breaths. Breathe in slowly, filling your lungs with air. Hold your breath for a moment, feeling the air expand inside of you. As you breathe out, sense your body relaxing as you let go of all the stress and tension in your body. Inhale again while slightly arching your shoulders. Holding your breath, you feel the energy neutralizing. When you exhale, let your shoulders fully drop and release all the tension that has built up in your neck and shoulder muscles. Continue taking deep breaths until you feel in a state of peaceful relaxation.

Now in your mind's eye, imagine being out on a warm day, moving across a landscape of small hills covered with green grass. In the distance you see a larger hill, and you begin traveling toward it. A slight breeze bends the blades of grass, and cools you off as you continue to move closer to the large hill.

Along the way, you encounter a circle of stones that seem to grow up out of the earth. Looking toward the west, one of the stones is in perfect alignment with the Sun that is halfway between its zenith and the horizon. Touching one of the stones, you feel its coarse texture, which is the result of standing long years in the elements. Bidding farewell to the stones, you continue your trek to the large hill that now seems much closer.

Reaching the base of the hill, you begin your ascent to the top. Walking in a straight line, the task seems long and arduous. Although you expend much energy, the top still seems far away. For a moment you consider giving up and returning to the bottom, but something inside of you keeps you moving onward and upward.

Halfway up the hill, you encounter a path that curves off to the left around the hill. Instinctively you follow it and it begins winding around the hill, steadily moving upward toward the top. On your journey, you come across a shadowy creature that seems to mirror your every move. Though it tries to impede your progress, you continue on your chosen path, gaining momentum as you go.

Finally you reach the top of the hill and you sense a burst of energy that lights up your entire being. You sense yourself becoming in perfect health as the energy empowers you on every level. You have reached a pinnacle where your goals for wellness become reality. You are rewarded for the persistence of your efforts on your natural magic quest.

Begin bringing your body back into your present surroundings. Stretch your muscles and rub your hands together. Remember that you have the power to succeed as long as you stick with your plan as your awareness steadily moves back into your body. Relax for a moment before getting up. Before doing anything else, write down in your Natural Magic Empowerment Journal the impressions and insight that you had while meditating.

Natural Magic Ritual for Wellness

The purpose of the following ritual is to create a healing labyrinth. You will need a clear quartz crystal point, a bowl of the earth, an incense burner with a smudge stick, a beeswax candle and holder, a cup of well or spring water, and 13 stones. Follow these steps:

1. Bring the elemental powers into your sacred circle by doing the three steps of the natural magic ritual for relationships in Chapter 1. Invite the divine energies of Oneness into your space by standing in the middle of the circle and saying:

   Divine energies of Oneness
   Please bless my sacred space with your presence.

2. Place a stone in each of the four directions, and then one in the middle of the circle. Starting with the north, place two rocks equal distances apart, spanning from the north point to the center. If the distance from the north point to the center is six feet, you would place one rock two feet from the north and the second rock four feet away. After finishing with the north point, move to the east, south, and west and do the same thing until you have placed all 13 stones.

   Stand at the east point, midway between the outer stone at east point and the rock you placed a third of the way toward the center. Walk the circle in a clockwise motion, staying on the outer part of the circle until you reach the north point. From the north, move back to the east to a point midway between the second and third stone from the outside, and again travel the circle from this point, until you reach the north.

   Move to the east point, midway between the first stone and center stone. Walk in a circle, basically around the center stone, until you reach the north, and then move into the center of the circle.

3. Standing in the center of the circle, facing east, say:

   Divine and elemental powers of wellness
   Earth, Air, Fire, and Water
   Shine your healing light on my being
   So that I may know wisdom of your ways
   And follow your magical path of wellness.
   So be it! Blessed be!

Thank the energies of the elements and Oneness. Before leaving the area, pull up your circle and make sure your candle and smudge stick are fully extinguished.

Natural Magic Blessing for Wellness

Blessed Lady, Blessed Lord, please let your divine light shine as a beacon to guide me through the labyrinth of life so that I may attain my natural magic goal for wellness.

Natural Magic Exercises for Wellness

In the following natural magic exercise, you create a small classical three-circuit labyrinth for wellness. This labyrinth can be drawn out on paper, mud, or wet sand. Rather than walking this labyrinth, you will be tracing it with your index finger.

Begin by drawing the seed pattern. Make a cross by drawing a line that runs north to south, then intersect it with a line running west to east. Place a dot between each of these points, marking the northeast, southeast, southwest, and northwest points. Next, draw a half circle from the northeast to the north point. Draw a partial circle up from this half circle that reaches from the east to the northwest point. Circle counterclockwise around the top from the southeast to the west point. For the last step, draw a counterclockwise circle around the whole thing that reaches from the south to the southwest point. You should have what looks like a labyrinth with an opening between the south and southwest points.

Trace the labyrinth with your index finger and enter through the opening and begin moving through the labyrinth until you reach the center. As you do this, focus your thoughts on wellness. Feel all the barriers being brought down that stand in the way of completing your natural magic plans for wellness. Once you reach the center, move back around toward the entrance. Do this several times, sensing the calming effect it has on you body, mind, and spirit.

In this second natural magic exercise, you take a healing foot bath. Your feet are often the part of your body that winds up carrying you and moving you forward on your natural magic quest. Your feet have thousands of nerve endings that correspond to various parts of your body.

Begin by filling a pan or tub with enough warm water to cover your feet. Add three tablespoons of sea salt and a few drops of lavender oil, and mix the water around before putting your feet into it. Take a few deep breaths and think about all the benefits that completing your plan for wellness will bring you. As the water soothes your feet, repeat your wellness affirmation:

Today and every day I fill my mind with positive and empowering thoughts, and fill my life with positive and empowering actions that move me toward my natural magic goals for wellness.

After the bath, rub your feet with a natural moisturizer so that they feel fresh and ready to take you further on your path to empowered wellness.

Enrichment

Staying positive and keeping your sense of humor when everything around you seems crazy is a key to both staying sane and sticking with your natural magic plans for enrichment. Often people and events seem to test your patience and resilience. When this happens, the important thing is to stay on course and not get angry.

Anger is like fear; once it begins it feeds on your insecurities and ego. The result is that it stops your forward movement. As with fear, the best way to deal with anger is to step back from the situation and commence focusing on the positive aspects of your natural magic plan. Get out your Natural Magic Empowerment Journal and review the steps of your plan. Repeat the affirmations and blessings until the anger dissipates. Take a few moments to do a guided meditation, putting your mind, along with your body and spirit, in a positive and focused state of being.

Natural Magic Affirmation for Enrichment

Say the following affirmation aloud three times before writing it into your Natural Magic Empowerment Journal:

Today and every day I believe in myself and my abilities to see my natural magic plans for enrichment come to fruition.

Write the affirmation on a small note card. Place the card in your work area, and each time you see it, repeat it to yourself.

Natural Magic Meditation for Enrichment

Get comfortable and begin to relax by taking several deep breaths. Inhale and slowly fill your lungs with air and the golden light of the Sun. As you hold your breath for a moment, sense the light expanding out from your chest to every part of your body. Exhale and imagine the cells of your body being energized by the golden light. Also feel your muscles relaxing.

Again breathe in slowly, filling your lungs with air and the golden light. Still your breath for a few moments, and sense the light moving up and down the front of your body, over your chakras, until it reaches the top of your head and the bottoms of your feet. Release your breath and feel the light energizing your cells while your exhale and relax your muscles even more. Continue taking deep breaths until you feel wholly energized and completely relaxed.

Imagine that you are on a boat, sailing across the water to a distant land that holds all of your dreams for enrichment. The soft wind is with you, filling your sails and pushing you along toward the shore that continues to become closer. The water is calm and like glass. Looking down into it, you see your reflection along with that of the Sun, the blue sky, and the side of your boat. You feel a serenity that lingers long within the essence of your spirit.

As you move closer to your destination, you begin to see the sandy beaches and outlines of the rocks and trees further inland. You sense an anticipation moving through you as your mind starts reeling through the images of your upcoming enrichment. It feels as though you can reach out and touch it, taste it, and smell it. The sensations build within you, adding to your impending excitement.

Just offshore, a fog begins rolling in all around you and the wind becomes quiet, ceasing to fill your sails and move you forward. You find yourself in a cloud, drifting around and around. At first you sense a feeling a despair and confusion coming over you, but you soon replace it with a mantra, "I believe in myself. I know I can do it. I believe in myself. I know I can do it."

Grasping the rigging on the main sail, you pull it so that the boat begins to move again. Regaining your focus, you scan the fog for the outline of the shore. You see it and turn the boat so that it is once again sailing toward your destination. Moving closer to the shore, the fog gradually lifts and before you is a beautiful sight.

As your feet touch down on the land, you are overwhelmed with an empowering feeling of accomplishment. Magic abounds everywhere. You feel enriched in every way as you explore and become One with this new land. It is everything you ever dreamed about and hoped for in terms of enrichment.

Slowly begin returning your awareness back to your body and physical surroundings. Stretch your muscles, and rub your feet together. Take some time to bask in the empowering feeling of enrichment and to let your awareness fully return to your body. Before doing anything else, write in your Natural Magic Empowerment Journal any impressions and insights that the meditation may have stirred within you.

Natural Magic Ritual for Enrichment

The purpose of the following ritual is to build energy to help move you through the steps in your natural magic plans for enrichment. You will need a clear quartz crystal point, a bowl of the earth, an incense burner with a smudge stick, a beeswax candle and holder, and a cup of well or spring water. Follow these steps:

1. Bring the elemental powers into your sacred circle by doing the three steps of the natural magic ritual for relationships in Chapter 1. Invite the divine energies of Oneness into your space by standing in the middle of the circle and saying:

   Divine energies of Oneness
   Please bless my sacred space with your presence.

2. Go to the north point of your circle, and envision the steps of your natural magic plans for enrichment while saying:

   Empowerment, empowerment, empowerment
   Enrichment, enrichment, enrichment.
   So be it!

With the last "So be it!," raise both your arms in the air and imagine sending the energy toward your natural magic plans for enrichment. Move over to the east point, and envision the steps of your plan while saying:

Empowerment, empowerment, empowerment
Enrichment, enrichment, enrichment.
So be it!

With the last "So be it," raise both your arms in the air and imagine sending the energy toward your natural magic plans for enrichment. Move over to the south point, and envision the steps of your plan while saying:

Empowerment, empowerment, empowerment
Enrichment, enrichment, enrichment.
So be it!

With the last "So be it!," raise both your arms in the air and send the energy toward your natural magic plans for enrichment. Move around to the west point, and envision the steps of your plan while saying:

Empowerment, empowerment, empowerment
Enrichment, enrichment, enrichment.
So be it!

With the last "So be it!," raise both your arms in the air and send the energy toward your natural magic plans for enrichment.

3. Go to the center of the circle, raise your arms up and say:

Let the positive and helpful energies of Oneness
Be directed toward my natural magic plans for enrichment
Let all the obstacles be gone from my path
As I move closer and closer toward enrichment.

Thank the energies of the elements and Oneness. Before leaving the area, pull up your circle and make sure your candle and smudge stick are completely extinguished.

Natural Magic Blessing for Enrichment

Divine Mother and Divine Father, please bless every day of my life with your light so that I may always know my way to empowerment and enrichment.

Natural Magic Exercises for Enrichment

In the following natural magic exercise, you create a positive bedtime routine. Researchers have determined that a good night's sleep is essential to creativity and successful actions. Begin by setting aside a half hour before you go to sleep. This time is your private time when you can think about things and set the stage for the next day's activities. During this time, you can go over the positive things you did during the day, read inspiring stories about people who overcame obstacles to become successful, listen to music that is uplifting and positive, and be thankful for the abilities and things that you have.

At some point during this personal time, go over the positive things that you want to accomplish the next day. If you have a problem that you are working on, give yourself the suggestion that the answer will come to you in a dream and you will know it when you awaken. Many great ideas have come from sleep and dream, including inventions, such as the sewing machine by Elias Howe, and works of art, such as the song "River of Dreams" by singer/songwriter Billy Joel. It's important to be in a positive frame of mind when you go to sleep. It makes for a better night's sleep and more positive and beneficial dreams.

In this second natural magic exercise, you make a sweet apple potion for enrichment. Begin by selecting three bright red apples and peeling them, cutting them into four pieces, and coring them. Put them into a blender or food processor along with about a cup of spring or pure well water, a pinch of cinnamon, and a heaping tablespoon of honey. As you blend the ingredients, focus on your natural magic plans for enrichment.

Pour the mixture into a glass and bless it with the energy of God and Goddess by placing your hands, palms down, over the glass and saying:

God and Goddess of enrichment
Please fill this potion with your divine power
Let it represent the fruition of my efforts
In my natural magic plan for enrichment.

Drink the potion while focusing on positive thoughts, knowing you have the power to stick with your natural magic plans for enrichment until it bears fruit.

Chapter Ten

Manifesting Your
Natural Magic Goals

Here's an interesting true story. The fountain in the center of a town stopped flowing so the businessman who owned it called the architect who built it. The architect came out and after analyzing the fountain, explained to the businessman that the coins people tossed in the fountain were clogging up the filter. After cleaning the filter, the architect decided to put up a sign that read, "Do not throw coins into the fountain. It's bad for the mechanism."

A couple of weeks later the architect was greeted with another call from the businessman, complaining that the flow of the fountain was again at a trickle. After cleaning all the coins out of the filter, the architect decided to place the same signs on each of the four sides of the fountain. Watching from a distance, the architect saw a young couple walk up to the foundation, look at the sign, and then toss three coins into the flowing waters. From the looks of them, this couple was obviously not your classic type of vandal. But why had they disregarded the sign and thrown the coins in anyway? As he walked back to his car, he knew he was up against something greater than any kind of logic.

Sure enough, a couple of weeks later the phone again rang with the businessman at the other end, demanding a solution to the problem. At this point the architect decided rather than struggling with the situation, he would work with it. He designed a filter to fit over the fountain's filter so the coins wouldn't clog it up. The coins gathered from the fountain were then donated to a local charity, the initial amount totaling over $3,000.

The reason people throw coins in a fountain or wishing well heralds back to the idea that you give something of value to the divine (whether your idea of the divine is the Goddess or God, a saint, an angel, or whatever) when asking for a wish. This is archetypal concept that moves through every level of being. When it comes to archetypes, it's much more productive to work with their ancient natural power than against it.

The Waters of Creation

The practice of throwing coins and objects of wealth into water as a means of procuring luck or divine help dates back to the time of the ancient Celts, Greeks, and Romans. In particular, the holy spring at Brocolitia or Carrawburgh on Hadrian's Wall was the sacred well of the Celtic Goddess Coventina. People would pilgrimage to the spring with offerings to the Goddess that included coins, small stones, jewelry, and figurines. They would throw the offerings into the water to ask for a favor and help of the Goddess, especially by women asking for a safe childbirth.

Water has always been associated with divine creation and with manifesting. The primordial mass spawning all creation is often associated with a watery world without structure that awaits its transition into a physical, mental, and spiritual form. From the womb of the Mother, the seed of creation is created and nourished into life in divine manifestation.

The Mesopotamian creation myth begins with a universe composed of a watery chaos of salt and fresh waters mingled together into Tiamet, Goddess of saltwater and Abzu, God of freshwater. In one of the Hindu myths, Brahma creates primal water as the womb for a small seed. The seed grows into a golden egg that when split open becomes one half the heavens and one half the earth and nature.

In the Egyptian creation myth, in the beginning only a watery world existed known as the deity "Nu" or "Nun." It represents the beginning of everything, including life. Atum, the Sun God, created himself, using his thoughts and will.

Echoing the stories in the creation myth, the theory of evolution believes life originally came from the sea. Whenever scientists explore a distant planet for life, the first thing they look for are signs of water. Life as we perceive it must have water, again drawing a direct connection between water and life.

The nature of water is to resonate with the vibration of the energy and matter around it. Crystals and the bodies of plants and animals are mostly made up of water. The human body is over 90 percent water.

As an excellent conductor of energy, water is the ultimate balancing force. Bodies of water such as fountains, waterfalls, creeks, streams, lakes, seas, and oceans have an ionizing effect that balances energy, including the energy of the human body. In the form of a small amount such as a crystal or cup of holy water, the water can be energized and programmed with thought and energy. As such, it is an invaluable new age tool for manifesting things.

Kundalini Energy

In Hindu mythology, kundalini is symbolized by the energy of the serpent Goddess reaching up through the chakras to the crown chakra at the top of the head, where she is united with the God. In a biological sense, kundalini is linked with a warm liquid magnetic energy. When this energy moves up the chakras, it opens them up.

The manifestation of the kundalini energy frequency of vibration connects with the Sanskrit term "Chaitanya," relating to the integrated power of your physiological, mental, emotional, and spiritual bodies. It is this frequency of vibration that sends you to an enlightened level of awareness.

Kundalini literally means "coiling," and is the union of the curved feminine energy and straight male energy. The natural tendency of energy and consciousness is to move in a spiraling motion. In this sense, the spiral of kundalini is symbolic of the spiraling energies of consciousness. When these energies move as liquid energy up from the first chakra (root) to the seventh chakra (crown), they unite the many levels of your consciousness together into One.

Other names for kundalini include "esprit," "élan vital," "loosh," "prana," and bioelectricity. It relates to the concept of chi in Feng Shui (see Chapter 6). It also symbolizes the golden ratio of sacred geometry that I discussed in Chapter 3. In all its names, it represents the energy and potential waiting to be realized and manifested into matter. This means moving your goals from the unmanifested to the manifested.

Relationships

This is the point in the natural magic empowerment process when you manifest your goals into reality. Manifesting your natural magic goals means doing the steps you outlined in your plan. Natural magic doesn't just happen. You need to take the practical steps of your natural magic plan to successfully attain your goals. Using a garden analogy, this requires that you cultivate the soil, plant the seeds, water the plants, nurture the growing process, and then, and only then, do you harvest the empowering fruits of your labors.

Practical manifesting comes from doing the steps as you listed them in your natural magic plans for relationships. Moving natural energy toward your relationships helps, but ultimately you have to take the steps to nudge the relationship in the direction that you would like to go.

In terms of your relationship with nature and the earth, you have to go out and experience it first-hand by going to sacred places in nature. Just step outdoors and feel the breeze on your skin, the Sun on your face, or smell the fresh air on a spring morning. Take time to smell the roses! You will be pleasantly surprised that these simple acts of getting in touch with nature can be incredibly rewarding.

Natural Magic Affirmation for Relationships

Say the following affirmation aloud three times before writing it in your Natural Magic Empowerment Journal:

Today and every day, I manifest my potential and successfully actualize my natural magic goals for relationships.

Write the affirmation on a small note card. Place the card on your nightstand so that it's the first thing you see when you go to sleep and when you wake up.

Natural Magic Meditation for Relationships

Get comfortable and take several deep breaths. Inhale, totally filling your lungs with air and energizing your spirit. As you hold your breath for a moment, still your mind as much as possible.

Exhale all the air in your lungs while sensing every part of your body relaxing.

Now, breathe in again and fill your lungs full of air while filling your spirit full of energy. Hold your breath and sense a wave of tranquility wash through your mind. Release your breath while feeling your muscles and all the other parts of your body as they become relaxed.

Take another deep, complete breath, inhaling until your insides expand and your spirit has an energetic glow all around it. Your mind becomes more and more relaxed and calm as you hold your breath for a few moments before exhaling and feeling every cell in your body releasing any energetic tension and becoming completely relaxed.

In your mind's eye, imagine the light of the Goddess shining in a curved beam coming together with the light of the God that shines in a straight line. Their divine union produces a spiral of light, beaming down at your crown chakra at the top of your head. Just as your breath filled your lungs, the light fills and expands the energy vortex at the top of your head. Your awareness and connection to the divine blossoms and becomes One. You are a flower of creation and divine light.

Next, imagine the light moving down into your sixth chakra, your third eye, located just above your eyebrows, centered between them. The light fills and expands the eye of your spirit, and as a result, you perceive past the illusion of life into the energetic potential. You recognize the natural magic that exists on every plane of existence. You understand that you can move energy with thought and manifest it with action in the form of dynamic motion that moves energy into matter.

Spiraling, the light swirls down into your fifth chakra at the base of your throat. Intone "OM," sending a vibration cascading in waves throughout your being. Your throat expands with light and your voice to the world becomes clearer. Your communication with nature and the earth transcends words into pure thought moving faster than the speed of light. Everything happens in real time with no delay.

Continuing its spiral, the light descends into your fourth chakra also known as your heart chakra. Sense the light expanding and filling the chakra full of energy. Spirals of divine love beam throughout your being, and in your heart you know the meaning of "the perfect love of the Goddess and perfect peace of the God." Together they are the union of Oneness.

Downward, the light swirls and expands in your third chakra, located in your solar plexus, in the center between your chest and stomach. Your power vortex energizes in the glow of the light. Every part of you vibrates in harmony, raising the rate of your vibrations up in frequency. You feel in sync and balanced with the natural powers of the elements.

Take a deep breath and feel the light expand into the region around your navel and your second chakra. This vortex connects you to the forces of creation and manifestation. The stomach is the area where the seed comes into being, and nurtured by the womb, progresses through the stages that bring it to life. The light nourishes you, allowing you to grow as a living, evolving human being.

Generating spirals that grow larger with influx of natural energy. This is the area of the first chakra, the place where potential begins. Located at the base or root of your spine, in your pelvic area, this represents your primal tie to the forces of creation. The place where the beginning forces of life come together, to form a divine union that produces life, the manifestation of the seeds of creation.

Now take another deep breath and imagine the liquid light flowing across the layers of your being. You expand your awareness until you become One with all of the energies of natural magic. You become One with the trees, the sky, the earth, the rocks, the waterfall, the beach, the animals, and the magic of life. Each year with the advent of spring, you once again begin a cycle of creation that descends back into the beginnings of divine light and the creation of life in all its many forms.

Take another deep breath and bring this sensation back as you begin returning to your body. Take a moment to relax and bask in the glow of the light. You are the light manifested in physical, mental, and spiritual form. You are the child of Goddess and God, and as such, are a product of divine light.

Breathe deeply, feeling centered and connected with the light. Slowly come back to the room, moving your legs, feet, toes, arms, hands, and fingers around, and finally completely returning to your body and the present moment.

Open your eyes and take a few minutes to stretch your muscles and bring your awareness back to your physical body. Take a few minutes to think about your meditation experience and write your impressions and any insight you had down in your Natural Magic Empowerment Journal.

Natural Magic Ritual for Relationships

The purpose of the following ritual is to move the spiral of kundalini energy toward the manifestation of your natural magic goals for relationships. You will need a clear quartz crystal point, a bowl of the earth, an incense burner with a smudge stick, a beeswax candle and holder, a cup of well or spring water, and some lavender oil. Follow these steps:

1. Bring the elemental powers into your sacred circle by doing the three steps of the natural magic ritual for relationships in Chapter 1. Invite the divine energies of Oneness into your space by standing in the middle of the circle and saying:

   Divine energies of Oneness
   Please bless my sacred space with your presence.

2. Anoint your seven chakras with the lavender oil. Beginning at the north point dance in a clockwise spiral around the circle seven times. Each time you turn around the circle, direct the energy toward empowering one of your chakras, beginning at your first chakra. While doing this, say:

   Energies of natural magic
   Empower my first [through seventh] chakra.
   Ayea! Ayea! Ayea!

3. With your quartz crystal in your right hand, move to the center of the circle. Draw an energetic line of light from your first chakra up to your seventh chakra. Connect your chakras together as One power, working together. Hold your crystal up, and say:

   Divine powers of Goddess
   Please help me to create positive relationships.
   Divine powers of God
   Please help me to take the steps of my plan.
   Divine powers of Oneness
   Please help me to manifest my natural magic goals.

Thank the energies of the elements, Goddess and God, and Oneness, and pull up your sacred circle. Before leaving the area, make sure your smudge and candle are fully extinguished.

Natural Magic Blessing for Relationships

Divine Lady, Mother of creation, Divine Lord, Father of creation, please bless me with your powers to manifest positive, loving relationships each and every day and night.

Natural Magic Exercises for Relationships

In the following natural magic exercise, you make a conversation rock. Begin by finding a rock in nature that is easy to hold. Its exterior should be smooth so that you can run your fingers over it without cutting them. Clean the stone with cool water and salt, and dry it. Next, energetically clear the rock by smudging it with the smoke from your smudge stick.

To program the stone, hold it in both hands and imagine what it means to have successful communication and conversation in your mind's eye. This can be an image of two people having a great conversation, a successful speech to business people, a telephone, or computer e-mail program. As you imagine what it means to have communication and conversation in your mind's eye, take a deep breath in and then hold the image in your mind as you pulse your breath out through your nose. Imagine you are actually planting the image of communication and conversation into the stone itself with your mind's energy and your focused awareness.

The conversation stone can be passed around a circle of people, where each person takes the rock and adds anything they would like to the conversation. Between two people, the rock can be passed back and forth as a way of opening the lines of communication. You can also place it near your computer when you are e-mailing friends and family to encourage better communication. Be sure to wash, smudge, and reprogram the stone each time you use it to keep your channel of communication clear and positive.

In this second natural magic exercise, you plant a bulb garden to help you manifest your natural magic goals for relationships, and to continue encouraging you to manifest your goals in the future years to come. Begin by picking a spot in the fall where you can plant bulbs. You can plant them in a large pot if need be. This works especially well if you have a lot of bulb-loving gophers, moles, or squirrels in the area; it's harder for them to unearth the bulbs from a pot than it would be from the open ground.

Select an assortment of bulbs, such as irises, hyacinths, daffodils, and tulips. Till the soil well, and then use bulb food when you plant the bulbs to ensure a colorful display in the spring.

Hold each of the bulbs in your hands for a few minutes and bless them with the divine growing powers of the Goddess and God. Also imagine your natural magic goals for more loving relationships as you hold each of the bulbs. Then plant each bulb, all the while envisioning actually manifesting your goal for relationships. The bulb represents the seed of your goal, which you are planting in the earth. As it springs to life, you care for it. When it blooms in the spring, it represents all your seeds coming to fruition. This is a process that not only happens next spring, but every spring thereafter. In fact, you can add to the beauty and splendor of the flowers by adding more bulbs or by separating the mature bulbs and putting them in other spots to create even more beauty. The flowering bulbs mirror your goals, and manifesting your natural magic goals mirror the blooming bulbs!

Wellness

Setting a plan for wellness, and then carefully taking the steps you have set forth in your plan, is the key to manifesting your natural magic wellness goals. Your wellness goal needs to be something that you want to work toward for your own wellness, not something you struggle against. You need to take the time to think about your health and be honest with yourself. Set realistic natural magic plans for wellness, make the effort to follow the steps you have mapped out, and you will usually find that success, and better health, is right at your fingertips.

Natural Magic Affirmation for Wellness

Say the following affirmation aloud three times before writing it in your Natural Magic Empowerment Journal:

Today and each day, I make every effort to live more healthy, and to continue manifesting my natural magic goals for wellness.

Write the affirmation on a small note card. Place the card somewhere you cook and eat such as on the refrigerator, stove, microwave, dining table, or the back of your dining room chair.

Natural Magic Meditation for Wellness

Get comfortable and relax by taking several deep breaths. Breathe in and expand your lungs with air while feeling an energy charging your spirit with energy. Hold your breath for a moment and sense your mind floating on a still sea of tranquility. Exhale and sense the feeling of complete relaxation as it spreads out across your body.

Take another deep, complete breath and let go of all the tensions from the day. Relax every part of your body from the top of your head to the bottoms of your feet. Continue breathing deeply, energizing your being with your inhale, quieting your mind when you still your breath, and relaxing your muscles with your every exhale.

Now, in your mind's eye, imagine you are like an embryo bathing in the warm, womblike waters of creation. Warmth, security, and a sense of love surround you, nurturing your development from a seed to an egg to an embryo. With each new stage, your life energy becomes stronger and more vibrant. You can sense that the energy is reaching a peak level, and you will be moving into the next stage. Anticipation fills you as you wait for the coming change.

Arms and legs begin forming, and you use your new appendages to begin swimming around in the cosmic waters. You continue to grow as you swim through the water. In your travels, you encounter a surface just beneath the water that feels firm to the touch. Using your arms and legs, use this surface to move up out of the water onto a sandy beach, where the Sun shines warmly, filling you full of even more life energy. You can sense another stage getting ready to happen. You feel charged with anticipation as you wait for the coming change.

Take a deep breath and imagine you are a plant with a flower about to bloom. You feel your roots planted in the firmness of the soil, the water of life flows through your body and the light and warmth of the Sun shines on you.

Take another deep breath, and as you exhale sense the petals of your flower opening and expanding toward the light.

With each breath you take, you move into a greater level of fluorescence. After the first flower blooms, other flowers begin opening until their petals decorate every part of you. You have manifested your dreams into reality. And the beauty of it is that the blooms become seeds, ensuring that dreams will continue to become reality every year in your life and those of future generations.

Take a deep breath and sense your awareness moving back into your body and physical surroundings. As you move back into your body, imagine that the flower is within you, waiting to open to your full potential as a healthy and vibrant human being. You know deep within you that you can manifest your natural magic goals for wellness and make them real.

Before doing anything else, write down in your Natural Magic Empowerment Journal any impressions and insights that you had while meditating.

Natural Magic Ritual for Wellness

The purpose of the following ritual is to direct energy toward the fluorescence of your natural magic goals for wellness. You will need a clear quartz crystal point, a bowl of the earth, an incense burner with a smudge stick, a beeswax candle and holder, and a cup of well or spring water. Follow these steps:

1. Bring the elemental powers into your sacred circle by doing the three steps of the natural magic ritual for relationships in Chapter 1. Invite the divine energies of Oneness into your space by standing in the middle of the circle and saying:

   Divine energies of Oneness
   Please bless my sacred space with your presence.

2. Take the cup of well or spring water in your left hand and move to the center of the circle. Place your right hand over the cup, and say:

   Goddess and God of light and healing
   Empower this water with divine wellness
   So that all that it touches may be well
   And will be bathed in the fluorescence of health.

3. Beginning in the north point, take the water and sprinkle it around
   your circle. As you do this, envision your perfect state of wellness
   while saying:

   I am a flower of life
   My roots are in the Goddess of Earth
   My leaves reach up for the Sun God
   My body is filled with divine healing water
   My cells are filled with the healing breath of the God.

   Continue imagining your optimum state of wellness and manifesting your natural magic wellness goals for several minutes as you
   enjoy the divine healing energy of the circle. When you are done,
   thank the energies of the elements, Goddess and God, and Oneness,
   and pull up the circle. Before leaving the area, make sure the candle
   and smudge stick are completely extinguished.

Natural Magic Blessing for Wellness

*Divine energies and healing powers of Earth, Air, Fire, and Water, please
bless my natural magic plan for wellness, and help me to take the steps necessary to manifest my natural magic wellness goals.*

Natural Magic Exercises for Wellness

In the following natural magic exercise, you tie the successful manifesting of your wellness goals into your awareness. Begin by going outdoors
and finding a long piece of pliable grass or vine. Carefully tie a knot in
the grass in the middle to represent the first step on your wellness plan.
Then carefully tie another knot in the grass as you imagine taking the
next step toward manifesting your wellness plan. As you carefully tie
each knot, you are tying your awareness and focus into completing each
step in the plan. When you are done tying the knots in the grass, return
it to a moving body of water such as a creek, stream, river, lake, or
ocean to get the natural energies moving toward manifesting your wellness goals right now!

In this second natural magic exercise, you moisturize your skin with
honey. Begin by washing all the dirt and oil off of your face with a

natural complexion soap. Blot your skin dry, and then take three tablespoons of warm honey and begin rubbing it into your skin with your fingertips, a little at a time. Use the tips of your fingers to lightly massage the different areas of your face as you rub the honey into your skin. Be careful not to get any in your eyes.

After rubbing the honey thoroughly into your skin, rinse it off with warm water. Sense the waters of the Goddess, moisturizing and giving new life to your skin, and in turn energizing your spirit and your mind. Moisturize your skin with your favorite natural moisturizer, for example, one with essential oil of lavender, vanilla, or neroli.

Enrichment

Determining your natural magic goals' results is a direct experience of appropriate thought and action. Decide what you want to do and then do the steps that you mapped out for yourself. Keep in mind that you often have to adjust the equation so that it works for who you are, but that's all part of the empowerment process.

Manifesting is the point in the process where you move energy into matter and your goals into reality. One of the ways you can encourage this process is by assigning realistic completion dates to each of your goals. Things change and don't necessarily work out as planned, but completion dates give you a specific goal rather than a general one. They give you something tangible you can work toward and attain.

Natural Magic Affirmation for Enrichment

Say the following affirmation aloud three times before writing it into your Natural Magic Empowerment Journal:

Each and every day, I take the steps of my natural magic plans for enrichment and I joyfully manifest my goals for abundance.

Write the affirmation on a small note card. Place the card where you work, for example, on your desk, computer, tool chest, or the dash of your work vehicle. Read the affirmation aloud several times a day to remind yourself that you are moving forward and will indeed manifest your goals for enrichment.

Natural Magic Meditation for Enrichment

Rub a couple of drops of lavender essential oil on your forehead at your sixth chakra or third eye (be sure to keep it out of your eyes). Get comfortable and relax by taking several deep breaths. Slowly inhale, taking in as much air as you can. Hold your breath for a moment and sense everything expanding. Exhale and allow all the stress and tension flow out of your body with your exhaled breath.

Relax even more as you draw in another breath and fill your lungs with air and energy. As you still your breath, sense a peacefulness spread across your being. Exhale and move any residue stress and tension out with your exhaled breath, leaving your body, mind, and spirit in a relaxed, harmonious state of being.

Now in your mind's eye, imagine moving across the ground by wiggling your body up and down and scooting across to where you want to go. You climb the stalk of a lavender plant to a place just below the flower. There you begin spinning the stands of your cocoon, creating a safe haven where you will be secure during your time of natural transition.

Inside the sanctity of the sanctuary you have created around yourself, you transform into a different creature than the one you were before. You sense your body shifting shape. You grow arms that then become wings, waiting to be released into the sky. Inside your cocoon you await your moment of transcendence. You await to be released and allowed to shine brightly for your moment of fluorescence, when the fires of your life burn at their brightest.

With much effort, you split open the cocoon and free yourself from your safe haven. Your wings expanded for the first time, they glide in the wind and glisten in the sunlight. Away on the breeze, your wings take you wherever you want to go. They glitter with colors of yellow, orange, black, and iridescent blue, the colors vibrant in their hues. Everything seems to emanate with a brilliance that is everywhere you go. You are a reflection of your world, and it is a refection of you. All is divine. All is One.

Like the colors of the rainbow, you blend into white light. You become a divine spirit, flowing from the waters of creation. You flicker back and forth between full spectrum and Oneness. In the between points, they are the same. All is divine. All is One.

Now take a deep breath and bring that knowing that you are divine, that you are One, back with you as you bring your awareness back into your body and present physical surroundings. Stretch your muscles like a cat and rub your hands briskly together. Before doing anything else, write down in your Natural

Magic Empowerment Journal any impressions and insights you had while meditating, together with the sensations you had while becoming a butterfly.

Natural Magic Ritual for Enrichment

The purpose of the following ritual is to do a three-coin ritual to direct the energies of creation toward manifesting your natural magic goals for enrichment. You will need a clear quartz crystal point, a bowl of the earth, an incense burner with a smudge stick, a beeswax candle and holder, a cup of well or spring water, and three coins. Follow these steps:

1. Bring the elemental powers into your sacred circle by doing the three steps of the natural magic ritual for relationships in Chapter 1. Invite the divine energies of Oneness into your space by standing in the middle of the circle and saying:

   Divine energies of Oneness
   Please bless my sacred space with your presence.

2. Throw the first coin in your cup of well or spring water, and say:

   Mother of potential
   Please bring your energies together.

   Throw the second coin in the water, and say:

   Mother of here and now
   Please help me to manifest my enrichment goals.

   Throw the third coin in the water, and say:

   Mother of what will be
   Please shine your light on me through eternity.

3. Moving from the north point, go to each of the directions and empower the glass of water with each of the elements. Move to the center of the circle and hold the glass upward, saying:

   Divine powers of God and Goddess
   Enrich these waters with your powers
   Please help me to take the steps toward enrichment
   So that I manifest my empowerment goals.
   So be it!

Thank the energies of the elements, God and Goddess, and Oneness, and pull up the circle. Before leaving the area, be sure your candle and smudge stick are completely extinguished.

Natural Magic Blessing for Enrichment

May the blessed and divine powers of the Goddess and God come together as One, and help me manifest my natural magic goals for enrichment, today and every day.

Natural Magic Exercises for Enrichment

In the following natural magic exercise, you go out in nature and find a tree to bond with energetically. Stretch up toward the Sun, reach down to Earth, while utilizing water and air to maintain life. Pick a large tree and sense how immense the energy spirals in this being. Remember you are mostly made up of water so that you vibrate with the frequency that is around you.

You are the essence of all trees, connected in with the tree of life. You are the water of life, and the essence of energy becoming matter. You are the depository of knowledge and wisdom passed down through the ages. Write down any insights you may have while communicating with the trees.

In this second natural magic exercise, you create your personal dance for manifesting your enrichment. Use it to act out steps of your plan and how happy you are when everything works out in the end. If you like, use items such as rattles, bells, drums, tambourines, horns, squeakers, and whistles in your enrichment-manifesting dance. Every time you complete a step in your plan, you do the dance, celebrate, and build up the energy.

When you complete the last step of your plan, you *really* celebrate as you have manifested your goal and can now enjoy the harvest. When you manifest your goals into reality and live them, life becomes a little more to your liking and you become more empowered each and every time.

Chapter Eleven

Celebrating Your Natural Magic Empowerment

As I walk out outside my home on the first day of spring, I see the irises and daffodils and smell the fragrance of the hyacinths. Sugar peas line the fence, their jade green pods glistening in the sun. Backdrops of cherry trees fill out the landscape with their iridescent purple leaves, adding more color to the joyous celebration. The scent of fresh mint fills my senses as I step through it to the circles of budding multi-colored rose bushes that stretch out over the sunny hillside.

It's a time for enjoying and celebrating nature when you actualize your natural magic goals. It's a celebration that is ongoing with each natural seasonal cycle. Just as the seasons cycle, so does your life. With each step of your plan, and especially when you attain your goals, it's important to celebrate life and nature. Keep in step with nature's dance as it springs up around you every year, sprouts from the seeds of the year before, blooms with water and care in the sunshine, fades in the hot summer sun or cold autumn nights, and provides the necessary seed for the next cycle.

In nature, you plant a seed, nurture the sprouting plant, and then it flowers and bears fruit. When this happens, it's time to celebrate the harvest. Your bond and agreement with the plant is satisfied and you both have given to each other. You fertilize, give food to the plant, and make every effort to protect it. The plant, for example a fruit tree or flower, in turn, gives you food or beauty.

Celebrating your natural magic empowerment is comparable to the harvest festivals of European cultures. These great days of traditional celebration are when people gave thanks to nature for the annual harvest. They are the forebears of the idea of thanksgiving. It is symbolic of the cooperation of people and nature, and how this cooperation benefits all parties.

As I walk out on a summer's day, I see the bright red tomatoes, the yellow squash, the golden corn, and the green beans along with the fruiting blackberry bushes, crowned with shasta daisies. Celebrate attaining your empowerment goals by going outdoors and enjoying nature. After all, this is the essence of natural magic; experiencing the power and sublime beauty of nature.

Earth Day

Having one day a year to celebrate the earth and get people to become more aware of the environment started out in the early sixties as an idea of Sen. Gaylord Nelson of Wisconsin. The idea came to fruition on April 22, 1970, when 20 million Americans turned out in support of a healthy, sustainable environment. Since then, every year more and more people get together to celebrate and give thanks to the earth. Denis Hayes, who helped coordinate the first Earth Day, also coordinated Earth Day in 1990. This is when it went global, including 200 million people participating in 141 countries.

Earth Day has been a tremendous way of getting environmental concerns into the public consciousness. If we want nature to continue as something beautiful, it's time to start educating people and expanding our awareness in relation to the environment. Every year, April 22 is set aside as a day for celebrating and honoring the earth. But as the website www.earthday.net proclaims, Earth Day happens not only April 22, it happens every day of the year.

The Sierra Club

With John Muir as its first president, the Sierra Club was founded in May of 1892 with 182 charter members. Through the years the Sierra Club has championed many environmental causes, such as the damming of Hetch Hetchy valley, which has been said to be as beautiful as Yosemite Valley. A club motto passed down from the early days claims that members "climb the mountains and get their good tidings."

Ansel Adams, renowned for his black and white photography and wilderness preservation, was involved in the Sierra Club for over 50 years. Specifically he played a part in making people more aware of wilderness areas such as Yosemite, and how these areas needed to be preserved. This idea is echoed in the first sentence of the Sierra Club's mission statement, "Explore, enjoy and protect the wild places of the earth."

The members of the Sierra Club are still climbing the peaks of the Sierras to get the mountain's good tidings. With a current membership of over 700,000, the Sierra Club addresses issues as diverse as clean water and air, nonpolluting energy sources, and the preservation of animal species. The Sierra Club works within the legal system to stop industrial pollution as well as educating people as to how they can help keep the earth natural and magical for hundreds of years to come. Their website is www.sierraclub.org.

Championing Natural Magic

Actor Robert Redford, known for building the Sundance Village in the Wasatch Mountains of Utah and founding and hosting the annual Sundance Film Festival, was celebrated by having a building named after him. Not just any building, the Robert Redford Building houses the Santa Monica office of the Natural Resources Defense Council, and was named "Greenest Building in America" by the U.S. Green Building

Council. Using innovative environmental design and construction techniques the building uses 60 percent less water by capturing and filtering rain, shower, and sink water and using it to irrigate the landscape and flush toilets.

The Robert Redford Building also uses 60 to 75 percent less electricity, gets 20 percent of its power from photovoltaic cells, and is made entirely from recycled materials. The idea in constructing the building was as an example of how building can be made more environmentally friendly. These types of buildings are known as "green buildings," and are the way of the future of technology—working with nature rather than trying to control it.

Robert Redford is also a trustee, founding member, and fundraiser for the Natural Resources Defense Council (NRDC). Founded in 1970, the NRDC is one of the most well-known and respected, environmentally active organizations dedicated to preserving wildlife and wilderness areas. A nonprofit organization whose only reward comes from preserving wilderness areas and species of animals, the NRDC represents a rapidly growing number of people with the foresight to see that our future, our children's future, and our children's children's future lies in protecting and honoring nature rather than destroying its empowering splendor. For more, see the NRDC's website at www.nrdc.org.

Relationships

Celebrate the natural magic relationships you have with people, animals, and nature. These relationships are important in life and need to be cherished on an everyday basis. If you wait to let someone know you care, it often becomes too late. People change, move away, or die; animals grow older and pass away, and you are out there in the jungle, just trying to survive. Because life is so short, take some time each and every day to appreciate nature and your natural magic relationships with people, animals, and the divine spirit of the land around you.

Natural Magic Affirmation for Relationships

Say the following affirmation aloud three times before writing it in your Natural Magic Empowerment Journal:

Today and every day, I joyously celebrate successfully attaining my natural magic empowerment goals for more positive relationships.

Write the affirmation on a small note card. Place the card where you see it when you wake up and when you go to sleep. Also write the affirmation on a sheet of paper and tape it to your mirror. When you notice it, be sure to read the affirmation aloud or silently to yourself at least three times. Do this for at least 28 days, a full moon cycle.

Natural Magic Meditation for Relationships

Get comfortable, preferably in your power spot, and relax by taking several deep breaths. Breathe in, and feel your awareness expand in every direction. Hold your breath for a moment, and still your being with a peaceful quiet. Exhale and sense everything in your body releasing the stored up energy.

Again, inhale and expand your energy and awareness, moving farther and farther outward. Hold it while quieting your mind and focusing your energy. Breathe out all the old patterns that have been causing you stress. Sense all of your muscles relaxing. Continue taking deep breaths until all your muscles feel free of all stress and tension.

Now in your mind's eye, imagine walking into a garden that is in full bloom. Moving over to a circle of tomato vines, you pluck several beautifully red cherry tomatoes. As you bite down on them, the juices spread from your mouth throughout your being bringing vital energy to every cell. Standing in your garden with the Sun shining down, you celebrate every day you are alive. You celebrate your relationships to other people, and you celebrate your relationships with nature. You celebrate your relationships to the divine energy that connects everything into One.

Out on a bright summer day, the Sun shines brightly and life is everywhere. It's a celebration of life on every level of being. This is the time when the fires of action and celebration are most strong. Through the fields you see trees filled with fruit, vines covers with berries, and stalks bearing a multitude of fresh vegetables. You dance through the fields celebrating the harvest. It is a dance where you become One with the spirit of the earth.

Taking another deep, complete breath, you realize that every day you experience nature is a celebration. Now that you have a special place to go to both physically and mentally when events become stressful, you can charge your energies up and make better choices each and every day.

As you breathe in and out again, bring this natural magic power and knowledge forward with you to the present time and place.

Move your fingers and toes, and then stretch your muscles and gradually bring your awareness back to now. Before doing anything else, write your insights and impressions in your Natural Magic Empowerment Journal.

Natural Magic Ritual for Relationships

The purpose of the following ritual is to perform Earth-friendly nuptials and to celebrate your empowering relationship with your primary partner and the divine energies of nature. You will need a clear quartz crystal point; a bowl of the earth; an incense burner with a smudge stick; a beeswax candle and holder; a cup of well or spring water; nine items representing the Goddess, the God, Earth, Air, Fire, Water, Spirit, you, and your partner; and a ring representing your union. You also need a wooden box big enough to fit all nine items. Follow these steps:

1. Bring the elemental powers into your sacred circle by doing the three steps of the natural magic ritual for relationships in Chapter 1. Invite the divine energies of Oneness into your space by standing in the middle of the circle and saying:

   Divine energies of Oneness
   Please bless my sacred space with your presence.

2. Lay your nine items out on the natural magic altar and facing the altar, say:

   We are gathered together in this place and time
   To join together in love, peace, and joy
   We call upon the Goddess and God to witness our union
   And give us their blessings.

   Put the two items representing the Goddess and God in your relationship box. Pick up the item representing the element Earth and hold it up to the north point, saying:

   Sacred spirits of Earth, come into our circle
   Let your strength and wisdom be with us.

   Put the item representing Earth in your relationship box. Pick up the item representing the Air element and move to the east point. While standing in front of the east point, say:

226

Sacred spirits of Air, come into our circle
Let your breath of long life be with us.

Put the item representing Air in the relationship box. Move to the south point and hold up the item representing fire while saying:

Sacred spirits of Fire, come into our circle
Let your passion, ardor, and creativity be with us.

Put the item representing Fire in the box, and pick up the item representing water. Move to the west point and say:

Sacred spirits of Water, come into our circle
Let your divine, flowing love fill us.

Put the item representing the element of Water in your relationship box.

3. Stand before your altar with your partner, and each of you in turn put your object in the box while saying:

Together we are as One
By the powers of Earth, Air, Fire, Water, and Spirit
Blessed be our union!

Carrying the rings that symbolize your union and the relationship box, move to the center of the circle. Hold up the rings and box while saying in unison:

Goddess and God, please bless our union
Protect us and guide us each day
Please grant us love, beauty, and harmony
And please grant us abundance in our life together
Let our love be a shining light for all to see.
We ask this with our heart of hearts, blessed be!

Place the rings on one another's fingers, one at a time, and then say:

By the powers of Earth, Air, Fire, Water, and Spirit
We are joined together as One! So be it!

Thank the energies of the nature, the elements, Goddess and God, and Oneness, and pull up your circle. Before leaving your sacred space, be sure that the smudge stick and candle are completely extinguished.

+ + Natural Magic Blessing for Relationships +
+ *Divine Goddess and God, every day and every night, I celebrate my divine
relationship with you and thank you for your loving and uplifting blessings and
helping me attain my natural magic goals.*

Natural Magic Exercises for Relationships

In the following natural magic exercise, you celebrate your natural
magic empowerment for relationships. Select your favorite place in
nature and invite your primary partner. Bring some fresh fruits, vegetables, and breads along with a bottle of beer, wine, juice, and some
spring water, and a couple of glasses.

Enjoy your favorite spot in nature, feast on your natural foods, and
toast all who made it possible. Fill up your glasses and hold them up
saying this toast:

I toast all the divine energies of natural magic
Thank you for your continued help and blessings
May you be grow, be strong, and live long!

For the last part of the celebration, toast and give thanks to the individual energies that helped you on your natural magic quest. When you
are done, be sure to leave the area in the natural state you found it in.

In this second natural magic exercise, you go outside in nature and
give thanks for everything. Thank the air and the plants and trees every
time you breathe in and fill your lungs full of oxygen. Thank the earth
for providing the food you eat, and thank the rain for giving you the
water to live.

While outside, begin watching the relationships that things have with
one another as well as their role in nature as a whole. Ants can be a
problem at picnics, but if you study them you'll see that they work
together to basically clean up everything in nature without discrimination and malice. Spend as much time as you can observing the natural
flow of things. It's a great way to not only celebrate and learn about
nature, but to also celebrate and learn about parts of yourself.

Wellness

To have the sensory ability to experience life and nature is a divine gift that should be celebrated every moment. Every day you wake up and greet the sunlight pouring through the bedroom window, you are glad you are alive another day and you celebrate life.

The experience of life and natural magic is one that you need to enjoy, to live to its fullest in terms of "right now." This means staying in the present moment and enjoying the sensory experience as it happens. This is an important part of celebrating natural magic empowerment and your own wellness.

Natural Magic Affirmation for Wellness

Say the following affirmation aloud three times before writing it in your Natural Magic Empowerment Journal:

Today and every day, I am thankful for my life and filled with the healing energies of natural magic. I celebrate and enjoy successfully attaining my empowerment goals for wellness.

Write the affirmation on a small note card. Place the card where you can see it first thing in the morning and just as you go to sleep.

Natural Magic Meditation for Wellness

Get comfortable and begin relaxing by taking several deep breaths. Breathe in slowly, giving thanks for the breath of life. Feel it expanding in your lungs and give thanks for your ability to think and reason. Exhale and give thanks for the breeze that comes and takes away all of your tension and stress. Repeat the breathing exercise, giving thanks each time for the things in your life while at the same time becoming more relaxed.

Now in your mind's eye, imagine you are a hummingbird flying on a summer's day. You fly over to a large purple morning glory flower and you use your long beak to nestle in for the sweet nectar at the center of the flower. You move from flower to flower, drinking the nectar that overflows from the center of every circular grouping of petals. Everything exudes a sensation of the sweet, delightful celebration of summer.

Now in your mind's eye, imagine you are a dolphin skimming across the top the ocean water. You pop your head up above the waves and feel the warm glow of the summer sun before diving back into the cool ocean depths.

You move forward, gracefully through the sea, and your awareness continues to grow. Imagine that in the waters of creation, you have learned to manifest anything you can imagine, providing you have the intention and desire, and make the effort to bring your goals into reality.

Now, imagine you are the Goddess or God of your choice. Who would you be? What kind of world would you help to create? What if the choice was yours? What would you do? As a Goddess or God, these are questions you need to address. Everybody wants to know the answer. How would you make life different or the same? As Goddess or God, the choice is yours. What do you choose?

Next, imagine you are the fire-born phoenix, rising up and celebrating life. Your tears bring healing to all they touch. You celebrate life for five hundred years and then you die and are reborn for another five hundred years. It is the eternal cycle of birth, death, and rebirth. This mirrors the cycle of empowerment, where you gain empowerment, review and set new goals, and then re-empower yourself.

Now take a deep, complete breath and begin moving your toes and fingers, bringing your awareness back to your body and physical surroundings. Stay relaxed while you stretch your muscles and gradually return to the present time and place.

Before doing anything else, make a few helpful notes in your Natural Magic Empowerment Journal regarding your meditation experience.

Natural Magic Ritual for Wellness

The purpose of the following ritual is to celebrate attaining your natural magic empowerment goals for wellness. You will need a clear quartz crystal point, a bowl of the earth, an incense burner with a smudge stick, a beeswax candle and holder, and a cup of well or spring water. Follow these steps:

1. Bring the elemental powers into your sacred circle by doing the three steps of the natural magic ritual for relationships in Chapter 1. Invite the divine energies of Oneness into your space by standing in the middle of the circle and saying:

   Divine energies of Oneness
   Please bless my sacred space with your presence.

2. With your clear quartz crystal in your power hand, go to the north point and say:

Divine energies of Earth
You give my empowerment form
I thank you for your continued blessings.

Move to the east point and say:

Divine energies of Air
You give my empowerment breath
I thank you for your continued blessings.

Move to the south point and say:

Divine energies of Fire
You give my empowerment light
I thank you for your continued blessings.

Move to the west point and say:

Divine energies of Water
You give my empowerment life
I thank you for your continued blessings.

3. Step into the center of the circle and point your crystal toward the north. Move around clockwise while saying:

Goddess of love
God of peace
Thank you for filling me
With divine, healing light
I thank you for your continued blessings.

Thank the energies of the elements, Goddess and God, and Oneness, and pull up your circle. Before leaving the area, be sure your candle and smudge stick are completely extinguished.

Natural Magic Blessing for Wellness

Today I celebrate my natural magic wellness and give thanks to all of the divine energies who helped me on my quest.

Natural Magic Exercises for Wellness

In the following natural magic exercise, you adopt a wellness tree in celebration of your natural magic empowerment. Begin by finding a tree that to you symbolizes your natural magic wellness. Take a cup of spring or well water, and bless it by putting your power hand over the cup and asking for the blessings of the Goddess and God of wellness. Beginning at the north point, go around the tree clockwise three times while sprinkling the blessing water, and saying, "I bless you with healing water of wellness." Place your hands on the tree and imagine breathing the wisdom of the tree into your being. When you are finished, thank the tree and the spirit within it.

In this second natural magic exercise, you make an organic vegetable soup to celebrate your natural magic empowerment for wellness. If possible, use vegetables and spices that you grew in your garden; if that's not possible, choose organic vegetables from your supermarket. You will need the following ingredients:

- 3 TB. olive oil
- 1 yellow onion, peeled and chopped
- 3 cloves of garlic, peeled and chopped
- 3 carrots, peeled and sliced
- 1 stalk of celery, sliced
- 3 potatoes, peeled and diced
- 4 natural vegetable broth bouillon cubes
- 6 cups of pure spring or well water
- Sea salt, pepper, basil, thyme, or other seasonings, to taste

Heat a large soup pot with the olive oil. Add the onions and garlic and cook over low heat until the onion and garlic begin to brown. Add the carrots, celery, potatoes, bouillon cubes, and water, and bring to a boil. Reduce the heat and let your natural magic soup simmer for an hour or so. You may want to add some spices such as sea salt, pepper, basil, and thyme, and some flavorings such as tamari or Bragg's Amino Acids.

When your soup is done, enjoy it and savor its empowering nutrition and wonderful taste. Thank the Goddess and God for their gift of wellness.

Enrichment

Because enrichment comes in so many different forms, it can be celebrated in a number of different ways. Celebrate your physical empowerment by taking a bath in mineral springs or taking a walk on a beautiful spring day with everything in bloom. Mentally you can learn something new about the world and have a new experience that enlightens you and expands your awareness. Spiritually you can have energetic and divine experiences that connect you with the essence of the universe.

Natural Magic Affirmation for Enrichment

Say the following affirmation aloud three times before writing it into your Natural Magic Empowerment Journal:

Today and every day I celebrate successfully attaining my natural magic empowerment goals for enrichment. I thank the elements, the divine, and the universe for their enriching powers.

Write the affirmation on a small note card. Place the card where you can see it while you work. Remember every day is a celebration, so go outdoors and enjoy your natural magic surroundings.

Natural Magic Meditation for Enrichment

Get comfortable and relax by taking several deep breaths. Slowly inhale, filling your lungs full of air and spirit full of energy. Hold your breath for a moment, and still your mind of all thought. Exhale and let all the air out of your lungs while at the same time, releasing all the tension in your muscles.

Now, breathe in again and imagine your breath energizing your spirit, hold it for a moment while quieting your mind, and exhale, releasing all the stress and tension in your physical body. Do this breathing exercise three more times; energizing your spirit, quieting your mind, and relaxing your body.

Imagine celebrating nature by sitting next to a clear pool of water. The pool is fed by a series of small waterfalls created by larger rocks covered by a soft green moss. The water in the pool is clear with a mountain purity that makes it easy to see the large rocks and small pebbles that line its bottom.

Looking down into the water, you see an array of color gleaming from brown, gold, dark blue, deep red, to white, gray, pink, and jade green. Reaching down into the water, you pick up several of the stones, and as you do they begin to gently vibrate in your hands and the image around you begins to shift.

Now in your mind's eye, imagine sitting in a grove of giant cedar trees. When you breathe in, the air is filled with the aroma of fresh cedar, which has the effect of cleansing your energy. The giant trees whose roots run down deep into the earth, and whose trunks and limbs rise high into the blue sky, stand around in a sacred circle that celebrates all life and natural energies. Sitting inside this circle, you sense the sacred energy that begins to spin around the parameter of the circle. The magic of the trees reveals itself as the level of natural energy builds to a higher and higher degree. Once again the image around you begins to shift.

Now in your mind's eye, imagine sitting in a circle that has clear quartz crystals standing all around the outside of the ring. The crystals are aligned in such a way that the Sun as it travels through the sky, sends light down the tip of the circle, illuminating the whole circle with a spectrum of divine light. Each color swirls through you while healing, soothing, and charging your personal energy. A bright white light shines around your crown chakra at the top of your head. The light shimmers throughout your body, giving you a glow that enlivens every cell of your body.

Love and feelings of joy vibrate in waves across your being. You are One with all light and energy. You become the energetic essence and light of the earth. You shine your light and give your energy to all creation, and in turn all creation gives their energy to you. Like a latticework of light, it spreads out throughout the land. It's a divine web of light that connects all things together.

Sense your awareness moving back into your physical body and surroundings. Gently stretch your muscles while gradually coming out of the meditation. Take a moment to reflect on things. Before doing anything else, write down in your Natural Magic Empowerment Journal the impressions and insights you had while meditating.

Natural Magic Ritual for Enrichment

The purpose of the following ritual is to celebrate attaining your natural magic enrichment goals. You will need a clear quartz crystal point, a bowl of the earth, an incense burner with a smudge stick, a beeswax candle and holder, and a cup of well or spring water. Follow these steps:

1. Bring the elemental powers into your sacred circle by doing the three steps of the natural magic ritual for relationships in Chapter 1. Invite the divine energies of Oneness into your space by standing in the middle of the circle and saying:

   Divine energies of Oneness
   Please bless my sacred space with your presence.

2. With your crystal in your power hand, go to the north and say:

   Divine powers of Earth
   I celebrate my enriching relationship with you
   Thank you for your help
   Now and forever more.

   Move to the east point and say:

   Divine powers of Air
   I celebrate my enriching relationship with you
   Thank you for your help
   Now and forever more.

   Move to the south point and say:

   Divine powers of Air
   I celebrate my enriching relationship with you
   Thank you for your help
   Now and forever more.

   Move to the west point and say:

   Divine powers of Air
   I celebrate my enriching relationship with you
   Thank you for your help
   Now and forever more.

3. With your crystal in your power hand, go to the center of the circle. Beginning by facing the north point, slowly twirl in a clockwise circle and say:

   Divine powers of Goddess
   Divine powers of God
   Divine powers of Oneness
   I celebrate my enriching relationship with you
   Thank you for your help
   Now and forever more.

Thank the energies of the elements, Goddess and God, and Oneness for their help. Before leaving the area, pull up your circle and make sure your candle and smudge stick are completely extinguished.

Natural Magic Blessing for Enrichment

Thank you divine Lady and Lord for your bright blessings of enrichment and abundance. May you continue to help me in your miraculous ways today and every day.

Natural Magic Exercises for Enrichment

In the following natural magic exercise, you create something as an expression of your natural magic empowerment. Your creation can be anything, including planting a tree, flowing bush, or creating a medicine wheel from the rocks around your home. You can also create a song, poem, art, sculpture, a craft, or a dance of empowerment. The choice of your expression is completely yours to decide. As you craft it, envision the different parts of your empowerment. Make an effort to put this energy into your creation.

After you are done creating your expression of empowerment, present it to the energies of natural magic. Go outside where you will not be disturbed and express yourself. If it's a song, then play the song. If it's artwork, then place it on or near your altar in your natural sacred space. As you present it, say:

Divine energies of natural magic
I present this gift to you
As a way of saying thanks
For your eternal blessings.

In this second natural magic exercise, you do something to honor nature today. Select something you would like to do, such as plant a tree, bush, or seeds, water the plants in your garden or yard, clean up trash, save the life of a plant or animal, become a vegetarian, mail a check in support of an environmental or animal rights group of your choice, or send a letter or e-mail to your elected representatives expressing support of environmental legislation and animal rights.

As you do something nice for nature, remember it as a gesture of thanks for all of the natural magic moments and times of empowerment nature has bestowed upon you.

Chapter Twelve

Reflecting On Your
Natural Magic Process

Akin to the need of a human being to do certain things in order to evolve, humanity moves through periods where the focus is on one basic thing. During the Middle Ages it was religion, and in the subsequent period beginning with the Renaissance, the focus shifted to science. This focus and approach to life has brought great advances in technology and a more systematic view of nature. Science dissected and classified nature in every way possible.

The latest focus has been a blend of science and nature. The black-and-white world of science has had to allow for a lot of gray and phenomena that push the envelope beyond the ordinary. Some things defy conventional logic, but they nonetheless happen and are real.

Spiritual and mystical experiences are some of those things that defy logic. Progressive scientists such as Rupert Sheldrake have shown that thoughts have influence on matter and that people have a special energetic bond with their pets and animal allies.

The more directed your thoughts become, the more influence you can direct with them. Crystals help the process of directing your thoughts because they are vibrationally sympathetic to any energy they come into contact with or that programs them. In this way, crystals are incredible empowerment tools that can help you direct energy and help you see things more clearly.

Seeing things more clearly is the essence of reflecting on your natural magic empowerment process. When reflecting, your windows of perception need to be as clear as possible. It's important to see things as they are, so that you can more forward with the empowerment process and live a more enriched life.

Reflection is personal and introspective and is best done by yourself. It's often a good idea to ask the advice of someone who has had a similar experience, but the act of integrating your past with your future in a reflective moment is something you need to do with the least amount of influence from others as possible.

The Looking Glass

There comes a time in every process when you reflect on what you have done in the past. You peer into the looking glass and see how you have changed and what is in store for the future. This has been the traditional dual role of looking glasses:

- As something that mirrors the physical world at a present moment in time
- As something that within its depths reflects the future as well as the present

Lewis Carroll writes about how a young girl named Alice moves through the looking glass and suddenly has her world turned around. Being a reflection of life, looking glasses show many things depending on the person doing the looking. We as humans tend to see what we want to see. The idea is to step outside yourself. Put your conditioned ego aside for a few moments and observe who you are from afar as if you were observing yourself and your life. Only then can you begin to be objective about who you are, where you are going, and how you want to change.

The earliest looking glasses were crystal-clear and perfectly still pools of water. You could see your present reflection on the surface of the water at the same time that you asked for a gift of the future. The water melded the two images together into one image, giving you your wish.

These two aspects of looking glasses illustrate reflecting on your natural magic empowerment process. The process is twofold in that you are looking at your present situation, and then looking at the future and how your present situation can be improved. Reflection is something you can do at regular intervals in order to make better choices and move your life forward in a positive, empowering direction.

Seeds for the Future

One of the most beautiful aspects of nature is that one generation creates the seeds for the next generation. As flowers burst into bloom and create gorgeous displays of color, you don't have to feel regret as the blooms fade. Rather, look to the future as you collect the seeds for next year's blooms. Nature cycles rather than moves back and forth. Life sprouts, grows, blossoms, and then goes dormant and reseeds itself. This is the natural cycle of things.

Reflection is the part of the natural magic empowerment process where you put everything in perspective. This includes what your situation looks like now as well as your future prospects. This means keeping an optimistic view of things even when everyone around you is pessimistic, sarcastic, or cynical. For me, keeping a positive attitude and moving forward with each new day is a key to enjoying life.

With every project you do, you go through the natural cycles. You plant the seeds, they start growing and bloom, and then they wind up going to dormant or to seed. This is the natural cycle of nature. It's important to continually evolve your projects and goals to reflect the present and future.

In terms of relationships, some move you forward and others attempt to hold you back. Energetically you can sense the difference. In terms of wellness, positive relationships are those that leave you feeling better and spiritually give you light. Empowerment is an ongoing process. Positive energy is like an avalanche: Once it starts to build, there's no stopping it!

Reflections on Relationships, Wellness, and Enrichment

Empowerment and natural magic are processes that are always in progress. The last step is reflection, which is the link between the empowerment quest you are just finishing and the one you are about to begin.

The idea is to learn from your successes and failures. Now that you have moved through your natural magic quest, you have a better idea of your strengths and weaknesses. This information can be invaluable as you once again embark on your empowerment process.

Natural Magic Affirmation for Relationships, Wellness, and Enrichment

Say the following affirmation aloud three times before writing it in your Natural Magic Empowerment Journal:

Today I reflect on the direction of my life and I better understand what empowers me. From this understanding, each day I create more positive relationships, I feel healthier, and more enriched.

Write the affirmation on several small note cards that you put around your home and workplace. Every time you see one of the cards, read the affirmation aloud three times. Do this several times a day.

Natural Magic Meditation for Relationships, Wellness, and Enrichment

Anoint yourself with sandalwood or amber scented oil. (Dilute the oils with a carrier oil before using.) Get comfortable and relax by taking several deep breaths. Inhale and gradually fill your lungs full of air. Hold your breath for a moment and feel your being expand. Exhale and let all the stress and tension go out of your body. Inhale again and sense your spirit being energized. Hold your breath and feel a peaceful quiet spread across your being. As you exhale, take this sensation and move it throughout your physical body, relaxing all of your muscles. Do this breathing exercise three more times—energizing your spirit, quieting your mind, and relaxing your body.

In your mind's eye, imagine you are a ray of light being generated by an immense solar body. You incidentally beam through space until you make contact with mirrorlike objects that reflect your light, making you more than one ray. After a while your light is beamed throughout the dimensions of time and space, with each beam connected to your original ray of light.

Now, imagine one of the beams of light streaming out and eventually approaching and reflecting off of a giant multifaceted crystal that then lights up, getting brighter and brighter. The beam of light sets off a chain reaction that sends glowing light out through every facet and as it does so, the intensity of the light increases. The crystal goes from being a reflector of light to being a generator of light.

Imagine being a circle of light that has neither beginning nor end. You are because you are. Your rays light the darkness and make it so everything can see. Everything that can be seen is a reflection of your light. Every day you shine your rays of light for all to see. Other people who come into contact with you start out as reflectors of the light but soon become generators of light. In this way the ray of light continues to expand into many beams that eventually light the world.

Imagine standing arm and arm in a line of people that extends around the world. You are the protectors of the earth and guardians of nature. Everywhere you go you spread natural magic. You teach others to be One with Earth and nature. You are all part of the same family.

Gradually begin moving your awareness back to your body and physical surroundings. Stretch your muscles and rub your hands briskly together for a few moments. Take a moment to think about the meditation. Before doing anything else, write down your impressions and insights in your Natural Magic Empowerment Journal.

Natural Magic Ritual for Relationships, Wellness, and Enrichment

The purpose of the following ritual is to do a healing on the earth to help support more positive relationships on a global level, better health for the people of the world and global enrichment. You will need a clear quartz crystal point; a bowl of the earth; an incense burner with a smudge stick; a beeswax candle and holder; a cup of well or spring water; and patchouli, lavender, and amber scented oils (essential oils and resin added to a carrier oil). Follow these steps:

1. Bring the elemental powers into your sacred circle by doing the three steps of the natural magic ritual for relationships in Chapter 1. Invite the divine energies of Oneness into your space by standing in the middle of the circle and saying:

   Divine energies of Oneness
   Please bless my sacred space with your presence.

2. Anoint your wrists, ankles, throat, the back of your head, and your third eye with a few drops of the three scented oils. Face your altar at the north point and say:

   In this time of all times
   In this place of all places
   I stand at the crossroads of empowerment
   May Earth, Air, Fire, and Water bless, empower, and guide me
   May the divine Ones bless, empower, and guide me
   May my ancestors bless, empower, and guide me.
   Blessed be!

   Take the bowl of the earth from the altar and hold it up toward the north point of your circle and say:

   Divine Mother and Father
   Bless this bowl of Earth unto your service
   I call upon the empowering guardian energies of Earth
   Please fill me with your natural powers.

   Set the bowl back on the altar. Take the burning smudge from the altar and hold it up toward the east point of the circle and say:

   Divine Mother and Father
   Bless this burning smudge unto your service
   I call upon the empowering guardian energies of Air
   Please fill me with your natural powers.

   Set the smudge carefully back down upon the altar. Take the candlestick and burning candle from the altar and hold it up toward the south point of your circle and say:

   Divine Mother and Father
   Bless this burning flame unto your service

I call upon the empowering guardian energies of Fire
Please fill me with your natural powers.

Place the candle carefully back down on the altar. Take the cup of water from the altar and hold it upward toward the west point of the circle and say:

Divine Mother and Father
Bless this cup of water unto your service
I call upon the empowering guardian energies of Water
Please fill me with your natural powers.

Place the cup back down upon the altar.

3. With your crystal in your right hand, move to the center of the circle. Hold up both your arms upward and say:

Divine Mother and Divine Father
Please fill the earth with your loving powers
To help myself and others create more positive relationships
Please fill the earth with your healing power
To help myself and others live a healthier life
Please fill the earth with your abundant powers
To help myself and others live a more enriched life.

Point your crystal toward the north point and say:

Eternal blessings to the Divine Mother and Father
Blessed be the earth.

Point your crystal toward the east and say:

Eternal blessings to the Divine Mother and Father
Blessed be the winds.

Point your crystal toward the south and say:

Eternal blessings to the Divine Mother and Father
Blessed be the light.

Point your crystal toward the west and say:

Eternal blessings to the Divine Mother and Father
Blessed be the waters.

Move to the center of the circle and say:

I give thanks to the Divine Mother and Father
I give thanks to the helpful spirits of nature

I give thanks to the elements of Earth, Air, Fire, and Water
May the sacred Earth be loved, healed, and enriched
And may nature ever thrive, now and forevermore.
So be it! Blessed be Oneness!

Before leaving your sacred space, pull up your circle and make sure the candle and smudge stick are completely extinguished.

Natural Magic Blessing for Relationships, Wellness, and Enrichment

Dear God and Goddess, please bless me with the clear sight and common sense to see things as they are, so that I can better enjoy my life and all of nature's exquisite, empowering gifts.

Natural Magic Exercises for Relationships, Wellness, and Enrichment

In the following natural magic exercise, you make an energetic link between you and the earth. Begin by selecting a stone sphere (such as a marble) to represent the earth. Use your smudge stick to cleanse the sphere of any energy. Hold the sphere in your hands and imagine loving, healing, and enriching energy filling the stone, and in turn, the earth.

Carry or keep the sphere handy so that you pick it up often, sending loving, healing, and enriching energy to the earth. The sphere is also your connection to the powers of natural magic, something that will continue to play a greater part in your life. As the energy of the earth becomes stronger, your energy will also become stronger and the level of natural magic in your life will substantially increase.

In this second natural magic exercise, you save seeds for next year. In terms of flowers, you have to wait until the blossom wilts and dries. As far as vegetables such as corn and beans, let several of the ears and pods dry in the sun. Pick the seeds out after they dry. With pumpkins, you scrape the seeds out of the inside, and let they dry before storing them in a cool dry place until you are ready to plant them.

Label your seeds and keep them in a dark-colored container that can breathe, such as a brown paper bag. Make notes in your Natural Magic Empowerment Journal about particular generations of plants and their seeds. When planting, germinate and start the seeds in a seed tray or flowerpot before transplanting the plants. When they bloom and fruit, enjoy the beauty and natural splendor that they give you year after year.

Appendix A

Natural Magic Crystals and Stones

Crystals and stones are gifts from the earth, and as such, resonate with the energies of natural magic. Each crystal and stone has individual energetic properties that relate to relationships, wellness, and enrichment. The following is a listing of crystals and stones and their energetic properties as they relate to natural magic.

Agate   Natural magic energies: Grounding, longevity, self-confidence, best for balancing body, mind, and spirit, helps with digestion, grounding, building self-confidence, protection, self-honesty, reducing stress, and better blood circulation.

Amazonite   Natural magic energies: Soothes body, mind, and spirit, increases abundance, personal enrichment, creativity, truth, good luck, successful completion of projects, promotes psychic receptive ability.

Amethyst   Natural magic energies: Helps with divination, mental clarity, balancing temperament, peaceful sleep, relaxation, wellness, attracts love, wisdom, courage, promotes healing, better circulation, hormone production, psychic development, lucid dreaming, stone of protection that can help to overcome addictions.

Aquamarine   Natural magic energies: Protective and purifying stone that promotes peace of mind, wellness, relaxation, courage, creative inspiration, and mental clarity, helps with eyesight, to release grief and fear, keeps you centered and increases intuition.

Aventurine   Natural magic energies: Promotes positive action and adventures, safe travel, good luck, wellness, healing, activates your imagination, creativity, and awareness, strengthens eyesight, helps to soothe emotions, increases abundance, prosperity, and personal enrichment.

Azurite   Natural magic energies: A stone of wisdom with copper content, best for healing, wellness, amplifying energy, helps with insight, mental clarity, focus, concentration, and meditation.

Bloodstone   Natural magic energies: Helps with healing, wellness, cleansing body, mind, and spirit, detoxifying body, strengthens heart, increases creative dreaming, vitality, circulation of the body, divination, higher knowledge, and courage, puts you in touch with the elements.

Carnelian   Natural magic energies: Promotes positive relationships and sexuality, motivation, focus, fertility, purification, personal enrichment, increases fire element energy, builds personal strength, courage, and creativity, helps with lower back problems, protects against injury, and helps you to access past lives, ancestral powers.

Cat's Eye   Natural magic energies: Excellent stone for balancing body, mind, and spirit, promotes insight, wisdom, learning, seeing beyond illusions, confidence to attain natural magic goals, to access inner abilities, and helps in mental clarity, concentration, and shape-shifting.

Citrine   Natural magic energies: Stone of personal empowerment and learning that enhances motivation, mental abilities, clarity, insight, and logical thought, helps to relieve headaches, dispels negativity, and assists in natural magic goal actualization.

Clear Quartz   Natural magic energies: Promotes healing, wellness, balancing body, mind, and spirit, improves insight, clarity, lucid dreaming, higher consciousness, meditation, divine guidance, stores, releases, and regulates personal energies, purifies and unblocks stuck energy in your body, excellent for star walking and shape-shifting.

Diamond Natural magic energies: Promotes healing, wellness, personal power, positive and loving relationships, helps with insight, inspiration, mental clarity, stamina, memory, and altered states of awareness, protective stone of abundance, enrichment, and prosperity, amplifies your energy.

Emerald Natural magic energies: Promotes wellness, healing, personal growth, inspiration, psychic abilities, meditation, knowledge, lucid dreaming, divination, enhances sexuality, cleansing stone that helps with gastric problems, cultivating patience, balancing body, mind, and spirit, diabetes, back problems, and neutralizing radioactivity, boosts the immune system.

Fluorite Natural magic energies: Enhances harmony, balance, peace of mind, tranquility, sexuality, psychic abilities, and intuition, empowers female energy, helps with cancer remission, arthritis, benefits teeth and bones.

Garnet Natural magic energies: Promotes enrichment, prosperity, good fortune in business, and positive friendships, helps to better circulation, calm anger, and sharpen intuition, enhances physical strength, love, passion, compassion, imagination, shape-shifting, altered states of consciousness, and creativity.

Hematite Natural magic energies: Helps with grounding, body circulation, personal strength, vitality, self-esteem, healing, kidney problems, tissue regeneration, relieves headaches, hysteria, and fear, protective stone that enhances altered states of consciousness.

Jade Natural magic energies: A cleansing and protective stone that dispels negativity, calms nerves, and connects you energetically with the Earth element, promotes positive relationships, love, friendship, divine guidance, meditation, and spiritual awareness, helps with kidney and bladder problems and eases childbirth. Often used for amulets and talismans.

Jasper Natural magic energies: Protective stone that enhances mental clarity, quick thinking, concentration, meditation, relaxation, prayer, and endurance, promotes a calm, down-to-earth mental attitude when pursuing your natural magic goals.

Lapis Lazuli Natural magic energies: Enhances intuition, divination abilities, self-knowledge, and creativity, promotes wellness, personal enrichment and empowerment, shape-shifting, and altered states of consciousness, protective stone that amplifies thoughts and personal energy and acts as a defensive and offensive shield, helps with respiratory and nervous disorders, and boosts your immune system.

Malachite   Natural magic energies: Excellent stone for shape-shifting and communicating with the animal kingdom and all of nature, enhances enrichment, insight, peaceful sleep, divine guidance, clarity, healing, and wellness, promotes stronger willpower, emotional balance, tissue regeneration, stimulates the optic nerve.

Moonstone   Natural magic energies: Enhances moon/water energies, female energies, healing, wellness, receptivity, divination abilities, artistic creativity, dancing abilities, and altered states of awareness, helps to recognize true love, positive relationships, balance body, mind, and spirit, increases enrichment, good luck, fertility, intuition, clairvoyance, sensitivity to the elements, and is used in farming.

Obsidian   Natural magic energies: Protective stone that increases intuition, insight, past life experiences, divination abilities, enrichment, and good fortune, helps to let go of grief, fear, and troubling memories, often used for ritual tools.

Onyx   Natural magic energies: Helps to build strong patterns and attain your natural magic goals, promotes peace of mind, vitality, relaxation, and creativity, increases structure in your life, accesses ancestral powers and past memories.

Opal   Natural magic energies: Promotes harmony, insight, inspiration, altered states of consciousness, emotional balance, helps with eye problems, protects from negativity, enhances lucid dreaming, enrichment, business success, and personal wisdom.

Peridot   Natural magic energies: Enhances wellness, healing, digestion, tissue regeneration, peace of mind, insight, clairvoyance, intuition, empowerment, and mental clarity, promotes enlightenment, boosts confidence, and adds success power to your natural magic goals.

Rose Quartz   Natural magic energies: Promotes emotional balance, positive relationships and friendships, love, fertility, healing, wellness, creativity, and compassion, helps in spiritual prayer and divine guidance, forgiveness, building self-esteem, flexibility to change, and restores faith.

Ruby   Natural magic energies: Activates the elements, especially the Fire element, increases vitality, stamina, wisdom, mental clarity, personal empowerment, enrichment, and healing, promotes creativity, motivation, love, passion, friendship, and protection, helps with heart and circulatory problems.

Rutilated Quartz Natural magic energies: Promotes healing, continued wellness, centering, vitality, motivation, positive connection with the elements, boosts your immune system, enhances friendship, love, compassion, passion, sexuality, and self-esteem.

Sapphire Natural magic energies: Protective stone that promotes mental focus, concentration, meditation, prayer, astral projection, lucid dreaming, expanding awareness, healing, wellness, inner wisdom, enrichment, good luck, and creativity, increases intuition, divination abilities, relaxation, dispels negativity and fear, helps with eye problems.

Sodalite Natural magic energies: Promotes better wellness, healing, lymph circulation, mental clarity, focus, objectivity, insight, and clairvoyance, enhances immunities, neutralizes radiation, and balances your metabolism.

Tanzanite Natural magic energies: Enhances psychic development, divination abilities, divine guidance, and altered states of consciousness, calms and balances body, mind, and spirit, promotes insight and clarity.

Topaz Natural magic energies: Enhances peace of mind, artistic abilities, creativity, divine guidance, vitality, insight, wisdom, wellness, and healing, stone of loyalty, problem solving, and scientific discovery, promotes harmony, tranquility, and helps with eye problems.

Tourmaline Natural magic energies: Promotes creativity, motivation, healing, personal empowerment, regeneration of tissue, and divine guidance, helps to cleanse and purify the body, mind, and spirit, strengthens your energy, and boosts your immune system.

Turquoise Natural magic energies: Powerful ancestral and nature deva stone that promotes altered states of awareness, star walking, psychic development, elemental wisdom, and personal empowerment, stimulates healing (especially respiratory problems), wellness, stamina, endurance, and courage.

Zircon Natural magic energies: Promotes patience, tolerance, peace of mind, reflection, and harmony.

Appendix B

Natural Magic Essential Oils, Herbs, Flowers, Plants, and Resins

Herbs and flowers are available in all kinds of forms, from bulk to capsule, picked wild or grown in your backyard. Essential oils and resins are most often purchased, with some modestly priced, while others are relatively expensive.

A few words of caution: Always consult a knowledgeable herbalist, acupuncturist, naturopathic, or homeopathic professional, or physician before using herbs or essential oils in any form to treat a specific illness, disease, or if you are pregnant, epileptic, diabetic, or have a mental illness. Always do a patch test before using the herb or essential oil on your skin or in your bath water. Be aware that herbal medicine is not a substitute for seeing your doctor if you have a medical condition. It should be used in conjunction with standard medical care.

Aloe   Healing, balancing, rejuvenation, easing discomfort and pain, the aloe plant is easy to grow and use. To relieve skin infections, burns, sunburn, poison oak, or poison ivy, cut a leaf from the plant, and apply the gel to the problem area.

Put the cut leaf in a plastic bag in the refrigerator to use again when needed.

Amber   Used in merging and ritual, for protection and increased romance and passion. Put drops of amber scented oil or rub the resin on your third eye, wrists, and ankles to promote altered states of consciousness and spiritual development.

Angelica   Purifying, clarifying, warms the body and improves circulation, is a tonic and blood purifier for the body. Used as incense, sprinkle herb on ritual circle or alter, carry with you to encourage creativity.

Apple   Fruit of immortality and vitality, eating apples encourage wellness, symbol of love, fertility, romance, friendship, healing, and enrichment.

Basil (sweet)   Promotes higher states of awareness, stimulating, uplifting, opens the mind to creativity and the heart to love, reduces impotence and infertility, increases sexual interest, used to treat muscular cramps and respiratory infections. Basil essential oil, made from the flowering tops and leaves, has antiviral, anti-infectious, and antibacterial properties, helps heal acne, intestinal cramps, bladder problems, and helps heal wounds and insect bites. Best used with oil diffuser or in small amounts in bath blends and food. Soak the herb in water, strain, and put the mixture in a squirt bottle. Then spray the water here and there in your workplace and home for protection from unwanted energies and to bring good luck, success, and enrichment.

Barley   Used to attract wealth, enrichment, and prosperity, soothes the body's digestive system, used to rid unwanted energies from your sacred space, often scattered on the altar in honor of the Earth Mother.

Bay Laurel   A protective and purifying herb, used externally, inhaling the scent of a freshly torn bay leaf promotes endurance, intuition, and prophetic dreams. Often used in incense to encourage altered states of consciousness, promotes healing for chest colds and respiratory difficulties when used as a poultice.

Bergamot   This rich, sweet scented essential oil is made from the peel of nearly ripe fruit and is blended with other essential oils and diluted with a carrier oil and then used in baths, infusions, and massage. It promotes enrichment, love, harmony, restful sleep and dreams, and reduces tension, depression, and fatigue, neutralizes unpleasant odors, uplifting, stimulating, and healing, helpful for digestive problems and hiccups, respiratory infections, healing wounds, and treating acne. (Note: Bergamot makes your skin much more sensitive to UV light, so avoid prolonged sun exposure for up to 12 hours after using it on your skin.)

Blessed Thistle   Increases oxygen to the brain, strengthens memory and mental capacity, aids circulation, vitality, helps relieve headaches, and acts as a tonic for body, mind, and spirit. Encourages wellness, purifying, cleansing, divine communication.

Catnip   Calming, promotes harmony, love, friendship, happiness, joy, healing, wellness, restful sleep, pleasant dreams, quiets the nerves, an ideal herb for children when used in combination with chamomile, spearmint, and lemon balm as a tea. Cats are intoxicated by catnip.

Cayenne   A superior crisis herb, often used in herbal combinations and known as a catalyst for all herbs, it increases circulation, purifies your blood, and acts as a tonic for nervous system. Promotes healing, wellness, and relaxation, it is taken as a daily tonic and is nonirritating when uncooked. (Note: Handle cayenne with care as it can be irritating to your mucous membranes and causes a warm sensation in your stomach and even a burning sensation.)

Cedarwood   Considered sacred and healing throughout the world, made from the wood of the tree, this strong woodsy oil is one of the first essential oils made by the Egyptians and used in cosmetics and as an insect repellent. Also helps heal insect bites, promotes harmony and wellness, reduces stress, helps clear sinuses, relieves respiratory problems, helps clear acne and other skin problems, and relieves both dry and oily scalps. (Note: Do not use this oil on infants or small children. Always first dilute with a carrier oil as cedarwood is very irritating to the skin. Use a maximum of two or three drops of cedarwood essential oil in the bath.)

Chamomile (German)   One of my favorites! Made from the dried flowers, this sweet, soothing, scented, fruity essential oil encourages positive and harmonious relationships, wellness, and personal enrichment. The word chamomile means "Earth apple," and it is often taken in tea as a calmative, promotes better digestion, and reduces stress and insomnia. It has cleansing, anti-inflammatory, and antibacterial properties, and increases the production of white blood corpuscles which helps in healing and strengthens your immune system. Helps heal wounds, herpes, and skin irritations. Used in burners and steam baths to calm nerves and promote restful sleep. (Note: Mix with lavender and neroli oil when used in bath water.)

Clover (Red)   Relaxing, purifying, vitalizing, healing, tonic for your nerves, and a blood purifier, rids your body and space of negative energies, encourages harmony, love, fertility, centeredness, altered states of awareness, mental clarity, and clairvoyance. The trefoil clover shape (three leaves) is a ancient symbol of the threefold Goddess (maid, mother, crone) and the God (son, father, wise man), and the trinity (body, mind, spirit), a faery favorite.

Copal   Resin often burned in incense over charcoal, encourages purification, vitality, strength, passion and love, promotes better relationships, wellness, enrichment, and rids your sacred space of unwanted energies.

Coriander   A herb of love, sexuality, passion, desire, romance, lust, vitality, prowess, and rejuvenation. Often used in cooking. Sprinkle the loose herbs around your circle and on your altar when doing rituals regarding love and passion.

Dandelion   Encourages harmony, healing, wellness, relaxation, intuition, balance, and vitality. Drink in tea or sprinkle the herb around your natural magic circle and altar before doing rituals or blessings in honor of the Goddess and God.

Echinacea   Strength, healing, wellness, natural antibiotic, all-heal used for flu, respiratory problems, and to build your immune system.

Eucalyptus Australiana   This strong, citrus-like essential oil encourages healing, wellness, helps relieve digestion problems, powerful antiseptic that helps relieves skin problems such as acne, relieves respiratory problems, infection, fever, migraine headaches, neuralgia, and wards off insects when burned. (Note: Use only in small doses as high doses can be toxic.)

Fennel   A purifying herb that promotes healing, wellness, vitality, protection, and harmony, soothes your stomach and digestive system, used in essential oil, sachets, and in healing mixtures. Sweet fennel essential oil is made from the roots, seeds, and leaves, and is used for digestive troubles, suppressing your appetite, reduce cellulite, eliminates toxins from your body, helps stimulate the liver, encourages longevity, courage, and vigor. (Note: Use only in small amounts as high amounts are toxic.)

Flax   Promotes healing and wellness, a protective herb that rids your sacred space from negativity and unwanted energies. Scatter flax seed over healing areas, your sacred circle, and your altar to encourage the help of the Goddess.

Frankincense   A fragrant tree gum resin used for protection, purification, cleansing, and to communicate more readily with the divine. Promotes merging and successful meditation, encourages spiritual growth and psychic development. Frankincense essential oil is woodsy and spicy and used to treat respiratory infections and problems, speeds up healing, calms, harmonizes, and helps balance your emotions.

Garlic   A protective herb called a cure-all and spring tonic as the fresh juice (never boiled) promotes healing and wellness on many levels, encourages rejuvenation, cell growth and repair, detoxifies your system, and reduces blood pressure, also dispels negativity. Excellent herb to attract enrichment, prosperity, good advice, fortune, wealth, and success.

Geranium   This floral essential oil is considered a heal-all, encourages healing, wellness, enrichment, harmony, helps heal tumors, ulcers, toothaches, skin infections, digestive problems, and promotes wound healing.

Ginger   Encourages enrichment, love, personal power, healing, wellness, superior aid for digestive problems, strengthens and warms the body, mind, and spirit.

Ginkgo Biloba   A wellness and enrichment herb that improves mental functions, increases learning abilities, intuition, vigor, blood circulation, helps memory, focus, concentration, and reaction time, encourages healing energies and harmony.

Ginseng (Wild Siberian)   Used for longevity, healing, wellness, regenerates and restores sexual centers, encourages love, wishes, beauty, and protection. (Note: People with high blood pressure should not use ginseng in any form.)

Ginseng (American)   This cooling, summer tonic increases your strength, vigor, focus, concentration, promotes all mental activities, stimulating your entire body, helps you reduce tension and fatigue, nourishes your blood, enhances creativity, attracts positive energies, beauty, harmony, and peace of mind. (Note: People with high blood pressure should not use ginseng in any form.)

Gotu Kola   Encourages youth, rejuvenation, regeneration, this herb strengthens the heart, brain, and acts as a nerve tonic, promotes mental focus, clarity, and increases learning abilities. Burn Gota Kola over charcoal just before you meditate to encourage divine communication and help.

Honeysuckle   Use the scented oil to consecrate your ritual tools, or on your third eye to open that chakra, to enhance your psychic abilities, and encourage lucid dreaming. Promotes protection, merging, sexuality, beauty, and attracts positive relationships.

Jasmine   Encourages enrichment, prophetic dreams, and optimism. Spread jasmine flowers clockwise around your sacred space to increase the power of your natural magic rituals for love. The rich, sweet, floral essential oil symbolizes divine hope and love and encourages love, romance, compassion, lust, positive sexuality, and divine communication, helps heal skin problems, reproductive problems, and stimulates creativity. (Note: Use in small amounts and not when pregnant.)

Lavender   The sweet, floral essential oil is made from the flowering tops and leaves of the lavender plant and is used to help relieve headaches and depression, encourages love, peace, harmony, purification, protection, longevity positive sexuality, harmony, joy, happiness, enrichment, healing, and wellness. The oil has wondrous anti-infection properties when rubbed into the skin, helps relieve and heal insect bites, colds, and flu, speeds up healing of wounds and burns, used in incense, baths, in sachets, and sprinkle a few drops of the essential oil on your sheets and pillowcases to promote restful, pleasant dreams.

Lemon   This fresh, citrus essential oil and can be used to clean and purify, as a digestive aid and antiseptic, helps heal skin infections and insect bites, diminishes skin wrinkles and freckles, lightens hair, alleviates tension, promotes harmony, joy, and calm.

Marigold   Encourages lucid dreaming, altered states of awareness, second sight, intuition, psychic development, clairvoyance, and shape-shifting. The flowers are a faery favorite! The essential oil is called calendula.

Marjoram   This warm, rich, and spicy essential oil is used in cosmetics and medicines, dispels negativity, promotes fidelity, is used in marriage wreaths, restores joy, calm, and harmony, increases vitality, helps relieve muscle strains, reduces cramps and migraine headaches, helps relieve indigestion and respiratory problems such as bronchitis and asthma. (Note: Too much marjoram can stupefy. People with low blood pressure, depression, or women who are pregnant should not use this oil.)

Marshmallow   This herb promotes healing and wellness, soothes your nerves, as a tonic for body, purifies your blood, promotes cell repair and growth, encourages psychic abilities, dispels negativity, a magnet to the divine, used in sachets and burned as incense over charcoal.

Mint (Spearmint)   Used primarily in teas, this herb encourages healing, wellness, helps relieve headaches, soothes stomach and digestive system, promotes restful sleep, dispels negativity, protection, safe travel, mental focus and clarity, increases memory and learning abilities, enhances concentration.

Myrrh   A healing and antiseptic essential oil used in incense, perfumes, cosmetics, and medicines. It helps heal wounds and reduces inflammation, relieves skin problems such as eczema, helps relieve respiratory infections, encourages proper digestion, for protection, harmony, wellness, and spiritual development, also for purification and consecration, enhances stamina, strength, courage, vitality, and increases your energy.

Neroli   Used in cosmetics, perfumes, and medicines, this sweet, floral and citrus essential oil is made from the flowers of the bitter orange tree. It encourages harmony, joy, love, romance, peace of mind, and emotional balance, curbs anxiety attacks, relieves grief, reduces tension and stress, improves the elasticity of your skin (especially when blended with lavender essential oil). To sweeten things up, perfume yourself, your bathwater, sheets, and towels with neroli.

Patchouli   This rich, earthy, and musky essential oil has long been used in perfumes and encourages love, romance, passion, positive sexuality, enrichment, psychic development, mental clarity, clairvoyance, and shape-shifting, tonic for snake and insect bites, antidepressant, antiseptic, and astringent properties, helps relieve and heal skin problems.

Pine (Scotch)   Made from the dry twigs, needles, and cones and commonly used in soaps and cosmetics, pine essential oil is used in medicines to treat lung and respiratory problems, has antiseptic and decongestant properties, helps relieve infections and gallstones, stimulates circulation, relieves fatigue, speeds healing process, promotes mental clarity, creativity, encourages enrichment, abundance, protection, love, friendship, romance, fertility, wellness, and dispels negativity.

Rose   Fossils of roses grown more than 32 million years ago have been found in North America. Very gentle, rich, and sweet essential oil used in cosmetics, with the petals used in bathwater, stimulates your senses.

It relieves PMS symptoms, regulates menstruation, purifies the blood, liver, and spleen tonic, helps heal skin problems, balances female and male energies, encourages abundance, enrichment, fortune, clear divination, healing, true love, romance, passion, positive sexuality, protection, peace of mind, harmony, joy, good luck, a faery favorite.

Rosemary An herb of protection and purification, the pungent, woodsy essential oil encourages love, passion, mental clarity, strength, courage, healing, wellness, promotes vitality, vigor, cell growth and repair, speeds healing to open wounds and burns, nerve stimulant, helps relieve headaches and vertigo, increases memory, assists you in the successful completion of thought, bringing solutions and answers more readily. Used in small amounts in baths, essential oil, on charcoal as incense, and eaten in small amounts.

Sage The leaves and flowers are made into essential oil. Commonly used in medicines and perfumes, it encourages healing, wellness, longevity, mental clarity, wisdom, protection, purification, vitality, increases memory and learning abilities, dispels negativity and nervous tension before meditating, used as overall body tonic, helps relieve respiratory problems such as asthma, reduces night sweats, improves digestion when eaten in small amounts. (Note: Sage is stimulating in small doses, but sedating and toxic in large doses.)

Sandalwood This rich woodsy essential oil is used in baths, aromatic blends, and in incense. It encourages relaxation, harmony, joy, spiritual states of awareness, shape-shifting, massaged into the skin after being blended with a carrier oil, it helps relieve throat problems such as laryngitis, helps regulate your heart, helps heal skin problems, sedates your nervous system.

Vanilla Encourages love, romance, lust, passion, mental flexibility, clairvoyance, shape-shifting, peace of mind, harmony, nerve tonic, brings relaxation.

Ylang-ylang This strong, sweet, floral essential oil is commonly used in perfumes and massage blends and to scent bathwater. It promotes energies of love, romance, passion, lust, positive sexuality, good luck, harmony, fertility, peace of mind, regulates the flow of adrenaline and sedates your nervous system, helps heal skin problems, and encourages hair growth.

Appendix C

Bibliography

Anderson, Rosemarie. *Celtic Oracles*. Harmony Books, 1998.

Artress, Lauren. *The Sand Labyrinth*. Journey Editions, 2000.

Benson, Herbert, and Miriam Klipper. *The Relaxation Response*. Avon, 1976.

Birdsall, George. *The Feng Shui Companion*. Destiny Books, 1995.

Bluestone, Sarvananda. *How to Read Signs and Omens In Everyday Life*. Destiny Books, 2002.

Bord, Janet, and Colin Bord. *Mysterious Britain*. Paladin Books, 1974.

Borgman, Peggy Wynne. *Four Seasons of Inner and Outer Beauty*. Broadway Books, 2000.

Braden, Gregg. *The Isaiah Effect*. Three Rivers Press, 2001.

———. *Awakening to Zero Point*. Radio Bookstore Press, 1997.

Brennan, Barbara Ann. *Light Emerging*. Bantam Books, 1993.

Bricklin, Mark. *Positive Living and Health*. Emmaus: Rodale Press, Inc., 1990.

Bromley, Michael. *Spirit Stones*. Journey Editions, 1997.

Brown, Simon. *Practical Feng Shui*. Ward Lock Books, 1997.

Buhlman, William. *The Secret of the Soul*. HarperSanFrancisco, 2001.

Burrill, Richard. *Protectors of the Land, An Environmental Journey*. The Anthro Company, 1994.

Cabarga, Leslie. *Talks with Trees*. Iconoclassics Publishing Co., 1997.

Cameron, Julia. *Heart Steps*. Jeremy P. Tarcher/Putnam, 1997.

Canfield, Jack, Mark Victor Hansen, and Les Hewitt. *The Power of Focus*. Health Communications, Inc., 2000.

Chaline, Eric. *Tai Chi for Body, Mind, and Spirit*. Sterling Publishing Co., 1998.

Chopra, Deepak, M.D. *Unconditional Life: Mastering the Forces that Shape Personal Reality*. Bantam Books, 1991.

Cobelo, Carolyn. *The Power of Sacred Space*. Akasha Productions, 2000.

Coffey, Lisa Marie. *Getting There with Grace*. Journey Editions, 2001.

Coghill, Roger. *The Healing Energies of Light*. Journey Editions, 2000.

Cowan, Tom. *The Pocket Guide to Shamanism*. The Crossing Press, 1997.

Craze, Richard. *Feng Shui*. Conari Press, 1997.

Creasy, Rosalind. *The Edible Herb Garden*. Periplus Editions, 1999.

Crosse, Joanna. *Encyclopedia of Mind, Body, Spirit, and Earth*. Element, 1998.

Cruden, Loren. *Compass of the Heart*. Destiny Books, 1996.

Davich, Victor. *The Best Guide to Meditation*. Renaissance Books, 1998.

Devereaux, Paul. *Secrets of Ancient and Sacred Places*. Blandford Press, 1992.

Eliade, Micea. *Shamanism*. Bollingen Series, 1964.

Fischer-Rizzi, Suzanne. *The Complete Aromatheraphy Handbook.* Sterling Publishing, 1990.

Gannon, Linda. *Creating Fairy Garden Fragrances.* Storey Books, 1998.

Garrett, Michael. *Walking on the Wind.* Bear and Company, 1998.

Garrett, Michael, and J.T. Garrett. *Medicine of the Cherokee.* Bear and Company, 1996.

Gawain, Shakti. *Creative Visualization.* Whatever Publishing, 1978.

Gimbutas, Marija. *The Goddesses and Gods of Old Europe.* University of California Press, 1982.

Goldstein, Nikki. *Essential Energy, A Guide to Aromatherapy and Essential Oils.* Warner Books, 1997.

Gray, John, Ph.D. *Men Are from Mars, Women Are from Venus.* HarperCollins, 1992.

Harner, Michael. *The Way of the Shaman.* Bantam, 1986.

Hart, Francine. *Sacred Geometry Oracle Deck.* Bear and Company, 2001.

Hart, Mickey. *Drumming at the Edge of Magic.* Grateful Dead Books, 1990.

Hasnas, Rachelle. *The Pocket Guide to Bach Flower Essences.* The Crossing Press, 1997.

Hay, Louise. *You Can Heal Your Life.* Hay House, 1984.

Henderson, Helene, and Sue Ellen Thompson (Editors). *Holidays, Festival, and Celebrations of the World Dictionary.* Omnigraphics, Inc., 1997.

Hill, Julia Butterfly. *The Legacy of Luna.* HarperSanFrancisco, 2000.

Hoffmann, David. *An Elder's Herbal.* Healing Arts Press, 1993.

Hopman, Ellen Evert. *A Druid's Herbal for the Sacred Year.* Destiny Books, 1995.

Kabat-Zinn, Jon. *Wherever You Go, There You Are.* Hyperion, 1994.

Keville, Kathi, and Mindy Green. *Aromatherapy, A Complete Guide to the Healing Art.* Crossing Press, 1995.

Khor, Gary. *Living Chi.* Tuttle Publishing, 1999.

Knight, Sirona. *Celtic Traditions*. Citadel Press, 2000.

———. *Dream Magic*. HarperSanFrancisco, 2000.

———. *Exploring Celtic Druidism*. New Page Books, 2001.

———. *Empowering Your Life with Wicca*. Alpha Books, 2003.

———. *Faery Magick*. New Page Books, 2002.

———. *Goddess Bless!* Red Wheel, 2002.

———. *Love, Sex, and Magic*. Citadel Press, 1999.

———. *The Pocket Guide to Celtic Spirituality*. Crossing Press, 1998.

———. *The Pocket Guide to Crystals and Gemstones*. Crossing Press, 1998.

———. *The Book of Reincarnation*. Barron's, 2002.

———. *Wiccan Spell-A-Day*. Kensington Publishing, 2003.

Knight, Sirona, et al. *The Shapeshifter Tarot*. Llewellyn Publications, 1998.

Lake-Thom, Bobby. *Call of the Great Spirit*. Bear and Company, 2001.

Lawlor, Robert. *Sacred Geometry*. Thames and Hudson, 1989.

Lazarus, Arnold. *In the Mind's Eye*. The Guilford Press, 1984.

Leach, Maria (Editor). *Standard Dictionary of Folklore, Mythology, and Legend*. Funk & Wagnalls Co., 1950.

Leeds, Regina. *Sharing a Place Without Losing Your Space: A Couple's Guide to Blending Homes, Lives, and Clutter*. Alpha Books, 2003.

Lin, Jami. *Earth Design, The Added Dimension*. Earth Design, Inc., 1995.

Linn, Denise. *The Secret Language of Signs*. Ballantine Books, 1996.

———. *Sacred Space*. Ballantine Books, 1995.

Melchizedek, Drunvalo. *The Ancient Secret of the Flower of Life*. Light Technology Publications, 1999.

Molyneaux, Brian Leigh, and Piers Vitebsky. *Sacred Earth, Sacred Stones*. Laurel Glen Publishing, 2001.

Moran, Elizabeth, Joseph Yu, and Val Biktashev. *The Complete Idiot's Guide to Feng Shui, Second Edition*. Alpha Books, 2002.

Newkin, Ingrid. *Save the Animals*. Warner Books, Inc., 1990.

Nuzzi, Debra. *The Pocket Herbal Reference Guide*. The Crossing Press, 1992.

Oman, Maggie (Editor). *Prayers for Healing*. Conari Press, 1997.

Patton, Mary Lee. *Natural Health and Beauty*. Penguin Putnum, Inc., 2001.

Paul, Jordan, and Margaret Paul. *Do I Have to Give Up Me to Be Loved by You?* CompCare Publishers, 1983.

Pritz, Alan. *The Pocket Guide to Meditation*. The Crossing Press, 1997.

Rector-Page, Linda. *Healthy Healing*. Healthy Healing Publications, 1992.

Roberts, Stephanie. *The Pocket Idiot's Guide to Feng Shui*. Alpha Books, 2004.

Ryan, R.S., and J.W. Travis. *Wellness Workbook*. Ten Speed Press, 1981.

Ryan, Robert E. *The Strong Eye of Shamanism*. Inner Traditions, 1999.

Schiller, David, and Carol Schiller. *Aromatherapy Basics*. Sterling Publishing Co., 1998.

Scully, Nicki. *Power Animal Meditations*. Bear and Company, 2001.

Shapiro, Debbie. *Your Body Speaks Your Mind*. Crossing Press, 1997.

Simpson, Liz. *The Book of Crystal Healing*. Sterling Publishing, 1997.

————. *The Healing Energies of Earth*. Journey Editions, 2000.

Skafte, Dianne. *Listening to the Oracle*. HarperSanFrancisco, 1997.

Skinner, Stephen. *Feng Shui, Before and After*. Tuttle Publishing, 2001.

Stewart, R. J. *Earth Light*. Element Books, 1992.

Tart, Charles. *Altered States of Consciousness*. John Wiley, 1969.

Taub, Edward. *Seven Steps to Self-Healing*. DK Publishing, Inc., 1996.

Tolle, Eckhart. *Practicing the Power of Now*. New World Library, 1999.

Tribe, Ian. *The Plant Kingdom*. Bantam Books, 1970.

Weinstein, Marion. *Earth Magic*. Earth Magic Productions, 1998.

Wesselman, Hank. *Medicinemaker: Mystic Encounter on the Shaman's Path*. Bantam Books, 1998.

Wood, Nicholas. *Voices from the Earth: Practical Shamanism*. Sterling Publishing, 2000.

Worwood, Valerie. *The Complete Book of Essential Oils and Aromatherapy.* New World Library, 1995.

Ying, Wu. *Do-It-Yourself Feng Shui.* Element Books, 1998.

Zerin, Edward, Ph.D., and Marjory Zerin, Ph.D. *The "Q" Model for the Effective Management of Personal Stress.* Gardner Press, Inc., 1986.

Sirona Knight lives in Northern California with her family: Michael, her husband of 29 years; Skylor, their 12-year-old son; four beagles; and a family of cats. Sirona's ancestors include James Smithson, founder of the Smithsonian Institute, and she comes from a long line of the Daughters of the Revolution.

Sirona is also the award-winning creator and co-author of the best-selling *Shapeshifter Tarot*. She is Contributing Editor for the international magazine *Magical Blend* (www.magicalblend.com), and has interviewed notable New Age authors and musicians. She also has a special Master's degree in Stress Management from California State University, Sacramento (with honors), and is a Master Hypnotherapist.

Sirona maintains strong Internet visibility (www.sironaknight.com), answering e-mail from fans and chatting on websites across the United States. She also lectures and teaches workshops. She enjoys reading, spending time with her family, home-schooling her son, swimming, walking in the woods with her dogs and cats, watching classic movies, going to concerts, and tending her organic flower and vegetable gardens.

Published books by Sirona Knight:

- *Empowering Your Life with Dreams* (Alpha Books, 2003)
- *Empowering Your Life with Wicca* (Alpha Books, 2003)
- *Wiccan Spell A Day* (Kensington/Citadel, 2002)

- *The Book of Reincarnation* (Barron's, 2002)
- *The Cyber Spellbook* (New Page Books, 2002)
- *Goddess Bless!* (Red Wheel, 2002)
- *Faery Magic* (New Page Books, 2002)
- *The Wiccan Spell Kit* (Kensington/Citadel, 2001)
- *A Witch Like Me* (New Page Books, 2001)
- *The Wiccan Web* (Kensington/Citadel, 2001)
- *The Witch and Wizard Training Guide* (Kensington/Citadel, 2001)
- *Exploring Celtic Druidism* (New Page Books, 2001)
- *Dream Magic* (HarperSanFrancisco, 2000)
- *Celtic Traditions* (Kensington/Citadel, 2000)
- *The Little Giant Encyclopedia of Runes* (Sterling, 2000)
- *Love, Sex, and Magic* (Kensington/Citadel, 1999)
- *The Shapeshifter Tarot* (Llewellyn, 1998)
- *The Pocket Guide to Celtic Spirituality* (Crossing Press, 1998)
- *The Pocket Guide to Crystals and Gemstones* (Crossing Press, 1998)
- *Moonflower: Erotic Dreaming With the Goddess* (Llewellyn, 1996)
- *Greenfire: Making Love With the Goddess* (Llewellyn, 1995)

Index